Voice production in Singing and speaking

Based on scientific principles

Wesley Mills

Alpha Editions

This edition published in 2024

ISBN : 9789362998392

Design and Setting By
Alpha Editions
www.alphaedis.com
Email - info@alphaedis.com

As per information held with us this book is in Public Domain. This book is a reproduction of an important historical work. Alpha Editions uses the best technology to reproduce historical work in the same manner it was first published to preserve its original nature. Any marks or number seen are left intentionally to preserve its true form.

Contents

VOICE PRODUCTION IN SINGING AND SPEAKING .....- 1 -
PREFACE TO THE FOURTH REVISED AND
ENLARGED EDITION. ....- 3 -
PREFACE TO THE THIRD EDITION. ....- 4 -
PREFACE. ....- 5 -
CHAPTER I. ....- 6 -
CHAPTER II. ....- 14 -
CHAPTER III. ....- 26 -
CHAPTER IV. ....- 38 -
CHAPTER V. ....- 43 -
CHAPTER VI. ....- 51 -
CHAPTER VII. ....- 74 -
CHAPTER VIII. ....- 88 -
CHAPTER IX. ....- 101 -
CHAPTER X. ....- 110 -
CHAPTER XI. ....- 117 -
CHAPTER XII. ....- 128 -
CHAPTER XIII. ....- 139 -
CHAPTER XIV. ....- 145 -
CHAPTER XV ....- 151 -
CHAPTER XVI. ....- 159 -
CHAPTER XVII. ....- 162 -
CHAPTER XVIII ....- 172 -
CHAPTER XIX. ....- 181 -
CHAPTER XX ....- 185 -
FOOTNOTES ....- 191 -

VOICE PRODUCTION IN SINGING AND SPEAKING

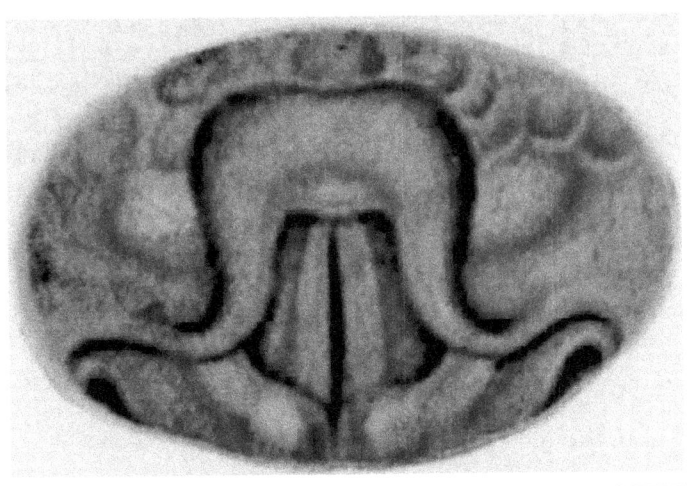

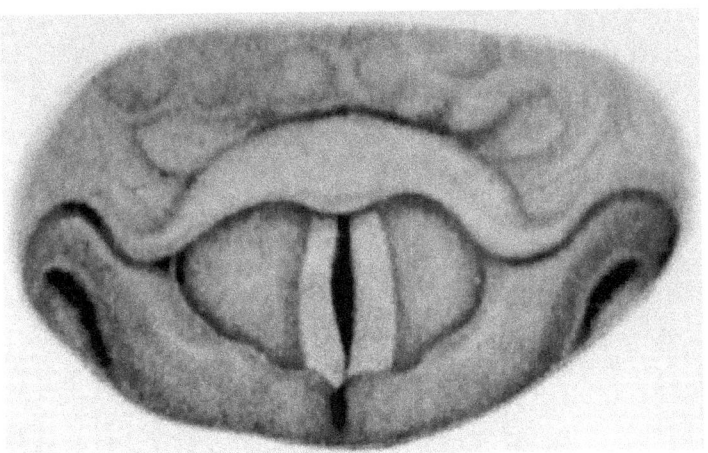

Illustrations of the appearance of the larynx during phonation in two special cases. (Grünwald.)

EXPLANATION OF THE COLORED ILLUSTRATIONS.

They contrast with each other in that the one (upper) is too red; the other, too pale. The upper represents appearances such as one gets with the laryngoscope when the subject has a very severe cold, or even inflammation of the larynx, including the central vocal bands. In this particular case, a young woman of twenty-five years of age, there was inflammation with a certain amount of weakness of the internal thyro-arytenoid muscles. Speaking was almost impossible, and such voice as was produced was of a very rough character. In the lower illustration we have the appearances presented in a man affected with tuberculosis of the lungs and larynx. The pallor of the larynx is characteristic. There is weakness of the internal thyro-arytenoid muscle on the right side, which results in imperfect tension of the vocal band on that side, so that the voice is uncertain and harsh. Such illustrations are introduced to impress the normal by contrast. The reader is strongly advised to compare these figures with others in the body of the work, especially those of [Chapter VII](#).

PREFACE TO THE FOURTH REVISED AND ENLARGED EDITION.

IN addition to certain emendations, etc., introduced throughout the work, I have thought it well to add a chapter in which the whole subject is treated in a broad and comprehensive way in the light of the latest scientific knowledge.

In this review the psychological aspects of the subject have not been neglected, and the whole has been related to practice to as great an extent as the character of the book permits.

It is significant that on both sides of the Atlantic there is a growing conviction that the foundations for speaking and singing as an art must be made as scientific as the state of our knowledge will permit.

THE AUTHOR.

January, 1913.

PREFACE TO THE THIRD EDITION.

NO preface to the Second Edition was written, so few were the changes that were made in the work, and the same might apply to this Third Edition. However, the fact that within a period of less than two years, a Second English and a Third American Edition have been called for, seems to the Author to be so conclusive an endorsement of the application of science to vocal art, that he may be entitled at least to express his gratification at the progress the cause, to which he has devoted his pen, is making. It would seem that the better portion at least of that public that is interested in the progress of vocal art has made up its mind that the time has come when sense and science must replace tradition and empiricism.

THE AUTHOR.

MONTREAL, September, 1908.

PREFACE.

THE present work is based on a life study of the voice, and has grown out of the conviction that all teaching and learning in voice-culture, whether for the purposes of singing or speaking, should as far as possible rest on a scientific foundation.

The author, believing that practice and principles have been too much separated, has endeavored to combine them in this book. His purpose has not been to write an exhaustive work on vocal physiology, with references at every step to the views of various authors; rather has he tried always to keep in mind the real needs of the practical voice-user, and to give him a sure foundation for the principles that must underlie sound practice. A perusal of the first chapter of the work will give the reader a clearer idea of the author's purpose as briefly expressed above.

The writer bespeaks an unprejudiced hearing, being convinced that in art as in all else there is but one ultimate court of appeal: to the scientific, the demonstrable—to what lies at the very foundations of human nature.

In conclusion, the author desires to thank those publishers and authors who have kindly permitted the use of their illustrations.

THE AUTHOR.

MCGILL UNIVERSITY, Montreal, October, 1906.

CHAPTER I.

THE CLAIMS AND IMPORTANCE OF VOCAL PHYSIOLOGY.

TO know consciously and to do with special reference to guiding principles are to be distinguished from carrying out some process without bearing in mind the why or wherefore. Science is exact and related knowledge, facts bound together by principles. Art is execution, doing, and has not necessarily any conscious reference to principles.

While every art has its corresponding science, their relation is in some cases of much greater practical importance than in others. While a painter may be the better for knowing the laws of light, there can be no question that he may do very good work without any knowledge whatever of the science of optics. He is at least in no danger of injuring any part of his person.

Entirely otherwise is it with the voice-user. He employs a delicate and easily injured vital apparatus. His results depend on the most accurate adjustment of certain neuro-muscular mechanisms, and one might suppose that it would be obvious to all who are concerned with this art that a knowledge of the structure and functions of these delicate arrangements of Nature would be at least of great if not of essential importance. The engineer knows the structure and uses of each part of his engine, and does not trust to unintelligent observation of the mere working of mechanisms which others have constructed. The architect studies not only the principles of design, etc., but also the nature and relative value of materials. In his own way he is a kind of anatomist and physiologist.

We do not trust the care of our bodies to those who have picked up a few methods of treatment by experience or the imitation of others. The doctor must have, we all believe, a knowledge of the structure and working of the animal body; he must understand the action of drugs and other healing agents. We expect him not only to diagnose the disease—to tell us exactly what is the matter—but also to be able to predict with, some degree of certainty the course of the malady. Even the nurse of the day must show some grasp of the principles underlying her art.

In connection with all the largest and best equipped universities in America there are officials to plan and direct the courses in physical culture. This matter is no longer entrusted to a "trainer," who has only his experience and observation to rely upon. It is realized that the building up of the mechanism which they are supposed to train in an intelligent manner rests upon well-established principles.

It would be just as reasonable for an engineer to point to the fact that his engine works well, as evidence of his ability, as for the teacher of voice-production to make the same claim in regard to the vocal mechanism. In each case there is a certain amount of justification for the claim, but such teaching cannot be called scientific. Is it even enlightened? It is just as rational to follow in medicine methods that seem to lead to good results, without any reference to the reason why, as to train for results in speaking and singing by methods which have for the student and teacher no conscious basis in scientific knowledge. The physician to-day who treats disease without reference to anatomy and physiology is, at best, but a sort of respectable charlatan. Why should students and teachers of voice-production be content to remain, in the advanced present, where they were hundreds of years ago?

Indeed, there is much more reason now than formerly why the vocalist, speaker, and teacher should have a theoretical and practical knowledge of the structure and workings of the mechanism employed. Many tendencies of the present day work against successful voice-training—worst of all, perhaps, the spirit of haste, the desire to reach ends by short cuts, the aim to substitute tricky for straightforward vocalization, and much more which I shall refer to again and again. They hurt this cause; and I am deeply impressed with the conviction that, if we are to attain the best results in singing and speaking, we must betake ourselves in practice to the methods in vogue at a time which may be justly characterized as the golden age of voice-production.

We have advanced, musically, in many respects since the days of the old Italian masters, but just as we must turn to the Greeks to learn what constitutes the highest and best in sculpture, so must we sit at the feet of these old masters. Consciously or unconsciously they taught on sound physiological principles, and they insisted on the voice-training absolutely necessary to the attainment of the best art.

However talented any individual may be, he can only produce the best results as a singer, actor, or speaker, when the mechanisms by which he hopes to influence his listeners are adequately trained. Why do we look in vain to-day for elocutionists such as Vandenhoff, Bell, and others? Why are there not actors with the voices of Garrick, Kean, Kemble, or Mrs. Siddons, or singers with the vocal powers of a score of celebrities of a former time? It is not that voices are rarer, or talent less widely bestowed by nature. It is because *we do not to-day pursue right methods for a sufficient length of time*; because our methods rest frequently on a foundation less physiological, and therefore less sound. Take a single instance, breath-control. In this alone singers to-day are far behind those of the old Italian period, not always because they do not know how to breathe, but because often they are unwilling to give the time necessary for the full development of adequate breathing power and control.

There was probably never a time when so much attention was paid to the interpretation of music, yet the results are often unsatisfactory because of inadequate technique. People seem to hope to impress us, on the stage, with voices that from a technical point of view are crude and undeveloped, and accordingly lack beauty and expressiveness. Speakers to-day have often every qualification except voice—a voice that can arrest attention, charm with its music, or carry conviction by the adequate expression of the idea or emotion intended.

Is it not strange that a student of the piano or violin is willing to devote perhaps ten years to the study of the technique of his instrument, while the voice-user expects to succeed with a period of vocal practice extending over a year or two, possibly even only a few months?

When the anatomy and physiology of the larynx are considered, it will be seen that the muscular mechanisms concerned in voice-production are of a delicacy unequalled anywhere in the body except possibly in the eye and the ear. And when it is further considered that these elaborate and sensitive mechanisms of the larynx are of little use except when adequately put into action by the breath-stream, which again involves hosts of other muscular movements, and the whole in relation to the parts of the vocal apparatus above the larynx, the mouth, nose, etc., it becomes clear that only long, patient, and *intelligent* study will lead to the highest results.

It should also be remembered that such an apparatus can easily acquire habits which may last for life, for good or ill, artistically considered. Such delicate mechanisms can also be easily injured or hopelessly ruined; and, as a matter of fact, this is being done daily. A great musical periodical has made the statement that thousands of voices are being ruined annually, in America alone, by incompetent teaching. My experience when a practising laryngologist made me acquainted with the extent of the ruin that may be brought about by incorrect methods of using the voice, both as regards the throat and the voice itself; and contact with teachers and students has so impressed me with the importance of placing voice-production on a sound foundation, not only artistic but physiological, that I have felt constrained to tell others who may be willing to hear me what I have learned as to correct methods, with some reference also to wrong ones, though the latter are so numerous that I shall not be able to find the space to deal at length with them.

The correct methods of singing and speaking are always, of necessity, physiological. Others may satisfy a vitiated or undeveloped public taste, but what is artistically sound is also physiological. None have ever sung with more ease than those taught by the correct methods of the old Italian masters; as none run so easily as the wisely trained athlete, and none endure so well. People in singing and speaking will, as in other cases, get what they work for, but have no right to expect to sing or speak effectively by inspiration, any more than the athlete to win a race because he is born naturally fleet of foot or with a quick intelligence. In each case the ideas are converted into performance, the results attained, by the exercise of neuromuscular mechanisms. I am most anxious that it shall be perceived that this is the case, that the same laws apply to voice-production as to running or any other exercise. The difference is one of delicacy and complexity so far as the body is concerned.

It will be understood that I speak only of the technique. For art there must be more than technique, but there is no art without good methods of execution, which constitute technique. The latter is nothing more than method—manner of performance. Behind these methods of performance, or the simplest part of them, there must be some idea. The more intelligent the student, speaker or singer, as to his art and generally, the better for the teacher who instructs scientifically, though such intelligence is largely lost to the teacher who depends on tradition and pure imitation. In the present work I shall be so concerned with the physical that I shall be able only to refer briefly to the part that intelligence and feeling play in the result.

The qualifications for the successful treatment of vocal physiology—that is, such a discussion of the subject as shall lead to a clear comprehension of the nature of the principles involved, and place them on a practical foundation, make them at once usable in actual study and in teaching—such qualifications are many, and, in their totality and in an adequate degree, difficult to attain. After more than twenty years of the best study I could give to this subject in both a theoretical and a practical manner, I feel that I have something to say which may be useful to a large class, and, so far as I know, that is my reason for writing this book.

For myself music is indispensable. The one instrument we all possess is a voice-mechanism. I am one of those who regret that so little attention is paid, especially in America, to pleasing and expressive use of the voice in ordinary conversation. Yet how much pleasure cannot a beautiful speaking voice convey! The college undergraduate rarely finds vocal study among the requirements, in spite of the fact that the voice is an instrument that he will use much more than the pen. The truth is, the home methods of voice-production are those we are most likely to carry with us through life, and, unfortunately, little attention is given to the subject.

Sometimes a love of sweet sounds may be a hidden cause for much that would otherwise be inexplicable in an entire career, as in my own case. It led to an early study of singers and actors and their performances; it gave rise to an effort to form a voice that would meet the requirements of an unusually sensitive ear; it led to the practice and teaching of elocution, and, later, to much communion with voice-users, both singers and speakers. In the meantime came medical practice, with speedy specialization as a laryngologist, when there were daily consultations with singers and speakers who had employed wrong methods of voice-production; this again led on to the scientific investigation of voice problems, with a view of settling certain disputed points; then came renewed and deeper study of music, both as an art and as a science, with a profound interest in the study of the philosophy of musical art and the psychological study of the musical artist, all culminating in this attempt to help those who will listen to me without prejudice. I do not think I know all that is to be known, but I believe I do know how to form and preserve the voice according to physiological principles; I at least ask the reader to give my teachings and recommendations a fair trial. He shall have reasons for what is presented and recommended to him.

Once more let it be said that I do not deny that good practical results may follow teaching that is not put before the pupil as physiology; but what is claimed for physiological teaching is that—

1. It is more rational. The student sees that things must be thus and so, and not otherwise.

2. Faults can be the better recognized and explained.

3. The student can the more surely guide his own development, and meet the stress and storm that sooner or later come to every professional voice-user.

4. Injured voices can be the more effectively restored.

5. The physical welfare of the student is advanced—a matter which I find is often neglected by teachers of music, though more so in the case of instrumental than vocal teachers.

6. The student can much more effectively learn from the performances of others, because he sees that singing and speaking are physical processes leading to artistic ends. This is perhaps one of the most valuable results, and I can testify to the greater readiness with which analysis of a performance can be made after even moderate advancement. The teacher who is wise will encourage the student to hear those who excel, and to analyze the methods which successful artists employ. The student can much more readily accomplish this than detect the mental movements of the artist, though the two really go hand in hand to a large extent.

The above are some of the advantages, but by no means all, of a method of study of voice-production which I must claim is the only rational one—certainly, the only one that rests on a scientific foundation.

It does not follow that such study, to be scientific, shall be made repellent by the use of technical terms the significance of which the reader is left to guess at, but finds unexplained. I fear such treatment of vocal physiology has brought it into disrepute. The aim of the writer will be to give a clear scientific treatment of the subject, which shall not be obscured by unexplained technical terms, and which shall be *practical*—capable of immediate use by student and teacher. If he did not believe the latter possible he would not think it worth while to attempt the former, especially as this has often been done before, he regrets to say, badly enough.

Although the author has not now the time to give regular lessons in voice-production, he is frequently consulted, especially when abroad, during his vacations, by speakers and especially singers who are anxious to learn how they may increase their efficiency in the profession by which they earn their livelihood and make their reputation; and the reader may be gratified to learn how, in such cases, the writer applies the principles he so strongly recommends to others.

Let two or three illustrations suffice:

1. A tenor of world renown consulted him in regard to the position of the larynx in singing, as he had a suspicion that his practice was not correct, inasmuch as his voice seemed to be deteriorating to some extent. The answer to his question need not be given here, as this subject is discussed adequately in a later chapter.

2. The second was the case of a young lady, an amateur singer, who was anxious to know why she failed to get satisfactory results. The author heard her in a large room, without any accompaniment (to cover up defects, etc.), and standing at first at some distance from her, then nearer. Her tones were delightfully pure and beautiful, but her performance suggested rather the sound of some instrument than singing in the proper sense. It was impossible to learn the ideas to be imparted, as the words could not be distinctly made out; there was a monotony in the whole performance, though, it must be confessed, a beautiful monotony, and there was a total lack of that vigor and sureness that both educated and uneducated listeners must be made to feel, or there results a sense of dissatisfaction, if not even irritation.

The beauty of tone was owing to a production that was to a certain extent sound, and this explained why the voice carried well in spite of its being small. This young lady was well educated, had heard much good music, possessed a sensitive ear and a fine æsthetic taste, and, perhaps most important of all, in this case at least, was able to think for herself. She was very slight of body, with an ill-developed chest, and, from her appearance, could not have enjoyed robust health. It was at once evident that this was an admirable case by which to test the views advocated. Accordingly, the author addressed the young lady as follows:

"Your voice is beautiful in quality, and carries well; you observe the registers properly; but your vocalization is feeble, and your singing is ineffective. This is due largely to the lack of robustness in your voice, but not wholly. You do not tell your story in song so that the listener may know what you have to say to him. The imperfections in your method of speaking, so common in America—an imperfect articulation and a limp texture of voice—are evident in your singing; you do not phrase well, and you paint all in one color. This is due chiefly to your breathing and your attacks. One may observe that at no time do you fill your chest completely. You use the lower chest and the diaphragm correctly, but you rob yourself of one half of your breathing power, and your chest is not at all well developed. You do not use the parts above your voice-box with vigor and efficiency, and you direct so much attention to the quality of the tone that you neglect its quantity and the ideas to be expressed. You have been correctly but inadequately instructed. Your teachers have evidently understood registers practically, as few do, but they have only half taught you breathing and attack. Their fidelity to that high ideal of quality of tone as the final consideration wins my respect."

The writer thought, but did not say, that they must have understood little of vocal physiology, or they would not have left this young lady so ill-developed physically, at least so far as the chest is concerned.

I then asked this earnest and intelligent student, as she proved to be, to take a full breath. She did not understand this, and was absolutely incapable of doing it. She had been taught to begin breathing below, to expand from the lower chest upward, and, as a natural result, she never filled the upper chest. She was at once shown how it was done, when she seemed greatly surprised, and said: "I never have done that in my whole life." "Did you not run and shout as a child?" "No, I never did run enough or shout enough to fill up my chest." The latter was small, and flat.

The method of attack was next explained and illustrated, first without reference to words, and then to show its importance in conveying ideas, and the causes of the defects in speaking were indicated, and the corrections named and illustrated. The lady was then asked to sing again, making the improvements suggested, with the result that it was clear that every principle set forth had been clearly apprehended, though of course as yet only imperfectly carried out. The student was recommended to take walking exercise, and to practice filling the chest in the manner to be explained later.

After six weeks she again asked to be heard. The change effected was wonderful; she was another type of vocalist now. Without any loss in quality her voice had a volume and intensity that made it adequate for singing in at least a small hall; her attacks were good, though not perfect; and at the end of a very large room it could easily be seen that her chest was, when necessary, filled full, so that she was able to produce a large and prolonged tone. But, best of all, her health had greatly improved, and she had gained in size and weight.

It is but fair to point out that, in the present case, the student was an unusually intelligent and thoughtful person. Had it been otherwise, more consultations would have been necessary, with probably many detailed instructions and much practice before the teacher. But the case sufficed to convince me afresh that only physiological teaching meets the needs of pupil and teacher. I do not claim, of course, that it is a panacea. It will not supply the lack of a musical ear or an artistic temperament. Vocalization does not make an artist, but there can be no artist without sound vocalization.

All the author's experience as a laryngologist tended to convince him that most of those evils from which speakers and singers suffer, whatever the part of the vocal mechanism affected, arise from faulty methods of voice-production, or excess in the use of methods in themselves correct. A showman may have a correct method of voice-production—indeed, the writer has often studied the showman with admiration—but if he speak for hours in the open air in all sorts of weather, a disordered throat is but the natural consequence; and the Wagnerian singer who will shout instead of sing must not expect to retain a voice of musical quality, if, indeed, he retain one at all.

Throughout this work it will be assumed that the speaker and the singer should employ essentially the same vocal methods. The singer should be a good speaker, even a good elocutionist, and the speaker should be able to produce tones equal in beauty, power, and expressiveness to those of the singer, but, of course, within a more limited range, and less prolonged, as a rule. To each alike is voice-training essential, if artistic results are to follow; neither rhetorical training on the one hand nor musical training on the other will alone suffice.

So that it may be clear that the same physiological principles apply to the vocal mechanism as to all others in the body, a short chapter dealing with this subject is introduced, before taking up the structure and functions of any part of that apparatus by which the speaker or singer produces his results as a specialist.

The laws of health known as hygiene follow so naturally on those of physiology that brief references to this subject, from time to time, with a chapter at the end of the work bearing specially on the life of the voice-user, will probably suffice.

CHAPTER II.

GENERAL AND PHYSIOLOGICAL CONSIDERATIONS.

THE principle that knowledge consists in a perception of relations will now be applied to the structure and functions or uses of the different parts of the body.

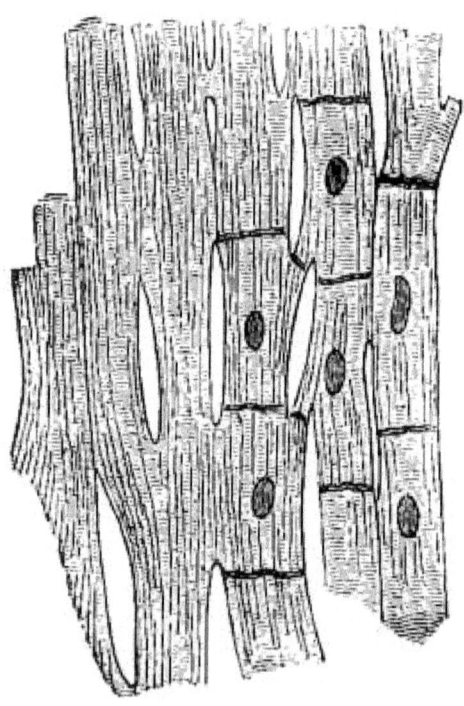

FIG. 1. Muscle-fibres from the heart, much magnified, showing cross-stripings, nuclei, or the darkly stained central bodies very important to the life of the cell, also the divisions and points of union. (Schäfer's *Histology*.)

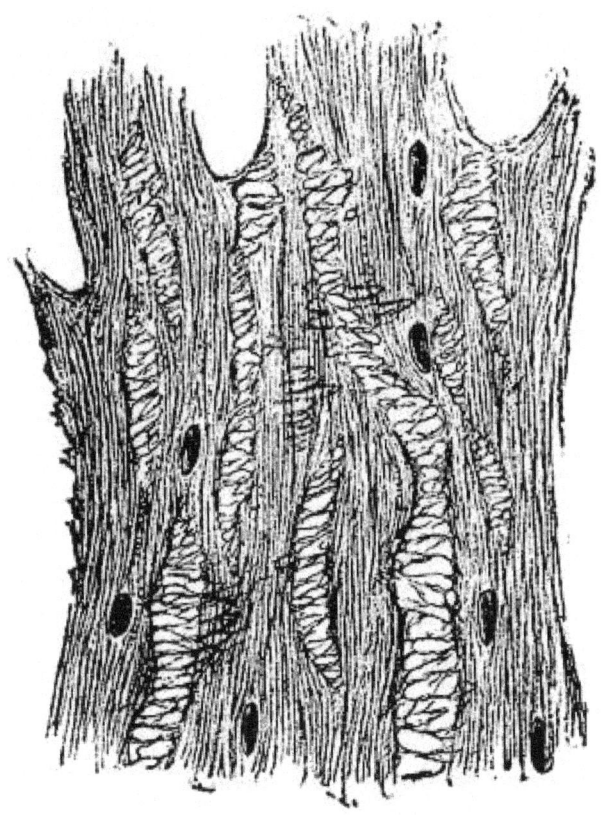

FIG. 2. Appearance of a small portion of muscle under a moderate magnification. Between the muscle-cells proper a form of binding tissue may be seen.

The demonstration that all animals, even all living things, have certain properties or functions in common is one of the great results of modern science. Man no longer can be rightly viewed apart from other animals. In many respects he is in no wise superior to them. The most desirable course to pursue is to learn wherein animals resemble and wherein they differ, without dwelling at great length on the question of relative superiority or inferiority. It may be unhesitatingly asserted that all animals live, move, and have their being, in every essential respect, in the same way. Whether one considers those creatures of microscopic size living in stagnant ponds, or man himself, it is found that certain qualities characterize them all. That minute mass of jelly-like substance known as protoplasm, constituting the one-celled animal amœba, may be described as *ingestive, digestive, secretory, excretory, assimilative, respiratory, irritable, contractile,* and *reproductive*: that is to say, the amœba must take in food; must digest it, or change its form; must produce some fluid within itself which acts on food; must cast out from itself what is no longer of any use; must convert the digested material into its own substance—perhaps the most wonderful property of living things; must take up into its own substance oxygen, and expel carbonic acid gas (carbon dioxide); and possess the power to respond to a stimulus, or cause of change, the property of changing form, and, finally, the ability to bring into being others like itself.

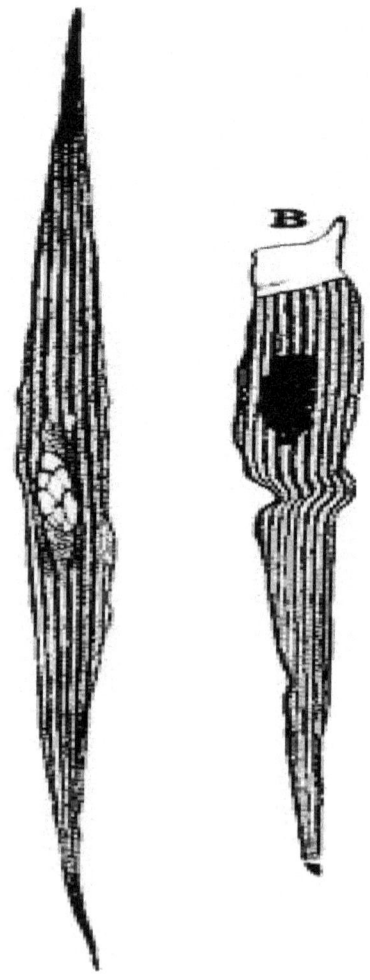

FIG. 3. Muscle-cells isolated from the muscular coats of the intestine. Similar cells are found in some part of most of the internal organs, including the bronchial tubes. These cells are less ready in responding

to a stimulus, contract more slowly, and tend to remain longer contracted when they pass into this condition than striped muscle cells. (Schäfer.)

Before justifying these statements in detail it will be desirable to say something of the anatomy or structure of a mammal, and we may select man himself, though it is to be remembered that one might apply exactly the same treatment to a dog, pig, mouse, or any other member of this group of animals. The amœba and creatures like it live immersed in water; man, at the bottom of an ocean of air. Both move in their own medium, the amœba creeping with extreme slowness, man moving with a speed incalculably greater. In each case the movements are determined by some cause from without which is termed by physiologists a *stimulus*. The slightest movement of the thin cover-glass placed over the drop of water in which an amœba is immersed, on a microscopic slide, suffices to act as a stimulus, and serves much the same purpose as an electric shock to the muscles of a man. In man an elaborate apparatus exists for the process known as respiration, but in this and in all other cases the mechanism is composed of what is known technically as *cells*, the latter being the units of structure, the individual bricks of the building, so to speak; and just as any edifice is made up of individual pieces some of which differ from one another while others do not to any appreciable extent, so is it with the body. The individual cells of a muscle are alike in structure and function, but they differ widely from those of a gland or secreting organ, as the liver. But it is to be ever remembered that the statements with which we set out hold: that is, that however cells may differ, they have in all animals certain properties in common. Of the muscle-cell, the liver-cell, and the one-celled animal we may affirm the same properties, but the difference is that while all are secretory the liver-cell is eminently so, and produces bile, which other cells do not; that while it is but feebly contractile, or susceptible of change of form, the muscle-cell is characterized by this property above all others.

The lower we descend in the animal scale the more simple are the mechanisms by which results are attained. The one-celled animal may be said to breathe with its whole body, while the man employs a large number of muscles, not to speak, at present, of other arrangements. But when a muscle is examined under the microscope, it is found to consist of cells, each one of which is physiologically in all essentials like an amœba, so that we may say that a muscle or other tissue or organ is really a sort of colony of cells of similar structure and function, all working in harmony like a happy family. We actually do find colonies of unicellular animals much like amœba, so that the muscle-cells and all other cells of the body may be compared to amœba and other one-celled animals.

But while in such unicellular creatures all functions are properties of the individual cell, among higher forms *systems* take the place of the protoplasm of the single cell. There is a circulatory system, a respiratory system, etc.; but we must once more point out that such systems are made up of cells, so that every function of the highest animal may be finally reduced to what takes place in the unicellular animal. A circulatory system consists of a heart and blood-vessels, all filled with blood, which latter is "the life," as was known from the earliest times; yet this same blood is of no more use for the nourishment of the body while it is contained in those tubes which constitute the blood-vessels than is bread locked up in a pantry to a hungry boy. That which really provides the nutriment for the body is a fluid derived from the blood, a something like the liquid part of blood and known as *lymph*. This latter is to the cells of any tissue, as a muscle, as is the water filled with the food on which an amœba lives. In like manner, in spite of the complicated apparatus which supplies oxygen and removes carbon dioxide, the respiratory system, respiration is finally the work of the cell, as in amœba; a muscle-cell respires exactly as does the one-celled animal.

When we consider the marvellous complexity of structure of one of the higher animals, and the amazing variety of its functions, the question naturally arises as to how all this is brought about without any sort of clashing of the interests of one part with those of another. Why is it that the stomach has enough and not too much blood? By what means has Nature solved the problem of supplying more oxygen to parts in action than to those at rest? How is it that one set of muscles acts with instead of antagonizing another set, as in any complicated series of movements, such as walking?

To bring about this harmonization, or *co-ordination*, the nervous system has been provided. As the nervous and muscular systems are of preëminent importance in voice-production, they will now be considered with more detail than it is necessary to give to other systems.

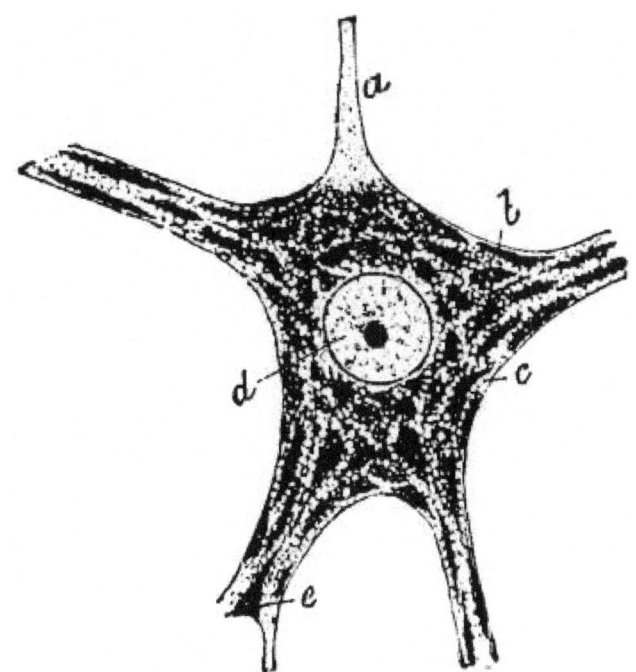

FIG. 4. Body of a nerve-cell of the spinal cord, specially stained so as to show the minute structure. (Schäfer's *Histology*.)

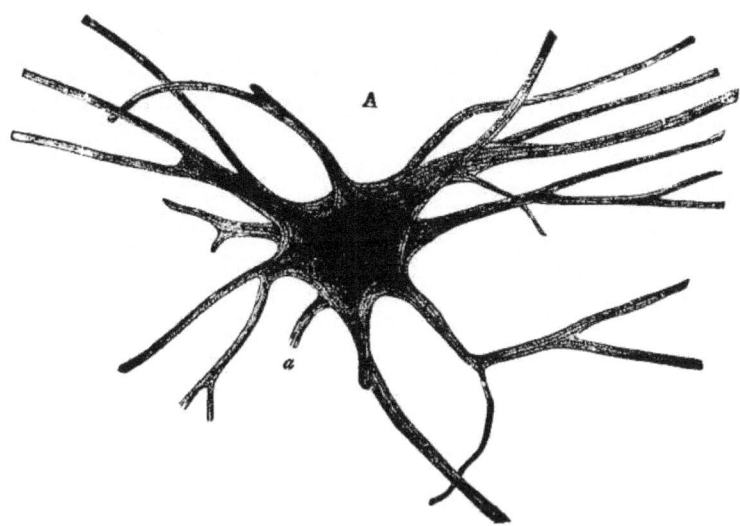

FIG. 5. A large nerve-cell from the spinal cord of the ox, magnified 175 diameters. (Schäfer.)

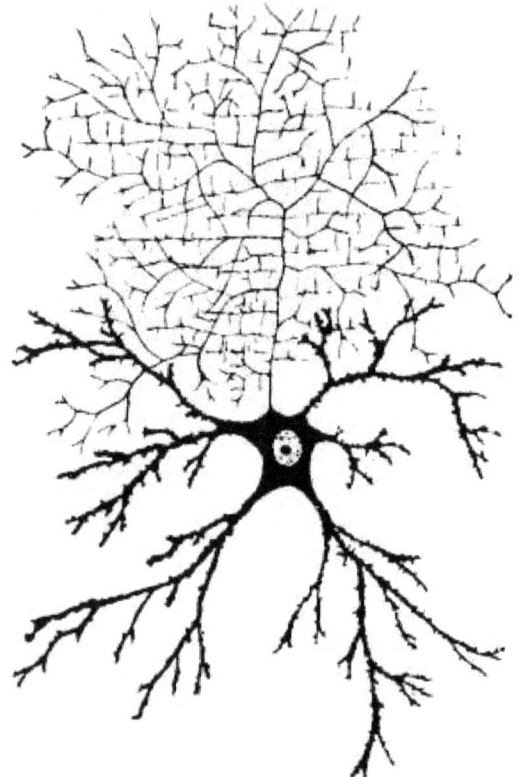

FIG. 6. A cell of another form, from the superficial or outer part of the greater brain (cortex cerebri). The great amount of branching is suggestive of the power to receive and to transmit nervous influences (impulses) from various other cells; in other words, complexity of structure suggests a corresponding complexity of function.

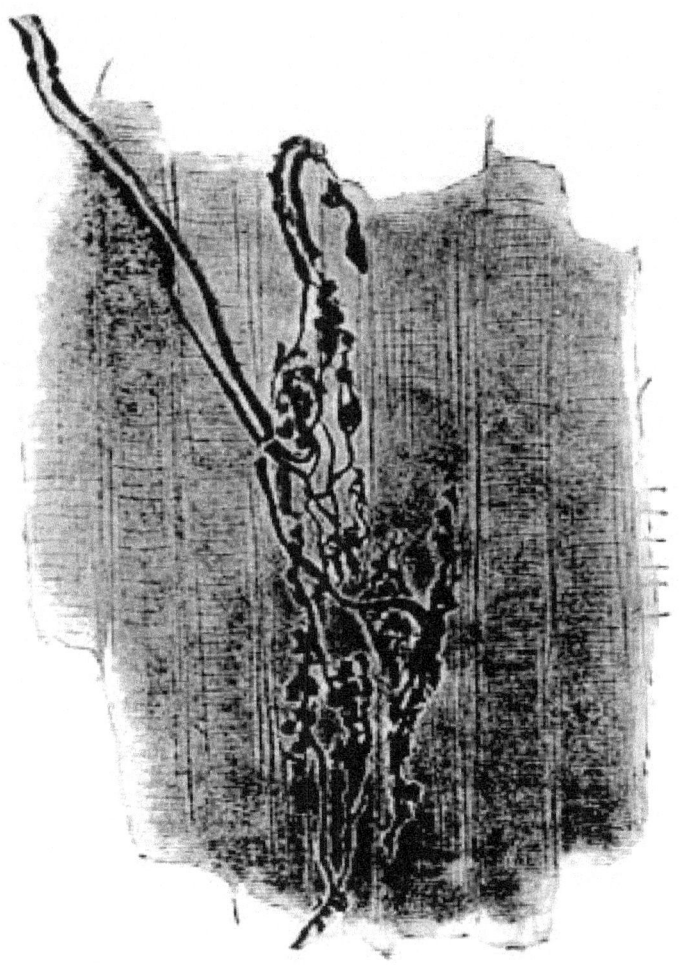

FIG. 7. Representation of the manner in which a nerve is seen to terminate in a muscle, such ending being one form of "nerve-ending" termed a "muscle plate." It tends to emphasize the close relationship existing between muscle and nerve, and to justify the expression "neuro-muscular mechanism," the nervous system being as important for movements as the muscles. (Schäfer's *Histology*.)

Complicated as is the nervous system, modern advances in the sciences of anatomy and physiology have made the comprehension of the subject easier. It is now known that the nervous system, in spite of its wide ramifications, is also made up of cells which are structurally and functionally related to each other, and make connection with every part of the whole community, the body. A nerve-cell, or *neurone*, may be very complicated in its structure because of its many branches or extensions from the main body of the cell.

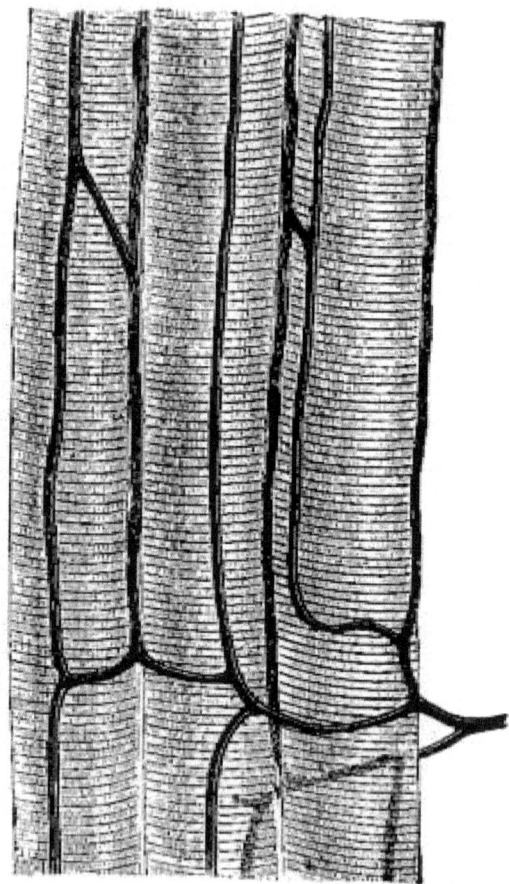

FIG. 8. **Three muscle-fibres lying beside each other, with the small blood-vessels (capillaries) around and between them. Such are the appearances presented under the microscope by skeletal or striped muscles such as those of the larynx. (Schäfer.)**

It may be said, in general terms, that the nervous *centres*, the brain and the spinal cord, which are parts of one anatomical whole, are characterized by the presence of the cell-bodies as well as their extensions, while nerves consist only of the extensions or arms of the cell-bodies. The nerve-cell whose body is in the top of the brain may have an extension or arm which may reach practically to the end of the spinal cord, and there make communication with another cell whose arm, in turn, may reach as far as the toe. Such nerve arms or extensions constitute the *nerve-fibres*, and bundles of these *nerves*, or *nerve-trunks*.

Usually nerve-fibres make connection with the cells of an organ by a special modification of structure known as a *nerve-ending*. A nervous message or influence (*nerve-impulse*) may pass either to the centre—*i.e.*, toward a cell-body—or from it; in other words, a nervous impulse may originate in the centre or in some organ more or less distant from it; a nervous impulse may be *central* or *peripheral*. Nearly all central impulses, we now know, arise because of the peripheral ones. One may illustrate this important relation by a telegraph system. The message a railroad operator sends out—*e.g.*, that which determines whether a train is to be held at a certain station or sent on—might depend wholly on information received from another office. The extra flow of blood to the stomach when food enters it is owing to such a relation of things. The food acts as a stimulus to the ends of the nerve-fibres, and, in consequence, there is an ingoing (*afferent*) message or impulse, and, by reason of this, an outgoing (*efferent*) one to the muscle-cells of the small blood-vessels, owing to which they contract less strongly and the calibre of these vessels is increased; hence more blood reaches the smallest vessels of all (*capillaries*.) Such a physiological relation of things is termed *reflex action*. For such reflex action there are required structurally at least two neurones or nerve-cells, and functionally a stimulus of a certain strength and quality. Of course, if more blood passes to the stomach there must be less somewhere else, as the total volume of the blood is limited. The value of the knowledge of such a fact is obvious. It must be unwise to exercise vigorously immediately after meals, for this determines blood to the muscles which would serve a better purpose in the digestive organs. For a like reason the singer who would do his best before the public will refrain from taking a large meal before appearing.

As this subject of reflex action is of the highest importance, the reader is advised to make himself thoroughly familiar with the principles involved before perusing the future chapters of this work. Fig. 16 shows the structural relations for reflex action. It also indicates how such nervous relations may be complicated by other connections of the nerve-cells involved in the reflex action. It will be seen that they make many upward connections with the brain, in consequence of which consciousness may be involved. Ordinarily one is more or less conscious of reflex action, though the will is not involved; in fact, a willed or voluntary action is usually considered the reverse of a reflex or involuntary action. But for a reflex action the brain is not essential. As is well known, a snake's hinder part will move in response to a touch when completely severed from the head end; and movements of considerable complexity can be evoked in a headless frog.

Herein, then, lies the solution of the problem. This is Nature's way of bringing one part into harmonious relations with another. As by a telegraphic system the most distant parts of a vast railway system may be brought into harmonious working, so is it with the body by means of the nervous system. The nerve-centres correspond to the heads of the railway system, or, perhaps more correctly, to the various officials resident in some large city who from this centre regulate the affairs of the whole line.

The muscular system is made up of cells of two kinds, those characteristic of the muscles used in ordinary movements, and those employed for the movements of the internal organs. The muscles of the limbs are made up of striped muscle-cells; those of the stomach, etc., of unstriped cells. These latter are slower to act when stimulated, contract more slowly, and cease to function more tardily when the stimulus is withdrawn.

The muscular mechanisms used by the singer and speaker are of the skeletal variety.

If it be true that the welfare of one part of the body is bound up with that of every other, as are the interests of one member of a firm with those of another, in a great business, it will at once appear that the most perfect results can follow for the voice-user only under certain conditions. However perfect by nature the vocal mechanism, the result in any case must be largely determined by the character of the body as a whole. The man of fine physique generally has naturally more to hope for than one with an ill-developed body.

In the natural working of the body the stimulus to a muscle is nervous; hence we may appropriately, and often to advantage, speak of *neuro-muscular* mechanism, the nervous element being as important as the muscular.

In a later chapter it will be shown that the work of the singer and speaker when most successfully carried out must be largely reflex in nature—a fact on which hang weighty considerations with regard to many questions, among them methods of practice, the influence of example, etc.—be he ever so much the natural artist. It will be the writer's aim, however, to give such warnings and advice as may assist each reader in his own best development. Many who began with a comparatively poor physical stock in trade have surpassed the self-satisfied ones who trusted too much to what nature gave them. Singers as well as others would do well to believe that *Labor omnia vincit*.

SUMMARY.

The same fundamental physiological principles apply to the lowest and to the highest animals. To all belong certain properties or qualities. As structure is differentiated, or as one animal differs from another owing to greater or less complexity of form, there is a corresponding differentiation of function, none, however, ever losing the fundamental properties of protoplasm. Each organ comes to perform some one function better than all others. This is specialization, and implies advance among animals as it does in civilization.

The neuro-muscular system is of great moment to the voice-user. He is a specialist as regards the neuro-muscular systems of the vocal mechanism. But the same laws apply to it as to other neuro-muscular mechanisms. It is of great theoretical and practical importance to recognize this, and that one part of the body is related to every other, which relationship is maintained chiefly by the nervous system, and largely through reflex action.

CHAPTER III.

BREATHING CONSIDERED THEORETICALLY AND PRACTICALLY.

IF the old orator was right in considering *delivery* as the essence of public speaking as an art, it may with equal truth be said of singing, the term being always so extended in signification as to imply what Rossini named as the essential for the singer—*voice*.

Looking at it from the physiological point of view, we may say that the one absolutely essential thing for singers and speakers is breathing. Without methods of breathing that are correct and adequate there may be a perfect larynx and admirably formed resonance-chambers above the vocal bands, with very unsatisfactory results. The more the writer knows of singers and speakers, the more deeply does he become convinced that singing and speaking may be resolved into the correct use of the breathing apparatus, above all else. Not that this alone will suffice, but it is the most important, and determines more than any other factor the question of success or failure. Breathing is the key-note with which we must begin, and to which we must return again and again.

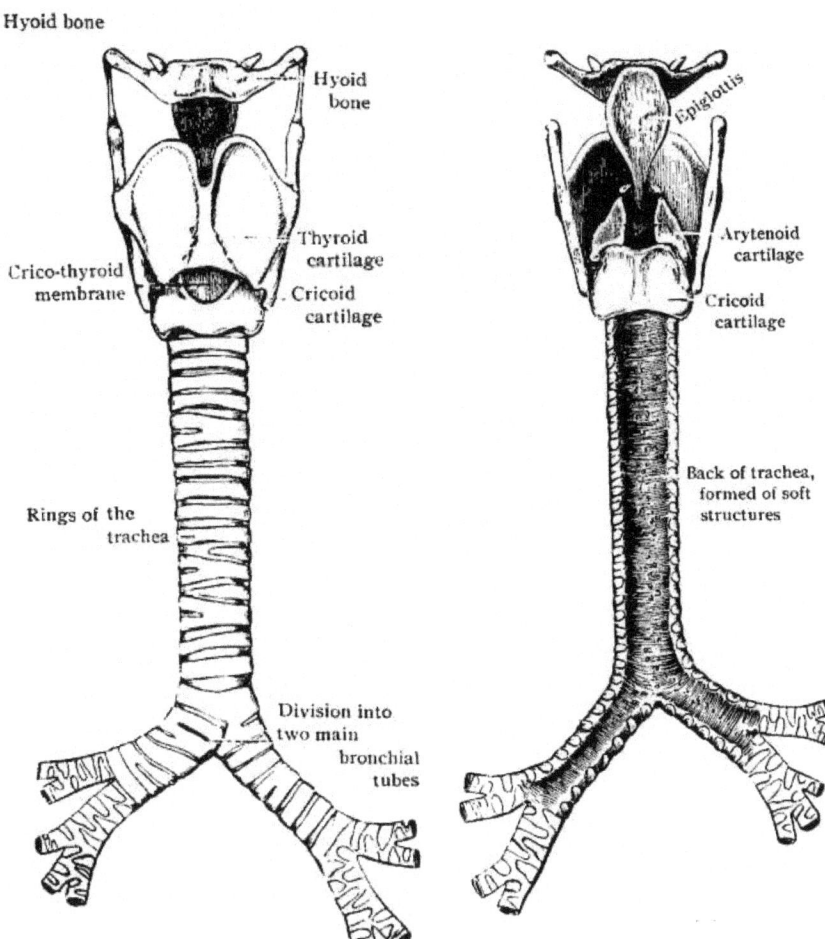

FIG. 9. A front view of parts of the respiratory apparatus. (Halliburton's Physiology.)

FIG. 9. A back view of the parts represented in Fig. 9. (Halliburton's Physiology.)

The extent to which this subject has been misunderstood, misrepresented, and obscured in works on the voice, and its neglect by so large a number of those who profess to understand how to teach singing and public speaking, are truly amazing. That many should fail to fully appreciate its importance in attaining artistic results is not so surprising as that the process itself should have been so ill understood, especially as it is open to any one to observe in himself, or in our domestic animals, Nature's method of getting air into and out of the body.

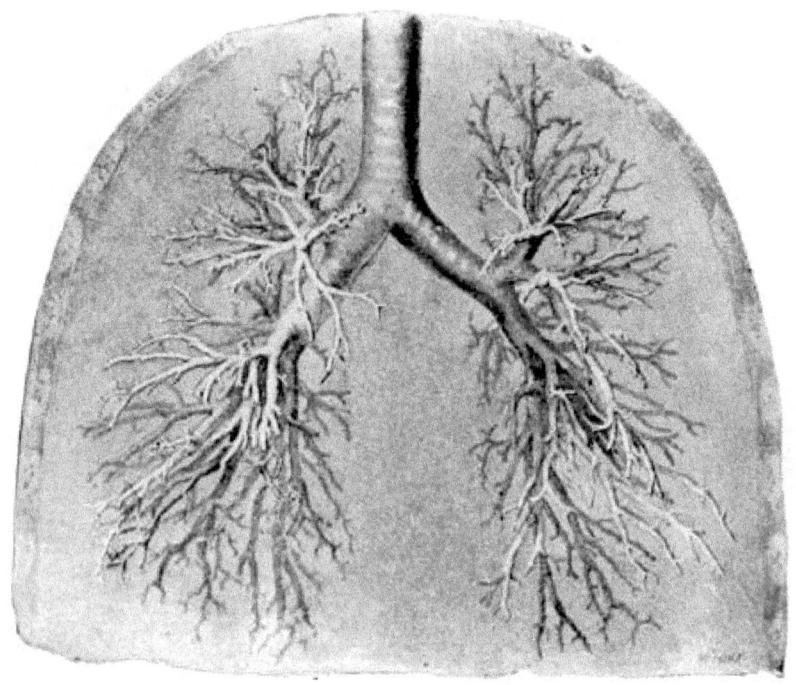

FIG. 10 (Spalteholz). A view of the lower part of the trachea, dividing into the main bronchial tubes, which again branch into a tree-like form. The air-cells are built up around the terminations of the finest bronchial tubes, of which they are a sort of membranous extension.

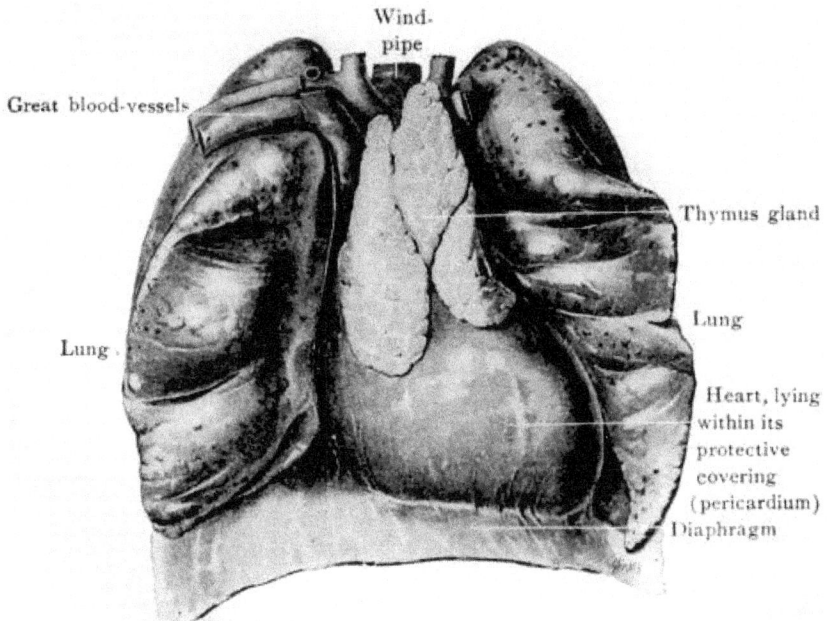

FIG. 11 (Spalteholz). Shows well the relations of heart, lungs, and diaphragm. The lungs have been drawn back, otherwise the heart would be covered almost wholly by them. It will be noted that the heart-covering is attached to the diaphragm. The fact that the stomach and other important organs of the abdomen lie immediately beneath the diaphragm is a significant one for the voice-user. Manifestly, a full stomach and free, vigorous breathing are incompatible.

This misapprehension is in all probability to be traced to the dependence of the student and teacher on tradition rather than observation—on authority rather than rational judgment. If a great teacher or singer makes any announcement whatever in regard to the technique of his art, it is natural that it should be considered with attention, but it may prove a great misfortune for the individual to accept it without thoughtful consideration. The author will illustrate, from time to time, the truth of the above.

In this and all other chapters of this work the student, by which term I mean every one who is seriously interested in the use of the voice, is recommended to give attention, before reading on any subject, to the illustrations employed, perusing very carefully the explanatory remarks beneath them.

The author considers the summaries at the conclusion of the chapters of much importance. They not only furnish exact and condensed statements of the main facts and principles involved, but afford the reader a test of the extent to which the foregoing chapter has been comprehended. As the author has a horror of what is termed "cramming," he expresses the hope that no student will use these synopses, which have been prepared with much care, for so great a misuse of the mind as cramming implies.

Breathing is essential for life. The oxygen of the air is, of all food-stuffs, the most important. Without it a mammal will perish in less than three minutes; hence there is no need of the body so urgent as that of oxygen. It is also of great moment that the waste—the carbon dioxide, or carbonic acid gas—should be got rid of rapidly; nevertheless, it is not this gas which kills when the air-passages are closed, though it is highly deleterious. The body is a sort of furnace in which combustions are continually going on, and oxygen is as essential for these as for the burning of a candle, and the products are in each case the same.

Whether the voice-user respires, like others, to maintain the functions of the body, or whether he employs the breathing apparatus to produce sound, it is to be borne in mind that he uses the same physical mechanisms, so that the way is at once clear to consider the anatomy and physiology of the breathing organs.

It has been already pointed out that respiration is in all animals, in the end, the same process. The one-celled animal and the muscle-cell respire in the same way, and with the same results—oxidation, combustion, and resulting waste products. In the animal of complicated structure special mechanisms are necessary that the essential oxygen be brought to the blood and the useless carbon dioxide removed. The respiratory organs or tract include the mouth, nose, larynx, trachea, bronchial tubes, and the lung-tissue proper or the air-cells.

The mouth, nose, and larynx, in so far as they are of special importance in voice-production, will be considered later.

The air enters the trachea, or windpipe, through a relatively narrow slit in the larynx, or voice-box, known as the *glottis*, or *chink of the glottis*, which is wider when air is being taken in (*inspiration*) than when it is being expelled (*expiration*). Life depends on this chink being kept open. The windpipe is composed of a series of cartilaginous or gristly rings connected together by softer tissues. These rings are not entire, but are completed behind by soft tissues including muscle. It follows that this tube is pliable and extensible—a very important provision, especially when large movements of the neck are made, during vigorous exercise, and also in singing and speaking.

The bronchial tubes are the tree-like branches of the trachea, and extend to the air-cells themselves, which may be considered as built up around them in some such fashion as a toy balloon on its wooden stem, but with many infoldings, etc. (Fig. 10). The air-cells are composed of a membrane which may be compared to the walls of the balloon, but we are of course dealing with living tissue supplied by countless blood-vessels of the most minute calibre, in which the blood is brought very near to the air which passes over them.

Throughout, the respiratory tract is lined with mucous membrane. Mucous membranes are so named because they secrete mucus, the fluid which moistens the nose, mouth, and all parts of the respiratory tract. When one suffers from a cold the mucous membrane, in the early stages, may become dry from failure of this natural secretion; hence sneezing, coughing, etc., as the air then acts as an irritant.

At no time do we breathe pure oxygen, but "air"—*i.e.*, a mixture of 21 parts of the former with 79 parts of an inert gas, nitrogen; and there is always in the air more oxygen than the blood actually takes from it in the air-cells.

The intaking of air is termed by physiologists *inspiration*, and its expulsion *expiration*, the whole process being *respiration*. Expiration takes a very little longer than inspiration, and the rapidity of respiration depends on the needs of the body. The more active the exercise, the more rapidly vital processes go on, the more ventilation of the tissues is required and the more is actually effected. When one is at rest breathing takes place at the rate of from 14 to 18 inspirations and expirations in the minute; but of all the processes of the body none is more variable than respiration, and of necessity, for every modification of action, every movement, implies a demand for an increased quantity of oxygen. It is not surprising, therefore, that the very exercise of singing tends in itself to put one out of breath.

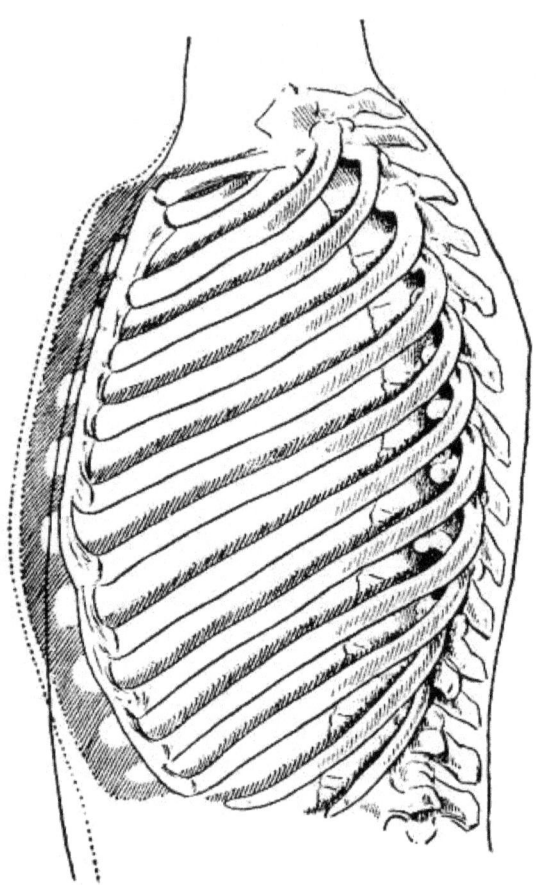

FIG. 12. In the above, the shaded outlines indicate the shape of the bony cage of the chest during inspiration, and the lighter ones the same during expiration. The alterations in the position of the ribs and in the diameters of the chest, giving rise to its greater capacity during inspiration, are evident.

Attention will now be directed to some facts that it is of the utmost importance to clearly understand, if one is to know how to breathe and the reasons for the method employed. The lungs are contained in a cavity the walls of which are made up of a domed muscular (and tendinous) structure below, and elsewhere of bony and cartilaginous tissues filled in with soft structures, chiefly muscles. This cage is lined within by a smooth membrane which is kept constantly moist by its own secretion. The lungs are covered by a similar membrane, both of these fitting closely like the hand to a glove, so that there are two smooth membranes in opposition. It cannot be too well remembered that these two, the inner surface of the chest walls and the outer surface of the lungs, are in the closest contact. This is so whatever the changes that take place in the size and shape of the chest. The lungs are concave below, and so fit accurately to the fleshy partition between the chest and the abdomen which constitutes the lower boundary of the chest, if we may use the term "chest" somewhat loosely. Above, suiting the shape of the chest, the lungs are somewhat conical.

The pressure of the air tends of itself to expand the lungs, which are highly elastic, even when one does not breathe at all. But if more air is to enter there must be additional space provided; hence greater expansion of the lungs can only follow an enlargement of the chest cavity in one or in all directions. These are spoken of as *diameters*. It follows that it is possible to conceive of the chest being enlarged in three, and only three, directions; so that it may be increased in size in its vertical, its transverse, and its antero-posterior diameter, or diameter from before backwards.

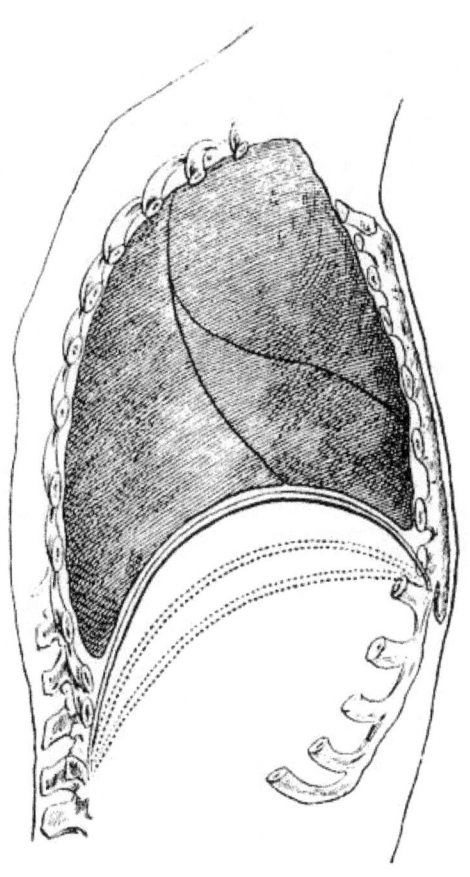

FIG. 13. This figure is intended to indicate, in a purely diagrammatic way, by dotted lines, the position of the diaphragm (1) when inspiration is moderate, and (2) when very deep. The unbroken curved line above the dotted ones indicates the position of the diaphragm (only approximately, of course) after expiration.

This expansion, as in the case of all other movements, can be effected only by muscles, or, to speak more accurately, by neuro-muscular mechanisms. Exactly what muscles are employed may be learned from the accompanying illustrations and by observation. While it is highly important to know in a general way which muscles are chiefly concerned, or, rather, where they are situated, it cannot be deemed essential for every reader to learn their names, attachments, etc., down to the minutest details, as in the case of a student of anatomy proper. The author does, however, deem it of the highest importance that the student should learn by actual observation on his own person that his chest does expand in each of the three directions indicated above.

It is not necessary to dissect to observe muscles; in fact, they can be seen in action only on the living subject. All who would really understand breathing should study the chest when divested of all clothing and before a sufficiently large mirror. He may then observe the following during a fairly deep inspiration:

1. The chest is enlarged as a whole.

2. The abdominal walls move outward.

3. The ribs pass from a more oblique to a less oblique position, and may become almost horizontal; their upper edges are also turned out slightly, though this is not so easy to observe.

4. Again, in the case of a very deep and sudden inspiration, the abdomen and the lower ribs also are drawn inward.

The changes above referred to are brought about in this way:

1. The total enlargement is due to the action of many muscles which function in harmony with each other.

2. The chief changes are brought about by those muscles attached between the ribs (*intercostales*); but these act more efficiently owing to the coöperation of other muscles which steady the ribs and chest generally, such as those attached to the shoulder-bones and the upper ribs; indeed, the most powerful inspiration possible can only be effected when most of the other muscles of the body are brought into action. One may observe that even the arms and

legs are called into requisition when a tenor sings his highest tone as forcibly as possible, though this is often overdone in a way to be condemned. Art should not be reduced to a gymnastic feat.

The most important muscle of inspiration is the *diaphragm*, or midriff, because it produces a greater change in the size of the chest than any other single muscle. Some animals can get the oxygen they require to maintain life by the action of this large muscle alone, when all other respiratory muscles are paralyzed. As it is so important, and above all to the voice-user, it merits special consideration.

In studying the action of a muscle it is necessary to note its *points of attachment* to harder structures, either bone or cartilage. Nearly always one such point is more fixed than the other, and from this the muscle pulls when it contracts.

The diaphragm is peculiar in that it is somewhat circular in shape and is more or less tendinous or sinew-like in the middle. Being attached to the spinal column behind and to the lower six or seven ribs, when the muscle contracts it becomes less domed in shape—less convex upward—and of course descends to a variable degree depending on the extent of the muscular contraction. As to whether the ribs, and with them the abdominal muscles, are drawn in or the reverse, is determined wholly by the degree of force with which the contraction takes place and the extent to which it is resisted. Throughout the body muscles are arranged in sets which may either coöperate with or antagonize each other, as required. The forcible bending of one's arm by another person may be resisted by one through the use of certain muscles. In this the action of the muscles which bend the arm is imitated by the agent seeking to perform this movement for us. The muscles acting in opposition to certain others are said to be their *antagonists*.

Were the diaphragm to contract moderately the ribs would be but little drawn in, even if no muscles acted as antagonists. But, as a matter of fact, this domed muscle descends at the same time as the ribs ascend, because of the action of the muscles attached to them. The diaphragm being concave below toward the abdomen, the contents of this cavity fit closely to its under surface. There are found the liver, stomach, intestines, etc.—a part of great practical importance, as will be shown presently.

Naturally, in breathing, the organs of the abdomen, especially those above, are pressed down somewhat with the descent of the diaphragm in inspiration, and, in turn, push out the abdominal walls. If, however, the midriff contract so powerfully that the lower ribs are drawn inward, the abdominal walls follow them. Although the actual extent of the descent of the diaphragm is small in itself, since the total surface is large it effects a very considerable enlargement of the chest in the vertical diameter.

The capacity of the lungs for air is a very variable quantity:

1. The quantity of air taken in with a single inspiration in quiet breathing (*tidal air*) is about 20-30 cubic inches.

2. The quantity taken in with the deepest possible inspiration (*complemental air*) is about 100 cubic inches.

3. The quantity that may be expelled by the most forcible expiration (*supplemental air*) is about 100 cubic inches.

4. The quantity that can under no circumstances be expelled (*residual air*) is about 100 cubic inches.

5. The quantity that can be expelled after the most forcible inspiration—*i.e.*, the amount of air that can be moved—indicates the *vital capacity*. This varies very much with the individual, and depends not a little on the elasticity of the chest walls, and so diminishes with age. It follows that youth is the best period for the development of the chest, and the time to learn that special breath-control so essential to good singing and speaking.

When the ribs have been raised by inspiration and the abdominal organs pressed down by the diaphragm, the chest, on the cessation of the act, tends to resume its former shape, owing to elastic recoil quite apart from all muscular action; in other words, inspiration is active, expiration largely passive. With the voice-user, especially the singer, expiration becomes the more important, and the more difficult to control, as will be shown later.

It must now be apparent that such use of the voice as is necessitated by speaking for the public, or by singing, still more, perhaps, must tend to the general welfare of the body—*i.e.*, the hygiene of respiration is evident from the physiology. Actual experience proves this to be the case. The author has known the greatest improvement in health and vigor follow on the judicious use of the voice, owing largely to a more active respiration. It also follows, however, that exhaustion may result from the excessive use of the respiratory muscles, as with any others, even when the method of chest-expansion is quite correct. Before condemning any vocal method one does well to inquire in regard to the extent to which it has been employed, as well as the circumstances of the voice-user. A poor clergyman worried with the fear of being supplanted by another man, or a singer unable to secure employment, possibly from lack of means to advertise himself, is not likely to grow fat under any method of vocal exercise, be it ever so physiological; while the prima donna who has chanced to please the popular taste and become a favorite may "wax fat and kick."

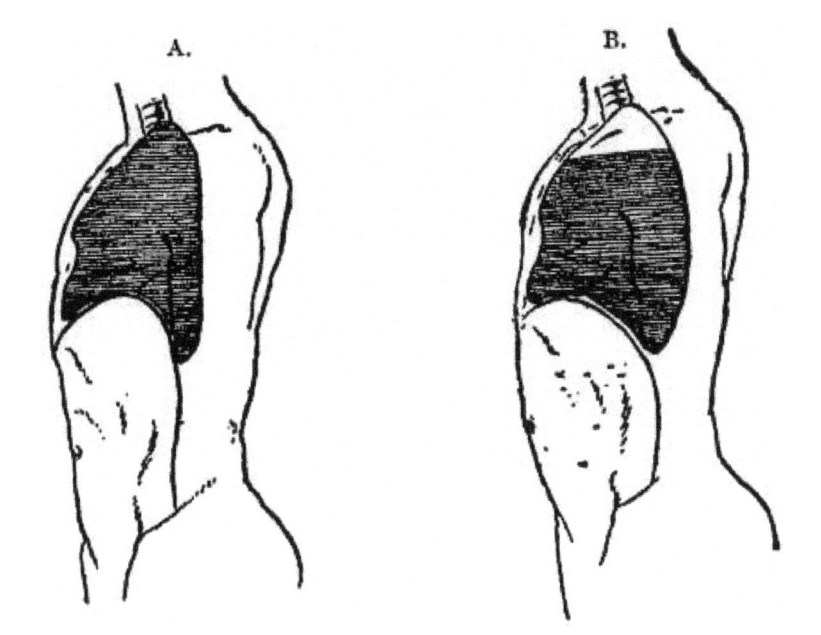

FIGS. 14, A and B, are to be compared: that on the left shows the position of the diaphragm, abdominal walls, etc., during expiration; the one on the right, during inspiration. The relative quantities of air in the chest in each case are approximately indicated by the shaded areas.

CHAPTER IV.

BREATHING FURTHER CONSIDERED THEORETICALLY AND PRACTICALLY.

WHEN one takes into account the large number of muscles employed in respiration, and remembers that these muscles must act in perfect harmony with each other if the great end is to be attained, he naturally inquires how this complex series of muscular contractions has been brought into concerted action so as to result in that physiological unity known as breathing.

It is impossible to conceive of such results being effected except through the influence of the nervous system, which acts as a sort of regulator throughout the whole economy. All the parts of the respiratory tract are supplied with nerves, which are of both kinds—those which carry nervous impulses or messages from and those which convey them to the nervous centres concerned; in other words, to and from the bodies of the nerve-cells whose extensions are termed nerves. These centres are the central offices where the information is received and from which orders are issued, so to speak.

The chief respiratory centre—*the* centre—is situated in that portion of the brain just above the spinal cord, in its continuation, in fact, and is known as the *medulla oblongata*, or *bulb*. But while this is the head centre, at which the ingoing (*afferent*) impulses are received and from which the outgoing (*efferent*) ones proceed, it makes use of many other collections of nerve-cells, or subordinate centres—*e.g.*, those whose nerve-extensions or nerve-fibres proceed from the spinal cord to the muscles of respiration.

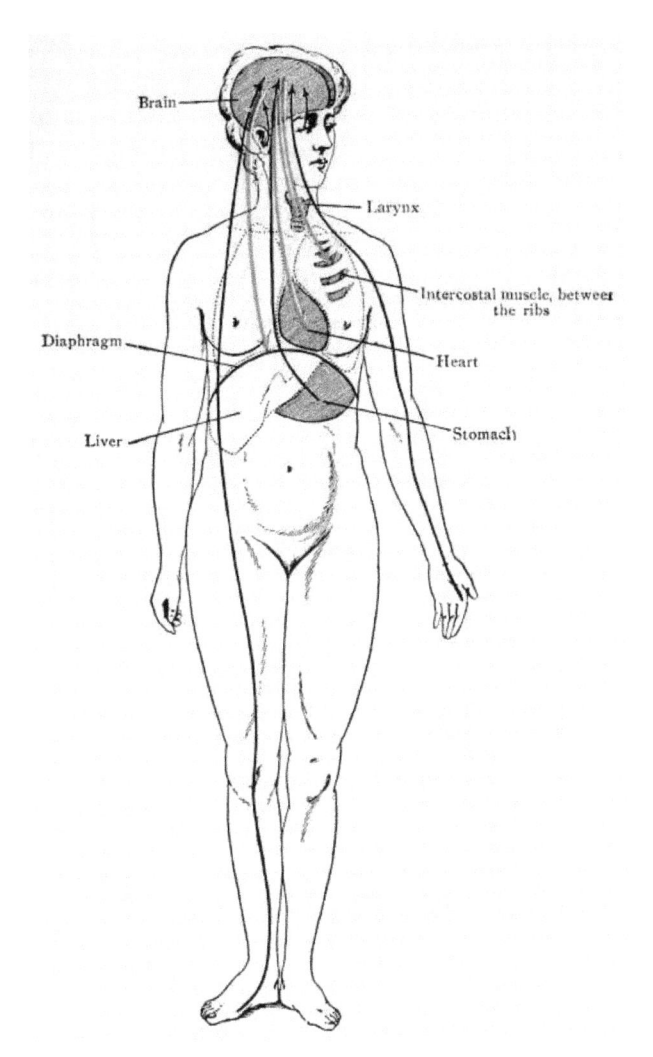

FIG. 15. The purpose of this diagram is to indicate the relation between ingoing (afferent) and outgoing (efferent) nervous influences (impulses)—in other words, to illustrate *reflex action*. The paths of the ingoing impulses are indicated by black lines, and those of the outgoing ones by red lines, the point of termination being shown by an arrow-tip. The result of an ingoing message may be either favorable or unfavorable. The nervous impulse that reaches the brain through the eye may be either exhilarating or depressing. The experienced singer is usually stimulated by the sight of an audience, while the beginner may be rendered nervous, and this may express itself in many and widely distant parts of the body. An unfavorable message may reach the diaphragm or intercostal muscles, and render breathing

shallow, irregular, or, in the worst cases, almost gasping. The heart or stomach, even the muscles of the larynx, the limbs, etc., may be affected, and trembling be the result. On the other hand, the laryngeal and other muscles may be toned up, and the voice rendered better than usual, as a result of applause—*i.e.*, by nervous impulses through the ear—or, again, by the sight of a friend. Even a very tight glove or a pinching shoe may suffice to hamper the action of the muscles required for singing or speaking. All this is a result of reflex action—*i.e.*, outgoing messages set up by ingoing ones—the "centre" being either the brain or the spinal cord. From all this it is evident that the singer or speaker must guard against everything unfavorable, to an extent that an ordinary person need not. The stomach, as the diagram is also meant to show, may express itself on the brain, and give rise, as in fact it often does, owing to indiscretion in eating, to unpleasant outward effects on the muscles required in singing or speaking. Of course, no attempt has been made in the above figure to express anatomical forms and relations exactly.

When all the ingoing impulses from the lungs, etc., are cut off, if respiration does not actually cease, it is carried out in a way so ineffective that life cannot be long sustained. It follows that as the muscular contractions necessary for the chest and other respiratory movements are dependent on the impulses passing in from the lungs, etc., breathing belongs to the class of movements known as reflex—chiefly so, at all events. It will thus be seen that respiration is a sort of self-regulative process, the movements being in proportion to the needs of the body. The greater the need for oxygen, the more are the nerve-terminals in the lungs and the centre itself stimulated, with, as a result, corresponding outgoing impulses to muscles.

As the respiratory centre is readily reached by impulses from every part of the body, like one who keeps open house, there are many different sorts of visitors, not all desirable. If, for example, a drop of a fluid that produces no special effect when on the tongue gets into the larynx, trachea, or lungs, the most violent coughing follows. This is one illustration of the *protective* character of many reflexes. This violent action of the respiratory apparatus is not in itself a desirable thing, because it disturbs if it does not exhaust, but it is preferable to the inflammation that might result if the fluid, a bread-crumb, etc., were to pass into the lungs.

In like manner, the deep breath and the "Oh!" that follow a fear-inspiring sight, a very loud noise, or a severe pinch of the skin, are examples of reflex action. They are quite independent of the will, though in some cases they may be prevented by it.

This reflex nature of breathing throws much light on many matters of great interest to the speaker and singer, some of which, as the formation of good habits of breathing, will be considered later. Unfortunately for the nervous débutant, his breathing is anything but what he could wish it. The pale face and almost gasping respiration, in the worst cases, are not unknown to the experienced observer. In such cases the preventive (*inhibitory*) influence of certain ingoing impulses is but too obvious. Such undesirable messages may pass in through the eyes when the young singer looks out on the throng that may either approve or condemn; or they may originate within, and pass from the higher part of the brain to the lower breathing centre. The beginner may have high ideals of art, and fear that they will be but ill realized in his performance. His ideals in this instance do not help but hinder, for they interfere with the regular action of the breathing centre. A few deep breaths after the platform has been reached greatly help under such circumstances. It is also wise for the singer to avoid those songs that begin softly and require long breaths and very evenly sustained tones. It is much better to begin with a selection that brings the breathing organs into fairly active exercise at once. One feeble, hesitating, or otherwise ineffective tone is in itself a stimulus of the wrong kind, sending in unfavorable messages which are only too apt to reach the breathing and other centres concerned in voice-production; but of this subject of nervousness again.

It is important to realize that sounds, whether musical or the reverse, are produced by the outgoing stream of breath, by an expiratory effort. Breath is taken in by the voice-producer in order to be converted into that expiratory force which, playing on the vocal bands, causes them to vibrate or pass into the rapid movements which give rise to similar movements of the air in the cavities above the larynx, the resonance-chambers, and on which the final result as regards sound is dependent. Important as is inspiration to the speaker and singer, expiration is much more so. Many persons fill the lungs well, but do not understand how to husband their resources, and so waste breath instead of converting every particle into sound, so to speak. After the larynx has been studied the importance of the expiratory blast will be better understood.

For the voice-user, it cannot be too soon realized that *all breath that does not become sound is wasted*, or, to express the same truth otherwise, the sole purpose of breathing is to cause effective vibrations of the vocal bands. In these two words, *effective vibrations*, lies the whole secret of voice production, the whole purpose of training, the key to the highest technical results, the cause of success or failure for those who speak or sing.

Before the larynx, the apparatus that produces sound-vibrations, can be effectively employed, the source of power, the bellows, must be developed. To some Nature has been generous—they have large chests; to others she has given a smaller wind-chest, but has perhaps compensated by providing an especially fine voice-box. Happy are they who have both, and thrice happy those who have all three requirements: a fine chest, a well-constructed larynx, and beautifully formed resonance-chambers. If with all these there are the musical ear and the artistic temperament, we have the singer who is born great. These are the very few. To most it must be—if greatness at all—greatness thrust upon them, greatness the result of long and patient effort to attain perfect development. Indeed, even those with the most complete natural outfit can only reach the highest results of which they are capable by long and patient application. Those who do not believe in attainment only through labor would do well to abandon an art career, as there is already a great deal too much poor speaking and bad singing.

CHAPTER V.

BREATHING WITH SPECIAL REGARD TO PRACTICAL CONSIDERATIONS.

THE first great requisite for a voice-user is a well-developed chest; the next, complete control of it, or, to put it otherwise, the art of breathing, as briefly explained above.

The chest may be large enough, yet not be, in the physiological sense, developed. The voice-user is a sort of athlete, a specialist whose chest muscles must be strong and not covered up by very much superfluous tissue in the form of fat, etc. Whatever the public may think of the goodly form, the singer must remember that fat is practically of no use to any one in voice-production, and may prove a great hindrance, possibly in some cases being a coöperative cause of that *tremolo* so fatal to good singing.

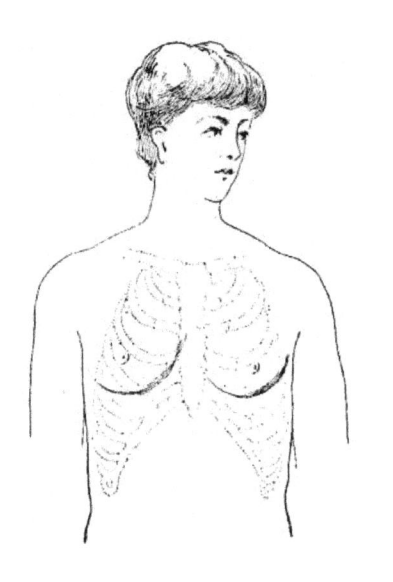

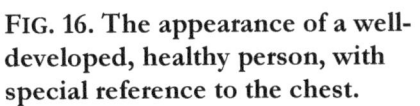

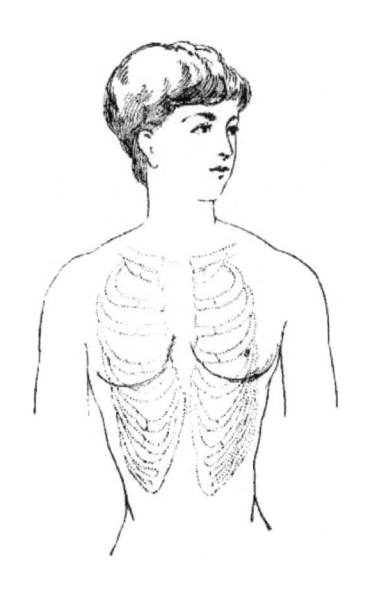

FIG. 16. The appearance of a well-developed, healthy person, with special reference to the chest.

FIG. 17. The appearance of the chest after undue compression, as with corsets.

The voice-user should eschew ease and take plenty of exercise, but most of all must he use those forms of exercise which develop the breathing apparatus and tend to keep it in the best condition. Walking, running, and hill climbing are all excellent, but do not in themselves suffice to develop the chest to the utmost.

To the beginner the following exercises are strongly recommended. They are highly important for all, whether beginners or not, who would have the best development of the breathing apparatus.

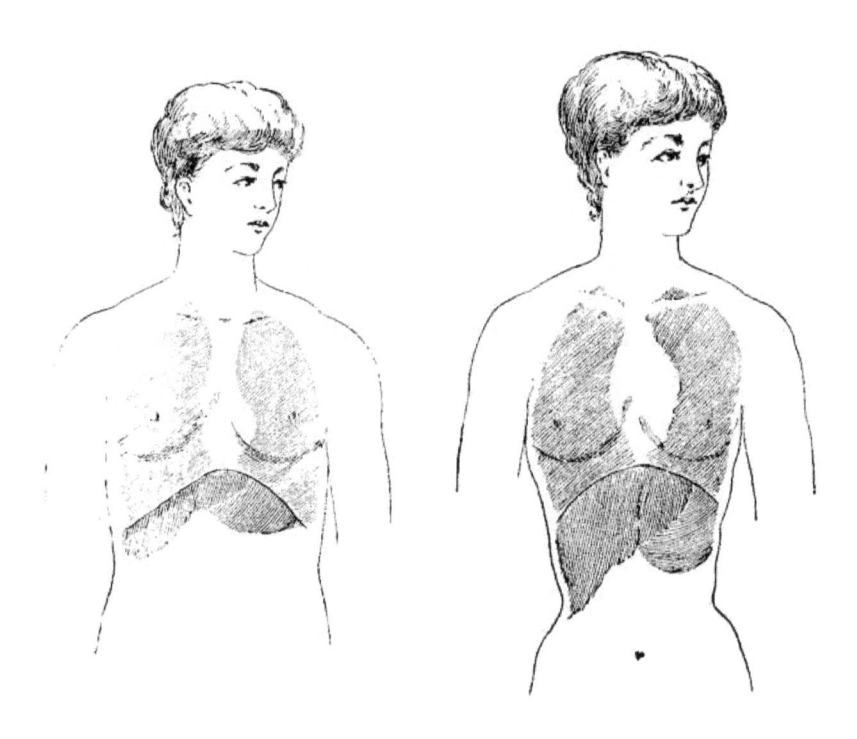

FIG. 18. In this figure, the dark curved line in the middle is meant to represent the position, etc., of the diaphragm, beneath which, and fitting closely to it, are the liver, stomach, and other abdominal organs, in this case not pressed upon or injured in any way. This represents the normal human being.

FIG. 19. A condition the reverse of that represented in the preceding. The vital organs are pressed upon, with results some of which are obvious; others equally serious are not such as appear to the eye.

Deep breathing, such a use of the respiratory organs as leads to the greatest possible expansion of the chest, should be learned and practised, if not absolutely before vocal exercises are attempted, at all events as soon after as possible. As in all cases where muscles are employed, the exercise should be *graduated*. It may be even harmful to attempt to fill the chest to its utmost capacity at once. It is better to breathe very moderately for several days. Any such symptoms as dizziness or headache accompanying or following the exercises indicate that they have been too vigorous, too long continued, or carried out under unsuitable conditions. Above all must the air be pure, and the body absolutely unhampered—most of all, the chest—by any form of clothing. Last century most ladies and some men applied to the chest a form of apparatus known as corsets, under the mistaken belief that they were for women a necessary support and improved the figure. They no doubt were responsible for much lack of development, and feeble health, and, as has been proved by examination of the body after death, led to compression of the liver and other organs. No voice-user should use such an effective means of preventing the very thing he should most desire, a full and free use of the breathing apparatus.

Before carrying out the exercises suggested or others equally good, the student is recommended to be weighed, and especially to have the chest carefully *measured*. This can be done with sufficient accuracy by the use of a tape-measure. It will be well to take the circumference a few inches above and below a certain point, so that it may be ascertained that the chest expands in every region. The measurements should be taken under the following conditions:

1. The chest should be almost or wholly divested of clothing.

2. Its circumference is to be ascertained—(*a*) when the breath has been allowed to pass out gently, and before a new breath is taken; (*b*) with the deepest possible inspiration; (*c*) after the deepest possible expiration, which has been preceded by a similar inspiration.

After about three weeks the individual should be again measured, by the same person, in exactly the same way, in order to learn whether there has been development or not, and, if so, how much. It is important that the measurements should be made at exactly the same horizontal planes, and with this end in view it is desirable to put a small mark of some kind on the chest, which may remain till the next measurements are made.

The method of breathing recommended is as follows:

1. Inhale very slowly through the nostrils, with closed mouth, counting mentally one, two, three, four, etc., with regularity.

2. Hold the breath thus taken, but only for a short time, counting in the same manner as before.

3. Exhale slowly, still counting.

After a few moments' rest the exercise may be again carried out in the same way. These exercises may be in series, several times a day.

The following warnings are especially to be observed:

1. Never continue any exercise when there is a sense of discomfort of any kind whatever. Such usually indicates that it is being carried out too vigorously.

2. Increase the depth of the inspirations daily, but not very rapidly.

3. The inspirations and expirations should both be carried out very slowly at first.

4. Cease the exercise before any sense of fatigue is experienced. Fatigue is Nature's warning, and should be always obeyed. It indicates that the waste products which result from the use of the muscles are accumulating and proving harmful.

After a week of such exercises the following modification of them is recommended:

1. Inhale with the lips slightly apart.

2. Gradually increase the length of the time the breath is held, but let it never exceed a few seconds.

3. Through open lips allow the breath to pass out, but with extreme slowness. The student should try to increase this last, somewhat, daily, as it is above all what is required in singing, and also in speaking, though to a somewhat less degree—a slow, regulated expulsion of the breath.

If when the chest is full of air the subject gently raises the arms over the head, or directs them backward, he will experience a sense of pressure on the chest. If this be carefully done, its effect is to strengthen, and it is especially valuable for those inclined to stoop. The recommendation to inspire through the open lips applies only when one is in a room, or in the open air when it is warm enough and free from dust. But the student should learn to inspire through the slightly open mouth, as to breathe through the nose in speaking, and especially in singing, is objectionable for several reasons which can be better explained later; so that the rule is to *breathe through the nose when not using the voice, and through the mouth when one does.*

Though all the exercises thus far referred to tend to develop the diaphragm and abdominal muscles, these may be strengthened by special exercises. The diaphragm is the soft floor of the chest, and must at once bear the strain of the air that acts on the approximated vocal bands, and assist in applying that pressure with just the amount of force required, and no more; hence it is important that this muscle be both strong and under perfect control. This large central muscle is probably not only the most generally effective of all the respiratory muscles, but has an action more precise and often more delicate, more nicely controlled, than that of any other. It is possible to make very powerful movements of this muscle, and an exercise that will cause it to descend deeply and remain in a tense condition is valuable. To effect this, one pushes it down as far as possible, and holds it there for a few seconds, then permits it to relax gradually. The extent to which this is successful can be inferred from the degree to which the abdominal wall bulges forward.

The sudden though slight movements required in those forms of vocalization that bear more or less resemblance to what vocalists term *staccato*, and which are so effective in dramatic speaking and singing, can be prepared for by larger but sudden movements of the diaphragm, as when one taking a full breath imitates coughing movements, but in a regular and measured way, the throat being used but little. At the same time, or separately, the abdominal muscles may be effectively exercised by being drawn in and thrust out with considerable force.

None of these movements are elegant—they scarcely put one in an artistic light; but they are highly effective in strengthening parts every voice-user must employ.

To furnish adequate support for the diaphragm and chest in a very vigorous use of the voice, as in the most trying passages a tragic actor has to speak or a vocalist to sing, the abdominal muscles must remain more or less tense, and to do so effectually they must have strength beyond that possessed by the corresponding muscles in ordinary persons; hence the desirability of employing special exercises to increase their vigor. Hill climbing and bicycling also tend to this end, but the latter is for many reasons not a form of exercise to be recommended to one who wishes to attain the highest results with the voice. Wind, dust, a stooping position, excessive heat of the body, etc., are all among the many factors of risk for the delicate vocal mechanism.

As the expiratory blast is so important in voice-production, the exercises above recommended should be followed by others in which this principle is specially recognized.

1. Inspire so as to fill the chest to the fullest with considerable rapidity; then allow the breath-stream to pass out with the utmost slowness.

2. Fill the chest with special reference to its lower or its upper part, as desired, and very rapidly, letting the breath flow out slowly.

SUMMARY.

The primary purpose of respiration in all animals is the same—namely, to furnish oxygen and remove carbon dioxide (carbonic acid). The lowest animals, as the amœba, breathe by the whole surface of the body. In all vertebrates the anatomical mechanism is essentially the same: a membrane (covered with flat cells) in which the blood is distributed in the minutest blood-vessels (capillaries). Respiration is finally effected in the tissues (cells) of the body. The more active the animal, or the higher in the scale, the more need of frequent interchange between the air, the blood, and the tissues.

The respiratory organs in mammals are the mouth, nose, larynx, trachea, bronchial tubes, and lung-tissue or air-cells proper. The windpipe is made up of cartilaginous rings completed by membrane, muscle, etc. (behind). The bronchial tubes are the continuation of the windpipe, and branch tree-like until they become very fine. The air-cells are built round these latter. The lung-tissue is highly elastic. The lungs are made up of an elastic membrane, covered with flat cells, and very abundantly supplied with a mesh-work of the finest blood-vessels. The whole of the respiratory tract as far as the air-cells is lined by mucous membrane.

The air consists essentially of 21 parts of oxygen and 79 parts of nitrogen, with a variable quantity of watery vapor. Only a small portion of the total oxygen of the air is removed before it is exhaled. The respiratory act consists of (1) inspiration, and (2) expiration; the latter is of a little longer duration than the former. The rate of breathing in man is from 14 to 18 per minute, in the resting state, or about one respiration to three or four heart-beats. The quantity of air inspired depends on (1) the size of the thorax, and (2) the extent of its movements. These are effected solely by muscular contractions, and give rise to an increase in all the diameters of the thorax. The lungs are closely applied (but not attached) to the inside of the chest wall, and remain so under all circumstances. When the chest cavity is enlarged by inspiration, the air, pressing down into the elastic lungs, expands them as much as possible, that is, as much as the chest walls will allow; but the lungs are never at any time either filled with or emptied of air to their utmost capacity. At most, the amount of expansion is very moderate.

The Quantity of Air in the Lungs.

1. The quantity of air inspired in quiet breathing is about 20-30 cubic inches.

2. The quantity that can be added to this by a deep inspiration is about 100 cubic inches.

3. The quantity that can be expelled by a forcible expiration is about 100 cubic inches.

4. The quantity that cannot be expelled at all is about 100 cubic inches.

The above are named: (1) The tidal air; (2) complemental air; (3) supplemental air; (4) residual air. The quantity that can be expelled by the most forcible expiration after the most forcible inspiration, that is, the air that can be moved, indicating the "vital capacity," is about 225-250 inches.

The chest is enlarged by the muscles of inspiration, the principal of which is the diaphragm or midriff. This muscle (tendinous in the centre) is attached to the spinal column (behind) and to the last six or seven ribs. When it contracts it becomes less domed upward, and is pressed down more or less on the contents of the abdomen; hence the walls of the latter move outward. During ordinary inspiration the lower ribs are steadied by other muscles, so that no indrawing of these ribs takes place, but a very forcible expiration makes such indrawing very noticeable. In addition to the enlargement of the chest by the descent of the diaphragm, the ribs are elevated and everted by the muscles attached to them, with the total result that the chest cavity is enlarged in all its three diameters during inspiration. The first rib is fixed by muscles from above. During extremely forced inspiration a large proportion of all the muscles of the body may act. Ordinary expiration is the result largely of the elastic recoil of the chest walls, only a few muscles taking part. The diaphragm ascends and becomes more domed. During forced expiration many other muscles are called into action. It is of importance for the singer and speaker to note: (1) That the chest cavity should be increased in all its directions; (2) that the muscular action should be easy and under perfect control, but also vigorous when required; (3) that the breath be taken through the nostrils when the individual is not actually vocalizing or about to do so; (4) that the breath be kept in or let out in the proportion required.

Breathing is a reflex or involuntary act. The respiratory centre, consisting of an expiratory and inspiratory division, is situated in the bulb, or medulla oblongata, the portion of the brain just above the spinal cord. All the ingoing nervous impulses affect respiration through the outgoing impulses that pass along the nerves to the muscles; that is, the ingoing impulses pass up by the nerves from the lungs to the centre, and thence along other nerves to the respiratory muscles. The condition of the blood determines the activity of the respiratory centre, but the incoming impulses regulate this activity. The respiratory centre can be approached from every part of the body.

Hygiene.

Every thing that favors the full and free expansion of the chest in a pure atmosphere is favorable, and the reverse unfavorable. Corsets are against the laws of beauty, are unnecessary for support, and may by compression injure and displace important organs, as the liver, stomach, etc.; and must interfere with the fullest expansion of the chest. They have militated against the physical, and indirectly the moral and mental advancement of the race.

Practical Exercises.

I. Measurements of the chest.

II. Exercises to strengthen muscles, promote complete expansion, regulate inflow and outflow of air, etc.

1. (*a*) Inspiring slowly, with counting.
(*b*) Holding.
(*c*) Expiring slowly, with counting.

2. The same, holding longer.

3. The same, with shorter inspiration and longer expiration. Gradually diminish first and lengthen last.

4. Breathing through open lips.

5. Exercises to strengthen diaphragm.

6. Exercises to improve shape of chest and strengthen muscles.

7. Exercises to strengthen abdominal muscles.

CHAPTER VI.

THE SPECIAL VOICE-PRODUCING MECHANISM, THE LARYNX.

THE larynx, or voice-box, is not the sole voice-producing apparatus, as is often supposed, but it is of great, possibly the greatest, importance. In describing the parts of this portion of the vocal mechanism the author deems it wiser to use the terms commonly employed by anatomists and physiologists, as others are awkward and inadequate. Moreover, there is this great advantage in learning the technical names of structures, that should the reader desire to consult a special work on anatomy in reference to this or other important organs, he will find in use the same terms as he has himself already learned. Such are, as a matter of fact, not difficult to learn or remember if one knows their derivation or other reason for their employment. All the muscles of the larynx have names which are not arbitrary but based on the names of the structures to which they are attached, so that one has but to know their connections and the names of the solid structures, which are few, to have a key to the whole nomenclature.

When one is not using the voice the larynx is simply a part of the respiratory apparatus, but when one phonates this organ assumes a special function for which specific structures are essential. As sound is caused by vibrations of the air, and these may be set up by vibrations of the vocal cords, it may with absolute correctness be said that the whole larynx exists for the vocal bands so far as voice-production is concerned. Such a view renders the study of the larynx much more interesting and rational; one is then engaged in working out that solution of a problem which Nature has accomplished.

The vocal cords, we can conceive, might be either relaxed or tightened, and lengthened or shortened, or both, and beyond that we can scarcely understand how they might have been modified so as to be effective in the production of sounds of different pitch. As a matter of fact, these are the methods Nature has employed to accomplish her purpose. For each vocal cord one fixed point, and only one, is required. We know of only one method in use by Nature to cause movement in living structures—viz., contraction, and muscle is the tissue which above all others has that property; hence the movements of the vocal cords are brought about by muscles. But both for the attachment of the muscles and the vocal cords themselves solid, relatively hard structures are required. Bone would prove too unyielding, but cartilage, or gristle, meets the case exactly. The entire framework of the larynx—its skeleton, so to speak—is made up of a series of cartilages united together so as to ensure sufficient firmness with pliability.

The cartilages have been named from their shape, as that appealed to the original observers, and the terms employed are of Greek origin. The largest and strongest is the *thyroid* (*thureos*, a shield) cartilage, which resembles somewhat two shields put together in front without any visible joint, and open behind but presenting a strongly convex surface externally, in front and laterally. "Front" (anterior) and "back" (posterior) always refer in anatomy to the subject described, and not to the observer's position. In observing another's larynx the subject observed and the observer naturally stand front to front, and it is impossible to see or touch the back of the larynx as it is covered behind by the other structures of the neck.

This thyroid, the largest of the cartilages, is attached to the hyoid or tongue bone above by a membrane, so that the whole larynx hangs suspended from this bone by a membrane, though not by it alone, for muscles are attached to it which also serve for its support. It is of practical importance to remember that the larynx is free to a very considerable extent, otherwise it would go ill with the voice-producer in the vigorous use of the voice, not to mention the advantages of mobility as well as pliability in the movements of the neck generally.

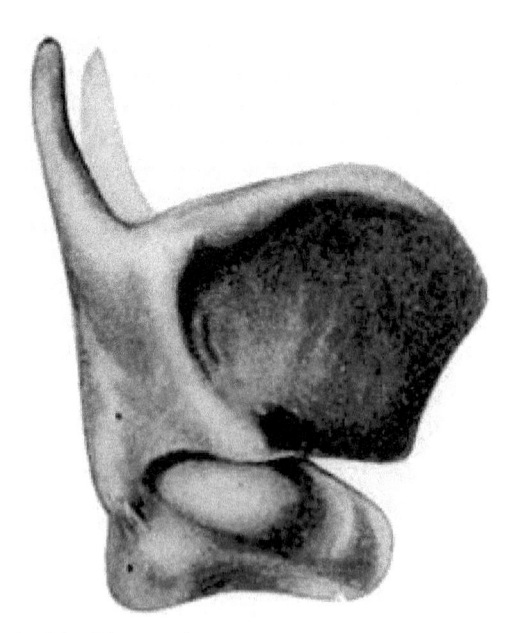

FIG. 20 (Spalteholz). Shows the thyroid cartilage above and the cricoid below both viewed from the side. The anterior surface is turned toward the right.

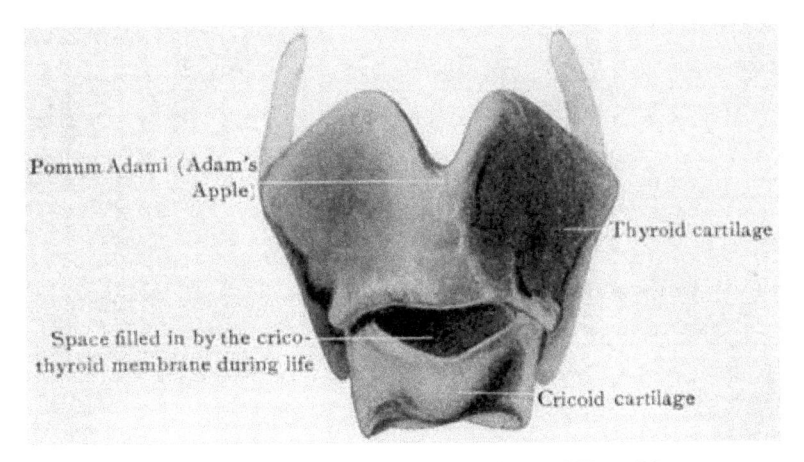

FIG. 21 (Spalteholz). A front view of FIG. 20.

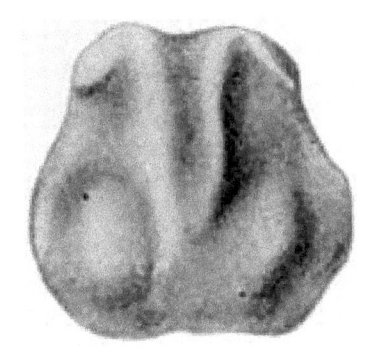

FIG. 22 (Spalteholz). The back or signet surface of the cricoid or ring cartilage, to which several muscles are attached.

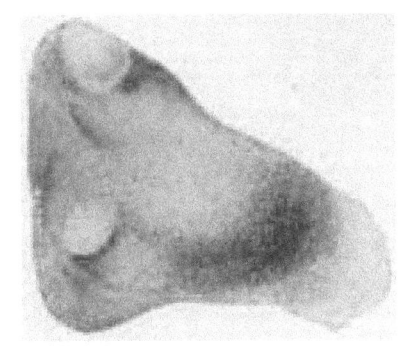

FIG. 23 (Spalteholz). The cricoid cartilage, seen from the side, and showing behind and laterally the articular or joint surfaces by which it connects with the thyroid below and the arytenoid cartilage above.

vocal process

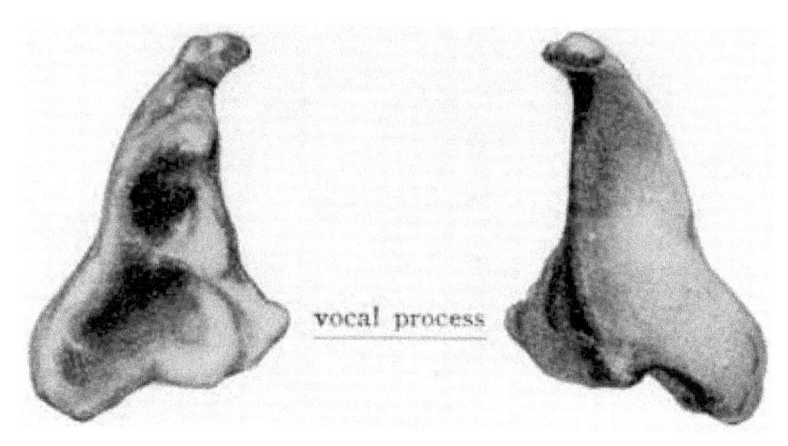

FIG. 24 (Spalteholz). Shows the arytenoid cartilages, the most important of all the cartilages of the larynx, inasmuch as to the part termed "vocal process" the vocal band is attached on each side. The movements of the vocal bands are nearly all determined by the movements of these cartilages, which have a swivel-like action. In the above the front surfaces are turned toward each other.

The *cricoid* (*krikos*, a signet-ring) is the cartilage next in size. It is situated below the thyroid cartilage, with which it is connected by a membrane, the crico-thyroid. The wider part of this signet-ring is situated behind, where it affords attachment to large muscles. It also furnishes a base of support for two very important structures, the *arytenoid* (*arutaina*, a ladle) cartilages. As the vocal bands are attached behind to them, and as they have a large degree of mobility, they are from a physiological point of view the most important of all the solid structures of the larynx.

There are two pairs of small bodies, the *cartilages of Santorini*, or *cornicula laryngis*, surmounting the arytenoids, and the *cuneiform*, or *cartilages of Wrisberg*, situated in the folds of mucous membrane on each side of the arytenoids; but these structures are of little importance.

The whole of the inner surface of the larynx is lined with mucous membrane, though that covering over the true vocal bands is very thin, and so does not cause them to appear red like the false vocal bands, which are merely folds of the mucous membrane. However, the true vocal bands may become red and thickened when inflamed, because of this same mucous membrane, which, though ordinarily not visible to the eye, becomes so when the condition referred to is present; for inflammation is always attended by excess in the blood supply, with a prominence of the small blood-vessels resulting in a corresponding redness. The same thing happens, in fact, as in inflammation of the eyes or the nose, both of which are more open to observation. Bearing this in mind one can readily understand why in such a condition, which is often approached if not actually present in the case of "a cold," the voice becomes so changed. Such vocal bands are clumsy in movement, as the arms or any other part would be if thus swollen. The plain remedy is rest, cessation of function—no speaking, much less attempts at singing. Like the nose the larynx, and especially the vocal bands, may be catarrhal, and such a condition may call for medical treatment before the speaker or singer can do the most effective vocal work.

While the *false vocal bands* have little or nothing to do with phonation directly, they do serve a good purpose as protectors to the more exalted true vocal bands. When coughing, swallowing, vomiting, holding the breath tightly, etc., these folds of mucous membrane close over the true bands, often completely, and thus shut up for the moment the whole of that space between the bands known as the glottis, or glottic chink, to which reference was made in a previous chapter as the space through which the air finally gains access to the lungs.

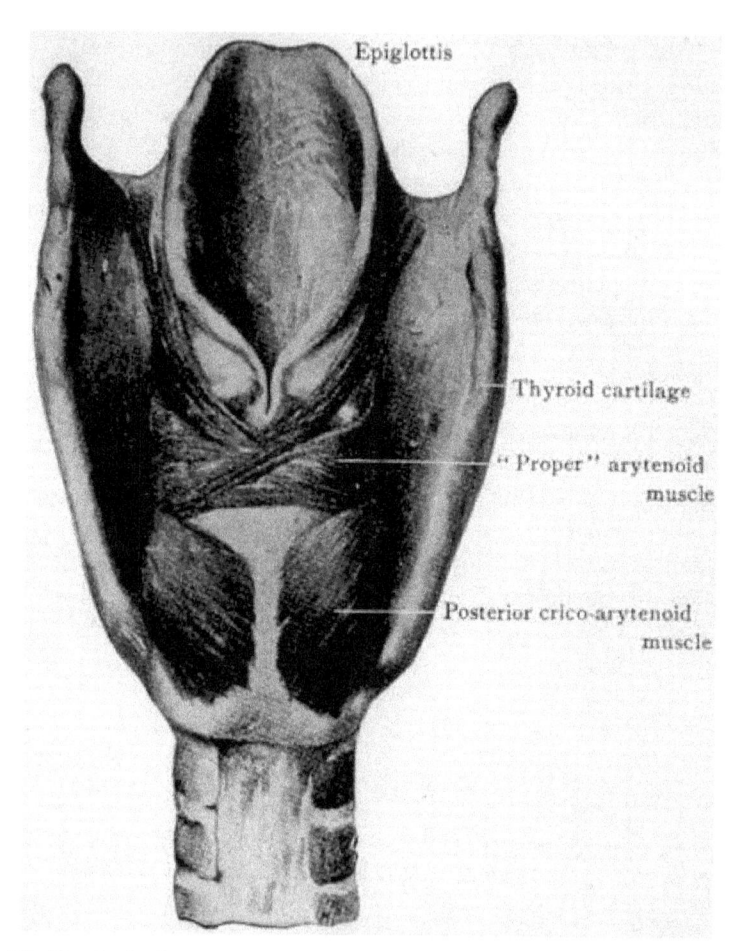

FIG. 25 (Spalteholz). A view of the larynx from behind. Several of the muscles are well shown, of which the two indicated above are of the most importance. The arytenoideus proprius tends to bring the cartilages from which it is named, and therefore the vocal bands, toward each other; while the posterior crico-thyroid, from its attachments and line of pull, tends to separate these and lengthen the vocal bands.

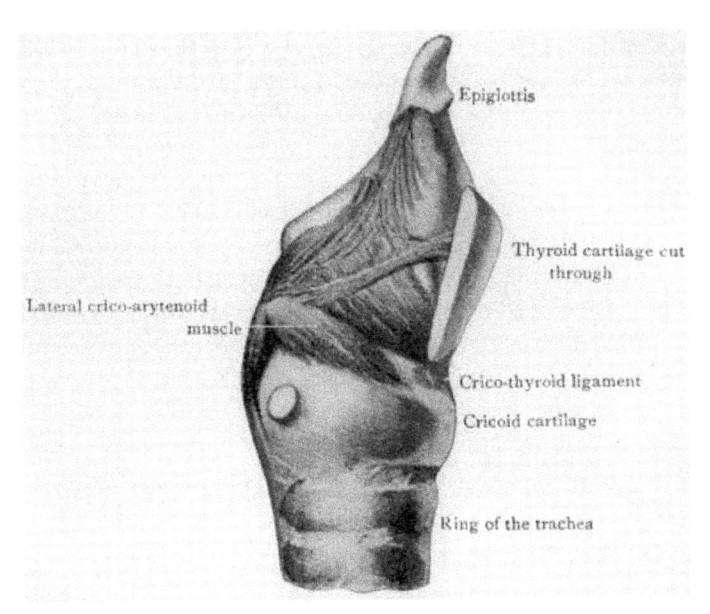

FIG. 26 (Spalteholz). Showing structures as indicated above. The mucous membrane, that naturally covers all parts within the vocal mechanism, has been dissected away to show the muscles.

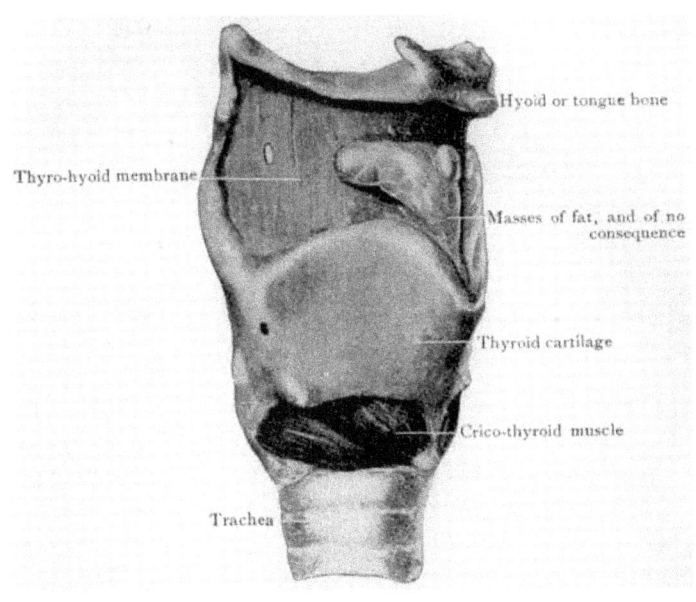

FIG. 27 (Spalteholz). Showing the parts indicated above; and of these the crico-thyroid muscle is to be especially observed. The oblique (especially so in the posterior part) direction of its fibres is evident, so

that when it contracts, it must pull up the ring cartilage in front, and so tilt back its hinder portion and with it the arytenoid cartilages, and so lengthen and tense the vocal bands, as in the utterance of low tones.

The true vocal cords (which, because of having some breadth and being rather flat, are better termed vocal bands) are composed largely of *elastic tissue*. The reader may be familiar with this structure, which is often to be found in the portions of the neck of the ox that the butcher sells as soup beef. It is yellow in color, and stretching it has furnished many a boy with amusement. It is so unmanageable when raw that when it falls to the dog he usually bolts it, the case being otherwise hopeless. Such elastic tissue is, however, the very material for the construction of vocal bands, as they require to be firm yet elastic.

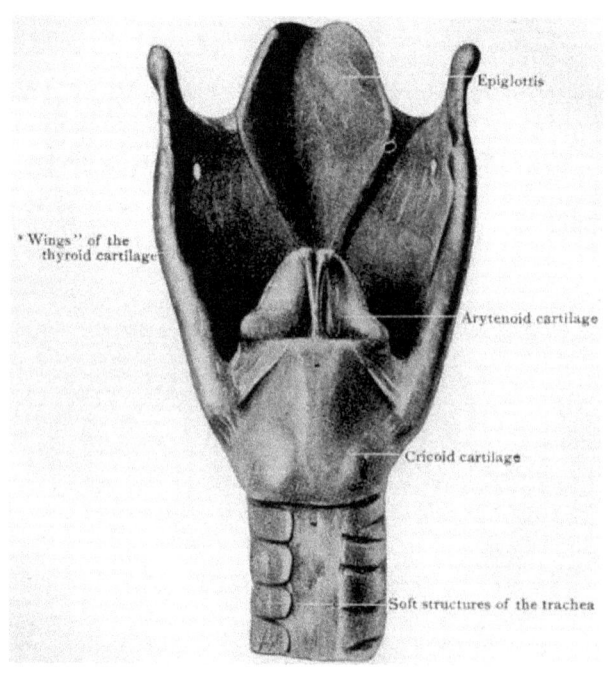

FIG. 28 (Spalteholz). A back (posterior) view of the larynx, etc. Note how the arytenoid cartilages rest on the cricoid; how the epiglottis overhangs, as its name implies, the glottis; and that the posterior part of the windpipe is closed in by soft structures, including (unstriped) muscle.

It is important to remember the relative position of parts and to bear in mind that most of the laryngeal structures are in pairs. To this last statement the thyroid and cricoid cartilages and the epiglottis are exceptions, being single.

Of the *epiglottis*, a flexible cartilage, it is necessary to say little, as its function in voice-production, if it have any, has never been determined. It hangs as a flexible protective lid over the glottis, and food in being swallowed passes over and about it. It no doubt acts to keep food and drink out of the larynx, yet in its absence, in some cases, owing to disease, no very great difficulty was experienced, probably because certain muscles acted more vigorously than usual and tended to close up the glottic chink.

The following simple diagram will, it is hoped, make the relative position of parts plain so far as the anterior (front) attachments of parts to the thyroid cartilage are concerned. It will be understood that the inner anterior surface is meant, and that by "middle line" is intended the middle line of the body, the imaginary vertical diameter passing like a plumb-line from the middle plane of the head, let us suppose, downward just in front of the larynx.

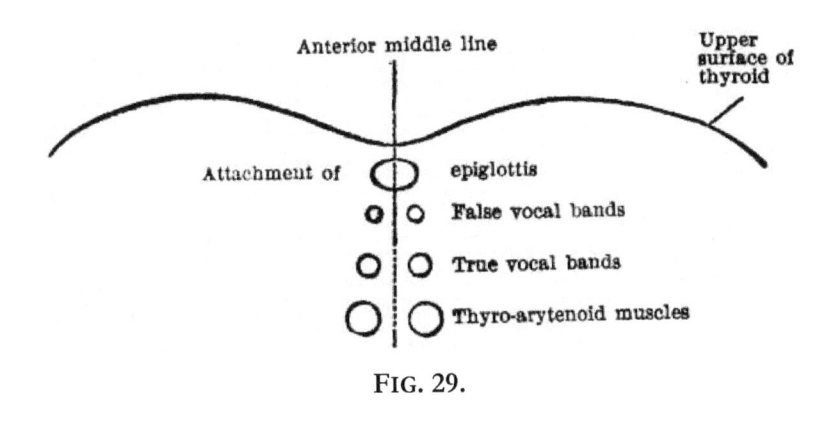

FIG. 29.

The angle made above and in front where the two wings of the thyroid cartilage meet is termed *Adam's apple* (*Pomum Adami*), and in some cases, mostly males, is very prominent. Adam's apple has in itself, however, no special significance in voice-production.

The little concavity between the false vocal bands above and the true vocal bands below is termed the *ventricle of the larynx*. It allows of more space for the free movements of the bands, especially those more important in voice-production.

The vocal bands are attached behind to the projecting angle of the base of the arytenoid cartilage, which is itself somewhat triangular in shape, the base of the triangle being downward and resting on the upper and posterior (back) surface of the cricoid cartilage, with which it makes a free joint, so that it can move swivel-like in all directions. This is most important, because through it is explained the fact that the vocal bands may be either tensed and lengthened or relaxed and shortened.

The muscles act on these movable cartilages, and nearly all the changes in the vocal bands are brought about through the alterations in position of the arytenoid cartilages, to which they are attached behind.

Before describing the muscles of the larynx, the reader is reminded of the order of structures from above downward, in front, which is as follows:

The hyoid bone.
The thyro-hyoid membrane.
The thyroid cartilage.
The crico-thyroid membrane.
The cricoid cartilage.
The trachea.

The latter is connected with the cricoid cartilage by its membrane.

All the above structures can be felt in one's own person, the more readily if he be thin and have a long neck. The hyoid bone, or tongue-bone, is that hard structure just above the cricoid cartilage, and which one may easily demonstrate to be much more movable than the larynx itself. The tongue muscles are attached to it above, and from it, below, the larynx is suspended, as already explained.

The muscles of the larynx are best understood if the principle of antagonistic action already referred to be remembered. Speaking generally, the muscles are arranged *in pairs* which have an opposite or antagonistic action—viz.: (1) Those that open and close the glottis; (2) those that regulate the tension, or degree of tightness, of the vocal bands.

1. The muscles whose action tends to approximate the vocal bands—the *adductors*—are the *arytenoidēus proprius* and the *thyro-arytenoidēus*. The former is attached to the posterior or back surface of both arytenoid cartilages; the latter, as its name indicates, to the anterior and inner surface of the thyroid and the anterior lower surface or angle (*vocal process*) of the arytenoid.

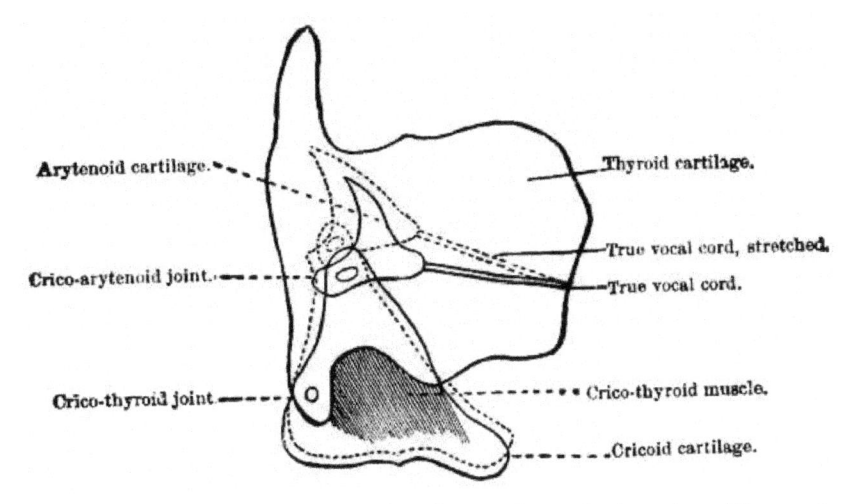

FIG. 30 (Chapman). Diagram showing action of crico-thyroid muscle, stretching of the vocal cords, and lengthening of them. The dotted lines indicate the position assumed when the muscle has contracted.

The opening or widening of the glottis is effected on each side (one muscle of the pair and its action being alone described in this and other cases) by the antagonist of these muscles, the *crico-arytenoidēus posticus*, whose attachments are exactly as indicated by the names—viz., to the posterior part of the two cartilages named. When reading the description of these or other muscles it is absolutely necessary to have a pictorial illustration or the real object before one. The pull of this muscle is from the more fixed point, as in all other cases; hence the force is applied in a direction from below and outward, with the result that the arytenoid cartilage is tilted outward, and with it the vocal band is moved from the middle line.

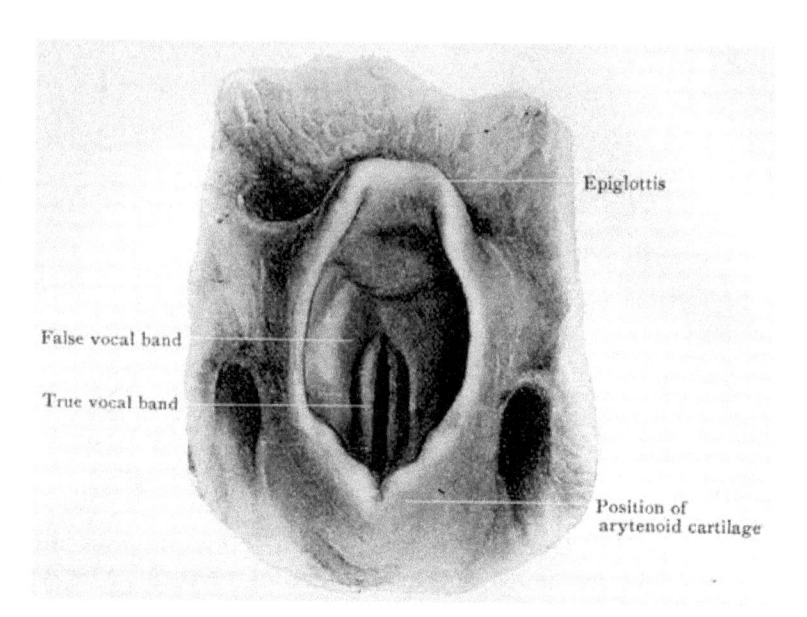

FIG. 31 (Spalteholz). View of the larynx as looked at from above. The illustration shows particularly well both the true and the false vocal bands. The true vocal bands are placed much as they are when a barytone is singing a very low tone. The part of the figure lowest on the page represents the back part of the larynx.

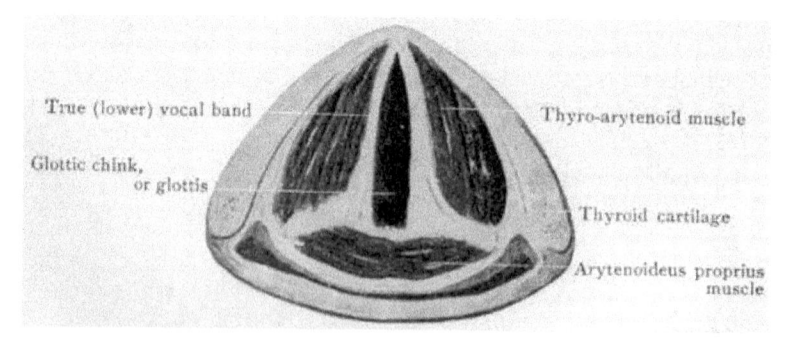

FIG. 32 (Spalteholz). A cross-section transverse to the larynx, such as can be readily made with a strong knife.

The *crico-thyroid* also tends to open the glottis. Just as the diaphragm is the most important muscle of breathing, so is the crico-thyroid the most important in ordinary speaking and in singing in the lower register. It is a relatively large and strong muscle with an oblique direction in the main, though it is composed in reality of several sets of fibres some of which are much more oblique in direction than others (Fig. 28). As its name indicates, its points of attachment are to the thyroid and the cricoid cartilages, but the most fixed point (*origin*) is its point of attachment to the larger cartilage; hence its direction of pull is from the thyroid, with the result that the anterior part of the cricoid is drawn up, the posterior part down, and the arytenoid cartilage, resting on the upper part of the cricoid, backward, so that the vocal band is rendered longer and more tense (see especially Fig. 29). It is important to note that this is the muscle most used in singing the lower tones of the scale, and that its action must necessarily cease, to a great extent, when a certain point in the pitch is reached, as there is a limit to the degree of contraction of all muscles; and, besides, the crico-thyroid space is of very moderate size, and the cricoid cartilage can ascend only within the limits thus determined. It thus follows that Nature has provided in the change of mechanism for a new register, which is nothing else than a change of mechanism with a corresponding change of function. It will be at once apparent that the claim that registers are an invention of men, and without foundation in nature, is without support in anatomy and physiology. The crico-thyroid is probably, however, of much more importance to tragic actors and barytones than to tenors or sopranos. This, however, is no excuse for the neglect of its development by the latter class, as often happens, for without it the best tones of the lower register are impossible. On the other hand, the elocutionists who prescribe for students practices that involve the excessive use of this muscle, with a cramped position of the vocal organs, the larynx being greatly drawn down, with the view of producing disproportionately heavy lower tones, must take no comfort from the above anatomical and physiological facts. Art implies proportion, and it was one of the ambitions of all the best actors in the golden age of histrionic art to have an "even voice"—*i.e.*, one equally good through the whole range required. The tragic actor, elocutionist, and public speaker, and the singer, whether soprano or bass, should neglect no muscle, though they may be justified in developing some in excess of others, but ever with a watchful eye on the weakest part.

2. The muscles which regulate the tension of the vocal bands are the following:

(*a*) The *thyro-arytenoidēus* (pair), which by tilting the arytenoid cartilages forward relaxes the tension of the vocal bands. When they act with the adductors—*e.g.*, the arytenoidēus proprius—the result must be relaxation and approximation behind, which implies a greater or less degree of shortening, as usually happens when a certain point in an ascending scale is reached in persons whose methods of voice-production have not been in some way modified, and a new register begins, which in most female voices is marked by a more or less distinct and abrupt alteration of the quality of the tone.

The crico-thyroids are the antagonists of the above-named muscles, and they may act either very much alone or, to some extent, in coöperation with the above, to regulate or steady their action; for in movements so complicated as those required for voice-production it is highly probable that we are inclined to reduce our explanations of muscular action to a simplicity that is excessive, and to appreciate but inadequately the delicacy and complexity of the mechanism and the processes involved. It is quite certain that in the production of the highest tones of a tenor or soprano several muscles coöperate, and one, especially, seems to be of great importance in the formation of such tones, most of all, perhaps, in high sopranos. The muscle referred to is the thyro-arytenoid already described. It is not only attached to the two cartilages indicated by its name, but also along the whole of the external or outer surface of the vocal band. It will be remembered that practically all the muscles are arranged in pairs, one on each side of the middle line. The muscle now under consideration, more, perhaps, than any other, is complex in its action. Apparently a very few of its fibres may act more or less independently of all the others at a particular moment and with a specific and very delicate result, a very slight change in pitch. Exactly how this is attained no one has as yet adequately explained; but it is doubtful whether any singer who does not possess a perfect control over this muscle can produce the highest tones of the soprano with ease and effectiveness. It is especially the muscle of the human birds of the higher flights.

(*b*) To these thyro-arytenoids, which for most singers and all speakers are probably chiefly relaxing in action, must be added as aiding in this function another pair, the *lateral crico-arytenoids*. They are situated between the cricoid and arytenoid cartilages, and the direction of action is obliquely from below and forward, upward, and backward, so that the arytenoids are brought forward and also approximated more or less, which involves relaxed tension, at least, possibly also shortening of the vocal bands.

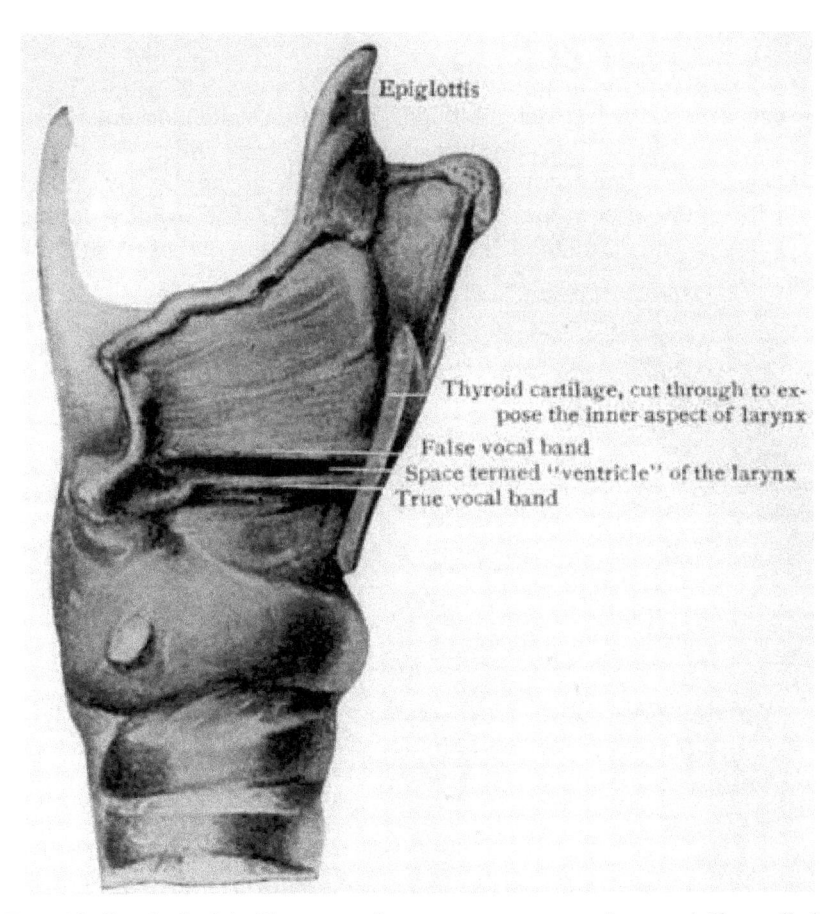

FIG. 33 (Spalteholz). Shows various structures, and especially well the false and the true vocal bands, with the space between them (ventricle of Morgagni), but which has no special function in phonation, unless it acts as a small resonance-chamber, which is possible. This space is a natural result of the existence of two pairs of vocal bands in such close proximity.

When a tenor or soprano singer reaches the upper tones, say about , or higher, there is considerable closing up in the larynx, much in the way in which the parts of the mouth are brought together in sucking. This is termed *sphincter action*, the mouth and the eyes being closed by such action, of which they are the most easily observed examples. As a result of this squeezing there is in some cases that reddening of the face and that tightness which is often felt uncomfortably, and which is *straining*, because when present in more than a very slight degree it is injurious, owing to congestion or accumulation of blood in the blood-vessels, with all the bad consequences of such a state of things. When the tightening does not go beyond a certain point it is normal—indeed, such sphincter action is inevitable; but it is the excess which is so common in tenors and others who strain for undue power, and to produce tones too high in pitch for their development or their method, which is so disastrous to the throat and to the best art also.

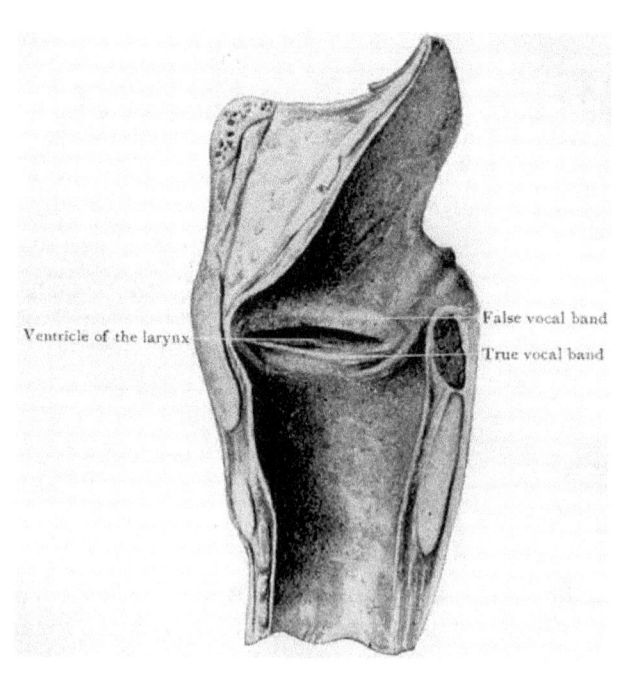

FIG. 34 (Spalteholz). Parts have been cut away to expose to view the whole of the inner surface of the larynx (lined with mucous membrane). An excellent view of the vocal bands and of the "ventricle" of the larynx, between them, is afforded.

When the vocal bands are in action their vibrations are accompanied by corresponding vibrations of the cartilages of the larynx—a fact of which any one may convince himself by laying his fingers on the upper part of the thyroid, especially when a low and powerful tone is produced. This vibration is not confined to the larynx, but extends to other parts—*e.g.*, the chest itself, for when one speaks or sings a distinct vibration of the chest walls can be felt, though the extent to which this is present is very variable in different persons. As an ascending scale is sung the larynx can be felt (by the fingers) to rise, and the reverse as the pitch is lowered. This is due partly to the action of those muscles attached to the larynx which are not connected with the movements of the vocal bands, and partly to the influence of the expiratory air-blast. The glottis, partially closed as it must be in phonation, presents considerable resistance to the outgoing stream of air, hence the upward movement of the larynx when it is left free, and not held down by muscular action.

In singing and speaking the larynx should be steadied, otherwise the "attack," or application of the air-blast to the vocal bands, cannot be perfect. On the other hand, it is obviously incorrect to attempt to hold the larynx always in the same position. Holding down this organ by main force, as in the production of the so-called "straw bass," is one of the surest methods of producing congestion and consequent disorders of the vocal organs; and the author wishes to warn all voice-producers against such unnatural practices. Students of elocution and young actors often sin in a similar way, and "clergyman's sore throat" is almost always due to this or some similar misuse of the vocal organs. One's own sensations and common sense should never be disregarded, however eminent the teacher who recommends unphysiological methods.

PRACTICAL CONSIDERATIONS.

When the student has read the above description of the structure and functions of the larynx, and studied the illustrations well, he will be prepared to deal with the subject in a practical manner, and without that it is feared his ideas will remain somewhat hazy.

First of all, he should try to find the parts mentioned in his own person, following this up by examinations of others, for which purpose children make good subjects, as they have usually necks that are not too deeply padded with fat, and they may be easily led to take the examinations as a sort of fun.

From above downward one feels in the middle line the parts in the order previously mentioned, beginning with the hyoid bone. One may learn that the larynx is movable and yielding, a hard structure covered with softer tissues, but what these are, and much more, can only be learned by examination of the larynx after it has been removed from some animal. Every butcher can provide the material for getting a sound, practical knowledge of the respiratory apparatus. He may be asked to supply the following:

1. A pig's "pluck"—*i.e.*, the "lights," or lungs, with the windpipe attached. The liver, heart, etc., are not required, though to observe the relations of the circulatory system—*i.e.*, the heart and large blood-vessels—to the respiratory system will be time well spent. Unless special instructions are given, the

larynx, which the butcher may term the "weezend," may be lacking or mutilated. It should be explained that this organ, with a part of the windpipe and the extreme back part of the tongue, and all below it, are required. For one sitting this single "pluck" will suffice, as it will serve for a general examination. The lungs may be dilated by inserting a tube into the windpipe, tying it in position, and blowing into it with greater or less force. It should be especially observed how suddenly the lungs collapse when the breath force is removed, as this illustrates well their *elasticity*. By cutting through the windpipe lengthwise and following it downward one learns how numerous are the branches of the bronchial tree, etc.

For a second sitting one should secure at least two specimens of the larynx of the pig or sheep, though the former is more like the human, and so the better on the whole. A case of dissecting instruments is not essential; a sharp pocket-knife will serve the purpose. In order that the student may have a clear idea of the cartilages, all the soft tissues must be cut or scraped away. It is necessary to exercise great care, or the membranes connecting the cartilages together will be cut through; and on the other hand, unless the work in the neighborhood of the arytenoids be cautiously done, these cartilages may be injured, and it is most important that their swivel-like action and their relations to the true vocal bands be observed. The glottic chink can be seen from above or below, and should be observed from both viewpoints. Its margins are formed by the true vocal bands.

Then, with the figures before him, the student should endeavor to isolate each of the muscles described. The muscles can always be recognized by their red color, but it is to be remembered that those on the inner surface of the larynx, such as the crico-arytenoid, are covered with mucous membrane, which after death is very pale. This can by careful dissection be removed, and if in doing this a small pair of forceps be employed, the work will be greatly facilitated. One must be very skilful indeed if he would get all the muscles "out," or well exposed to view as individuals, on a single specimen. Likely several will be required before entirely satisfactory results are reached, but these are well worth all the time and labor required. The action of the muscles can in some measure be demonstrated by pulling on them in the direction of their loosest attachment, though it must be confessed this is much more difficult in the case of most of the muscles of the larynx than in those of other parts of the body.

Should the specimens be very successfully dissected, it may be worth while to keep them for future observation, in rather weak alcohol (40 per cent.), in, say, a preserve jar.

All examinations of the vocal bands may leave the observer disappointed; he may fail to realize, most likely, how such wonderful results can be accomplished by structures so simple as those he sees before him. But when the laryngoscope is brought into use, then comes a revelation. This instrument will be described in the next chapter.

HYGIENE.

Some of the hygienic principles involved have already been referred to and illustrated, and others follow from the facts already set forth. It is very important for the voice-user to bear in mind that his larynx is a part of the respiratory tract, and that the whole of this region and the entire digestive tract, part of which is common to both, are lined with mucous membrane. If the nose be affected with catarrh, the throat does not usually long escape; and if the back of the mouth cavity (*pharynx*) be disordered, the vocal bands and other parts of the larynx are almost sure to be involved more or less.

The condition of the stomach is reflexly, if not by direct continuity through the mucous membrane, expressed in the throat generally; hence as experience shows, the voice-user cannot exercise too great care as to what and how much he eats, especially before a public appearance. He must know himself what best suits him, in this regard, to a degree that is necessary for few others.

When singing, more blood is sent to the organs used, hence the great danger of that excess of blood being retained in the parts too long, as might easily happen from pressure about the neck, etc. It is scarcely necessary to point out that draughts, cold rooms, etc., will also determine the blood from the skin inward, and set up that complicated condition of multiform evils known as "a cold." The obvious principle of prevention lies in keeping the body, and especially the neck, shoulders, and chest, warm after using the vocal organs in any way in public. To hand the singer a wrap after leaving the platform is always wise, and the judicious friend will see that conversation is not allowed, much less forced on the possibly breathless and wearied voice-user—a precaution that is probably more honored in the breach than in the observance, for in this as in other cases one's friends are sometimes his worst enemies.

SUMMARY.

The larynx is the most important organ in voice-production, and consists of cartilages, muscles, the vocal bands, true and false, membranes and ligaments, folds of mucous membrane, etc. It is situated between the hyoid (tongue) bone above and the trachea below. The cartilages are the (1) epiglottis, (2) thyroid, cricoid, arytenoid, the two small, unimportant cornicula laryngis, or cartilages of Santorini, surmounting the arytenoids, and the two cuneiform, or cartilages of Wrisberg, in the folds of mucous membrane on each side of the arytenoids.

The muscles are attached to the main cartilages. In addition to the muscles that are concerned with the movements of the vocal bands, others that hold the larynx in place or raise and lower it are attached *externally* to these, especially to the large thyroid cartilage. The epiglottis, the false vocal cords, the true vocal cords, and the thyro-arytenoid muscles are attached to the interior anterior surface of the thyroid in this order from above down.

The false vocal bands have no direct function in phonation. *The whole larynx, so far as phonation is concerned, may be said to exist for the true vocal bands.* They are attached close together to the internal and anterior surface of the thyroid in front and to the lower anterior angles (vocal processes) of the arytenoids behind. Between the false vocal bands above and the true vocal bands below there is a cavity (the ventricle of Morgagni). The false vocal bands are protective, and approximate closely during coughing, swallowing, etc.

It is very important to note that the arytenoid cartilages move freely on their base, swivel-like, so that nearly all the changes effected in the movements and tension of the vocal bands are brought about through alterations in the position of these cartilages; and this implies that all the muscles concerned are attached to them. From above down, in front, the order of structures is as follows:

Hyoid bone.
Membrane.
Thyroid cartilage.
Membrane.
Cricoid cartilage.
Trachea.

The hyoid bone is not a part of the larynx, but from it the larynx is suspended. The bone itself gives attachment to the muscles of the tongue. The glottis is the chink between the true vocal bands.

The muscles of the larynx may be divided into the following: (1) Those that open and those that close the glottis; (2) those which regulate the tension of the vocal bands. The latter include the (*a*) crico-thyroids, which tense and elongate them, (*b*) thyro-arytenoids, which relax and shorten them. The crico-thyroid may be considered the most important muscle of phonation, because it is so much used and so effective. By its action the cricoid is pulled up in front and down behind, so that the arytenoids are drawn back, and thus the vocal bands tensed and lengthened. The lateral crico-arytenoids and the thyro-arytenoids have the opposite effect—*i.e.*, they relax and shorten the vocal bands; hence when they come into play a new register begins. The thyro-arytenoids, attached along the whole length of the vocal bands externally, have a very important but not well-understood action in the production of the higher tones, and probably also of the falsetto.

The whole larynx is lined with mucous membrane, that covering the true vocal bands being very thin. The false vocal bands are made up chiefly of mucous membrane; the true vocal bands abound in elastic tissue. The larynx rises during the production of high tones, and during phonation its vibrations may be felt, as also those of the chest.

Practical.

1. Feel in your own person the parts of the larynx, etc., from above down.

2. Note the vibration of the larynx when a vowel is spoken or sung. A similar vibration of the chest walls may be felt by the hands laid over them.

3. Note the change of position of the larynx in singing a scale.

4. Dissect a pig's or sheep's pluck and some specimens of the larynx.

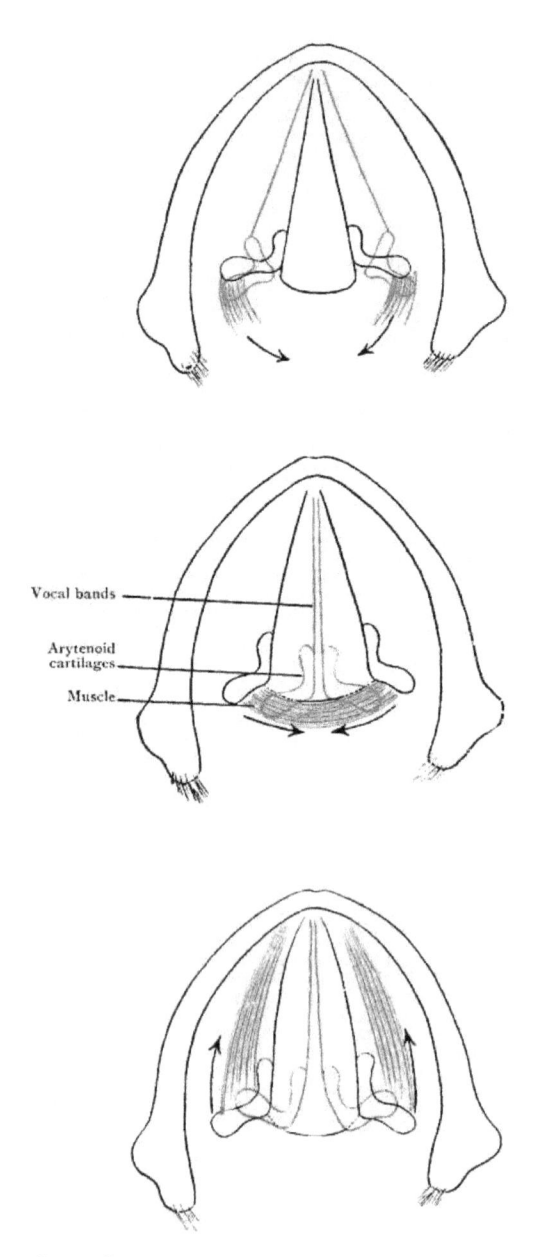

FIG. 35. These three figures illustrate perhaps more clearly the *action* of the muscles indicated FIGS. 26-34.

The arrows show the direction of the pull of the muscles. The result of this action is the new position of the cartilages and vocal bands, which is shown by red outlines. The muscle is also depicted in red. The heavier outer rim is to indicate the thyroid cartilage. By comparing the upper and the lowest figure it will be seen that they are opposites. Of course, in phonation the vocal bands are never so much separated as shown in the illustrations. Rather does the lower figure indicate a case of extreme separation due to a very deep inspiration. However, these illustrations are merely diagrams meant to indicate in a general way the manner of the working of parts. For exact pictures of the vocal bands and related parts, see Chapter VII.

CHAPTER VII.

SOUND—THE LARYNGOSCOPE—THE LARYNX RECONSIDERED.

BEFORE discussing our subject further it is desirable that some attention be given to a few of the fundamental principles of that department of physics termed *acoustics*, and which deals with the subject of sound. If the student has the opportunity to study this subject theoretically and practically, as it is set forth in some good work on physics, he will have no reason to regret the time spent. A deep knowledge of the laws of sound is not absolutely essential, or even highly necessary, for a sufficient understanding of the principles involved in voice-production. It is, however, all-important that a few facts and principles be thoroughly grasped.

For those who feel that they have the time for a study of acoustics, the author would especially recommend Tyndall's work on sound, in which the subject is treated with wonderful clearness and charm. What we endeavor now to bring before the reader we have found sufficient for nearly all the purposes of the voice-user.

An observer on the street, looking at a military band, notices certain movements of one member of the organization which result in what he termed the sound of the drum; but a deaf man by his side, though he sees the movements, hears nothing. This, being analyzed, means that the movements of the drummer's arm, conveyed through the drumstick to the membrane of the drum, give rise to movements in it which set up corresponding movements of the air within the drum, which again cause movements of the body of the instrument, the whole causing movements of the external air; and here the purely physical process ends. The movements other than muscular ones are not readily observed, but experiments not only prove that they exist, but demonstrate their nature, even to their exact rate of occurrence, their size, etc. These movements are termed *vibrations*, and, as has been indicated previously, they are the sole physical cause of sound. But that the latter is not due wholly to a physical origin is evident from the fact that sound for the deaf does not exist. It must, therefore, be a personal, a subjective experience, and as the sleeping, unconscious person does not necessarily hear a sound, the process is not wholly a corporeal or physiological process; it is finally an experience of the mind, the consciousness, and so is psychological as well as physiological.

The fact that sound has a physical basis in the vibrations of bodies, either solid, liquid, or gaseous, may be brought home to one in various ways. Concussion or shaking of some kind is essential to start these vibrations. The air is made up of its particles, and one being moved sets up, inevitably, movements in neighboring particles on all sides, hence vibrations travel in all directions; which explains why a sound in the street may be heard by those in every part of the street not too distant, and also in the upper rooms of the houses and below in the basements. This is an important fact for the singer or speaker to bear in mind. His purpose must be to set up vibrations that will travel with great perfection and rapidity in all directions.

The following experiments of a simple kind will serve to convince those who may not have given much attention to the subject that sound is due to movements of some object, which we term the sounding body, strictly that which starts the vibrations by its own movements or vibrations.

If a sufficiently flexible band of metal or a stiff piece of whalebone be fixed at one end in a vice, and then sharply pulled to one side and suddenly let go, a sound results. The same effect is produced when a tight cord or small rope is plucked at and then suddenly released. In each of these cases, if actual movements are not seen, a certain haze which seems to surround the object may be observed. The same can be seen when a tuning-fork is set into action by a bow, a blow, etc. In the case of the fork a graphic tracing (Fig. 36) can be readily taken on smoked paper, thus demonstrating to the eye that vibrations exist, that they occur with perfect regularity and with a frequency that can be measured.

FIG. 36 (Tyndall). **Illustrates how the vibrations of a tuning-fork are registered on a blackened (smoked) glass. In order that the movements of the fork shall be traced in the form of regular curves, the surface must be kept moving at a definite regular rate.**

A similar observation can be made in the case of stringed instruments. If pieces of paper be laid on the strings of a violin, and the bow then drawn across them, the bits of paper will fly off owing to the movements—*i.e.*, the vibrations—of the strings.

That a force applied at one end of several objects in a line or series causes an obvious effect at the other end, can be well illustrated in a simple way. If a number of individuals stand one behind another in a line, each with his hands laid firmly on the shoulders of the one next to him, and the person at the end be pushed, the force will be conveyed through all the intermediate individuals, and cause the unsupported person at the distant end to move. So is it with the particles of which the air is composed. The movements begun in the drum set up by contact corresponding movements or vibrations in the adjacent air, which ultimately reach the hearing subject's ear, thereby affect his brain, and are accompanied by that change in consciousness which he terms "hearing." It will be observed that these events constitute a chain, and a break anywhere will prevent a sound being heard; there is then, in fact, no sound.

Sounds are characterized by *pitch*, *volume*, and *quality*.

The *pitch* is determined by the number of vibrations that reach the ear within a certain time; the more numerous the sound-waves (vibrations) in a second, the higher the pitch.

FIG. 37 (Tyndall). Meant to illustrate vibrations. The impulse communicated by the ball pushed from the hand to all the intervening ones causes only the last to actually move bodily.

Animals differ a good deal as to the limits of hearing. Cats hear very high-pitched sounds, as of mice, that human beings may not notice, and it is likely that insects hear sounds altogether beyond the limit of the human ear. But it is wonderful how much human beings differ among themselves in regard to this matter. It has surprised the author to find that many persons cannot hear the high-pitched note of certain birds, as the wax-wing.

The lower limit, speaking generally, is for most persons 16 vibrations, and the highest 38000 vibrations a second, according to Helmholtz, hence the entire range of the human ear would be fully 11 octaves; but the practical range of musical sounds is within 40 and 4000 vibrations a second—*i.e.*, about 7 octaves—and, as is well known, even this range is beyond the appreciation of most persons, though as to this much depends on cultivation—attention to the subject extending over a considerable period of time.

The *volume*, or loudness, of a sound depends on the size of the vibrations, just as one feels a blow from a large object, other things being equal, more than from a small one. The ear drum-head is in the case of a large sound beaten, as it were, more powerfully. The singers that give us bigness of sound instead of quality belabor our ears, so to speak; they treat us as persons of mean understanding—dull intellects; the thing is essentially vulgar.

The *quality* of a sound is determined by the form of the vibrations. A sound of good quality is to the ear what a beautiful statue or picture is to the eye. As will be explained later, the form or quality depends largely on the shape, etc., of the resonance-chambers above the vocal bands.

Much discussion has taken place from time to time as to the nature of the larynx as a musical instrument, some being inclined to regard it as most closely allied to a stringed instrument, others to a wind-instrument. It has obviously points of resemblance to both, but the most recent researches make it clearer than ever that it is neither one nor the other, strictly speaking, but that it stands in a class by itself. It is, however, helpful, in considering many questions, to bear in mind its resemblances to both wind and stringed instruments. The vocal bands are not wholly free throughout their length, like the strings of a violin, nor do they bear any great resemblance to the reed of such an instrument as the clarinet, but as in the latter the force causing the vibrations is a blast of air. We have already pointed out that the vocal bands are set into vibration solely by the *expiratory* blast of air.

THE LARYNGOSCOPE.

The distinguished physiologist Johannes Müller demonstrated the working of the larynx by special experiments. He fixed into the windpipe a bellows, and showed, in the dead larynx, of course, that the blast from this source could cause the vocal bands to vibrate and thus produce sounds, which by varying the strength of the force, etc., were made to vary in pitch.

While such experiments indicate the essential principles of a possible voice-production, as the conditions in life were not and could not be fully met these results were rather suggestive than demonstrative of Nature's methods. These investigations served a good purpose, but they were manifestly inadequate, and this was felt by one thoughtful vocal teacher so keenly that he pondered much on the subject, in the hope of finding a method of observing the larynx during actual phonation. To this distinguished teacher,

Manuel Garcia, belongs the honor of inventing the means of observing the vocal bands in action. This was accomplished in 1854, and, soon after, Garcia read an account of his observations to the Royal Society of London; and though much in this paper required correction by subsequent observations, it remains to this day the foundation of our knowledge of the action of the larynx in voice-production.

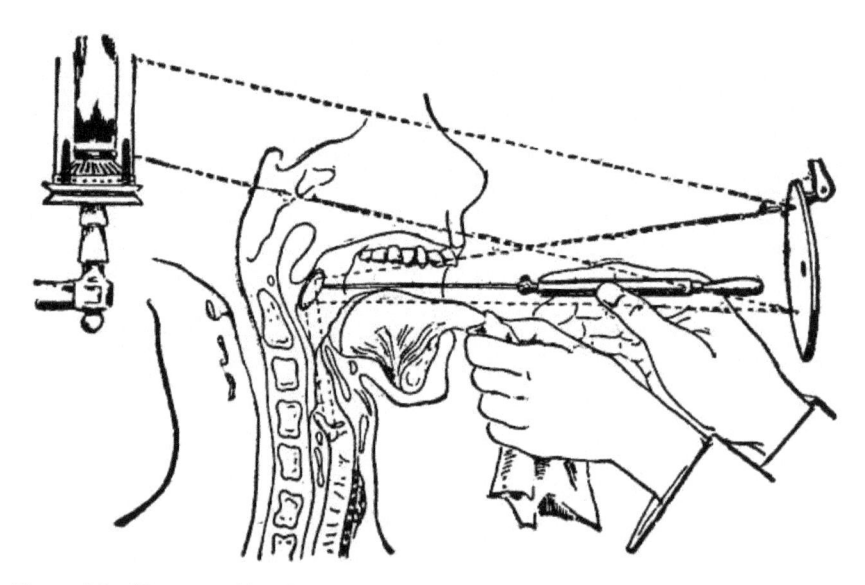

FIG. 38 (Bosworth). Intended to illustrate the optical principles involved and the practical method of carrying out laryngoscopic examination. The dotted lines show the paths of the light-rays.

As usually employed, the laryngoscope consists of two mirrors, the head-mirror, so called because it is usually attached to the forehead by an elastic band, and the throat-mirror, which is placed in the back part of the mouth cavity. The purpose of the head-mirror is to reflect the light that reaches it from a lamp or other source of illumination into the mouth cavity so perfectly that not only the back of the mouth, etc., but the larynx itself may be well lighted up; but inasmuch as this illumination may be accomplished, under favorable circumstances, by direct sunlight, the head-mirror is, though mostly indispensable, not an absolutely essential part of the laryngoscope. There is, indeed, one advantage in the use of direct sunlight, in that the color of the parts seen remains more nearly normal. Lamplight tends, because of its yellow color, to make parts seem rather of a deeper red than they actually are; but this to the practised observer, always using the same source of illumination, is not a serious matter—his standards of comparison remain the same. Moreover, this objection does not apply equally to electric light, now so much used.

FIG. 39. This illustration is meant to show more especially the relative position of observer and observed. The observer, on the right, is wearing the head-mirror, while two throat-mirrors seem to be in position—in reality, the same mirror in two different positions. One is placed so as to reflect the picture of the nasal chambers, especially their hinder portion. The walls of the nose, etc., may for the purposes of this illustration be considered transparent, so that the scroll (turbinated) bones, etc., come into view. The tongue is protruded. The light, not seen in this figure, is usually placed on the left of the subject, as in <u>Fig. 38</u>.

It being a fundamental law of light that the angle of reflection and the angle of incidence correspond—are, in fact, the same—it was necessary that the throat-mirror should be set at an angle to its stem, so that the light passing up by reflection from the larynx should, when striking on the surface of this plane throat-mirror, be reflected outward in a straight line to the eye, which must be in the same horizontal plane with it. This and all the other facts and principles involved can only be understood by a careful inspection of the accompanying figures, which it is hoped will make the subject plain. The throat-mirror is none other than the mouth-mirror of the dentists, and in use by them before Garcia discovered how it might be employed to throw light on the larynx, in a double sense.

The essentials, then, for a view of the interior of the larynx are: A source of illumination; a mirror to reflect the light reaching it from this source into the back of the throat and larynx; and a second mirror to reflect the light outward which is, in the first instance, reflected from below, from the interior of the larynx. The principles involved are few and simple, but their application to any particular case is not easy, and is sometimes well-nigh impossible.

The throat-mirror should be placed against that curtain suspended in the back of the mouth cavity known as the soft palate, so that it must be pushed back out of the line of view. But many persons find such a foreign object in the throat a sufficient cause of unpleasant sensations so that retching may be the result. Generally there is a tendency to raise the tongue behind in a way fatal to a view of the mirror and the picture reflected from it. These difficulties, however, can be overcome by a deft hand using the mirror brought to "blood heat" by placing it in warm water or holding it over some source of heat, as a small lamp, and directing the subject observed to breathe freely and *through the mouth*. This latter tends to quiet that unruly member, the tongue, and lead it to assume the flat position so important to an unobstructed view. It is for the same reason the author urges mouth breathing during speaking and singing. No other tends so well to put the tongue in the correct position.

The extent to which one feels the annoyance of a small mirror held gently in the throat depends really on the amount of attention directed to it, and the degree of determination with which he resolves to exercise self-control. The author has examined an entire class of students of voice-production and found only one person who did not succeed in at once giving him a view of the larynx. But it must be at once said that of all persons examined by the author during his experience as an investigator of voice-production and in special medical practice, none have been able to show their throats, the larynx included, so well as speakers and, above all, singers; which in itself indicates that speaking and singing do give control of the throat—that all its parts respond to the will of the observed person. The author must further, however, remark that he has found this control associated not so much with vocal power as with intelligent study. Intelligence tells in music a good deal more than many people have yet learned to believe; but on this point the reader will long since have learned the author's views—in fact, so deep are his convictions on this subject that he hopes he may be pardoned for frequent reference to them, in one form or another.

One anatomical fact may be so invincible that a view of the glottis cannot be obtained at all: the epiglottis may so overhang the opening to the larynx that a good view of its interior is absolutely impossible, in other cases only occasionally and under very favorable circumstances. Such cases are, however, of the rarest occurrence, while there are not a few persons in whom one may even see down the windpipe as far as its division into the two main bronchial tubes, and inflammation may thus often be traced from the vocal bands far down the mucous membrane common to the larynx, windpipe, etc.

As has been remarked previously, it is only by the use of the laryngoscope that one can see the vocal mechanism of the larynx in action, so that for investigation laryngoscopy is essential. Auto-laryngoscopy, or the use of the laryngoscope by the subject to observe his own larynx, has its special difficulties and advantages, the greatest of the latter being, perhaps, that the observer may use himself as often and as long as he will, while he would hesitate to make observations on others at great length or with frequent repetition. There are no new principles involved in auto-laryngoscopy. The observer must simply see that a good light is reflected into his own throat, and that the picture in his throat-mirror is reflected into another into which he may gaze, an ordinary small hand-glass usually sufficing.

Only rarely is the individual met who can himself so control his tongue that assistance from the observing laryngologist is unnecessary. In by far the greater number of instances the tongue, after being protruded, must be gently held by the left hand of the observer, a small napkin covering the tip of the organ. The auto-laryngologist must, of course, control his own tongue, and better if without any hand contact.

It is scarcely necessary to say that before placing the mirror in the mouth its temperature must be tested by touching it for a moment against the back of the hand.

Nearly all the facts of importance in phonation, several of which have already been referred to, or will be mentioned in the "Summary and Review" below, could only have been discovered by the use of the laryngoscope. The difference in the larynx in the two sexes and in different types of singers and speakers, though open to ordinary observation, dissection, etc., are still better brought out by the use of the instrument now under consideration.

One naturally expects any organ to be larger and heavier in the male than in the female, and to this the larynx is no exception; and individual differences are equally pronounced. There may be almost if not quite as much difference between the larynx of a barytone and of a tenor as between that of an ordinary man who is not a public voice-user and the larynx of the ordinary woman. The larynx of the contralto may in its size and general development remind one of the same organ in the male. The vocal bands of the bass singer may be to those of a soprano as are the strings of a violoncello to those of a violin—using these examples, it will be understood, merely as rough illustrations.

The change in the size of the larynx produced by even a few months' judicious practice may be astonishing. As already hinted, it is important that in bringing about this development exclusive attention should not be given, as is sometimes done, especially in the case of speakers, to the lower tones, though it is not so important for them as for singers to have an even development up to the highest range.

But again the author would urge the voice-user to aim at attaining that delicate control of muscles (neuro-muscular mechanisms, to speak more scientifically) so important for the finest vocal effects, rather than be satisfied with mere power. The vocalist and speaker must indeed be athletic specialists, but they should not aim at being like the ordinary athlete, much less mere strong men of the circus.

It is said that Madame Mara within her range of three octaves could effect 2100 changes of pitch, or 100 between each two tones of the twenty-one in her compass, which would represent a successive change in the length of the vocal bands of a small fraction, possibly not more than 1/17000 of an inch—something unapproachable in nicety in the use of any other instrument. Even if we make large deductions from the above, the performances of those who have reached the highest laryngeal control must remain marvellous, all the more when it is remembered that this control over the larynx, to be efficient for musical purposes, must be accompanied by a corresponding mastery of the art of breathing. Is it necessary to point out that such wonderful development and control can only be attained after years of steady work by the best methods?

At one period in the life of the individual changes of such importance take place in the entire nature, physical, mental, and moral, that he becomes almost a new being. This epoch is known as the period of puberty or adolescence, and may be considered that of the gravest moment during one's whole life; for then, for better or worse, great changes inevitably occur. It is incomparably the period of greatest development, and, unfortunately, there may also spring into being, with striking suddenness, physical and psychic traits which cause the greatest anxiety. In any case, the thoughtful must then regard the youth or maiden with feelings of the deepest interest, if not anxiety; and in the case of the voice-user, especially the singer, this period may come laden with the destinies of the future.

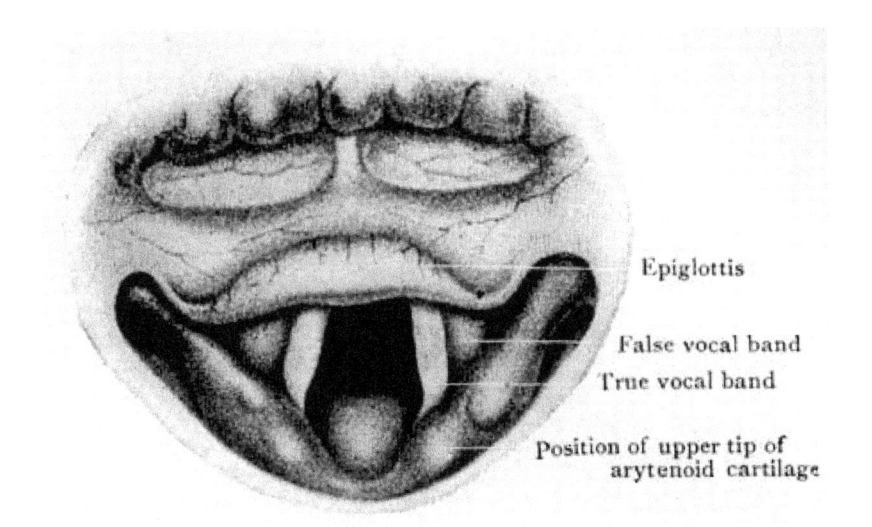

FIG. 40 (Grünwald). If this be compared with the next illustration (FIG. 41), some of the differences between the larynx of the male and that of the female may be noted. The vocal bands in FIG. 40, being those of a male, are heavier and wider. They are more covered by the epiglottis than in the other case—that of a female (FIG. 41). The false vocal bands are well seen in both cases, and by their redness (dark in the figures) contrast with the whiteness of the true vocal bands. In both illustrations the bands are in the inspiration position.

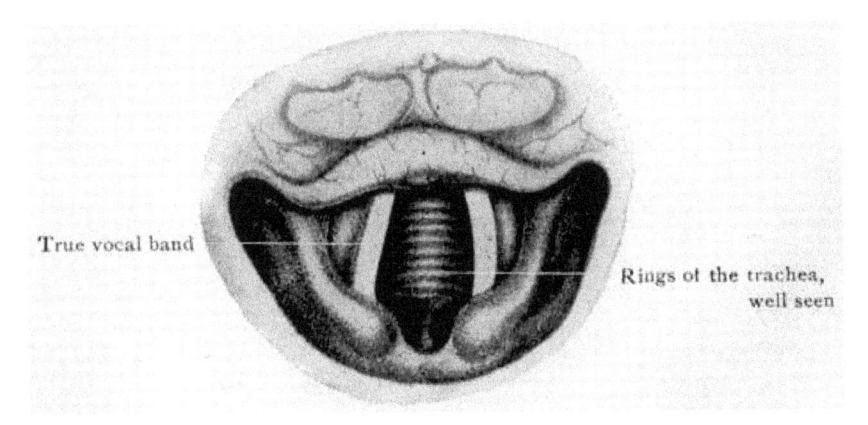

FIG. 41 (Grünwald). Laryngoscopic picture of the female larynx—to be contrasted with that of a male, shown in FIG. 40.

The vocal organs, especially in males, undergo very marked changes in relative proportions and actual growth. So marked is this that the boy soprano may actually become a barytone, or, unfortunately, no longer have a singing voice at all.

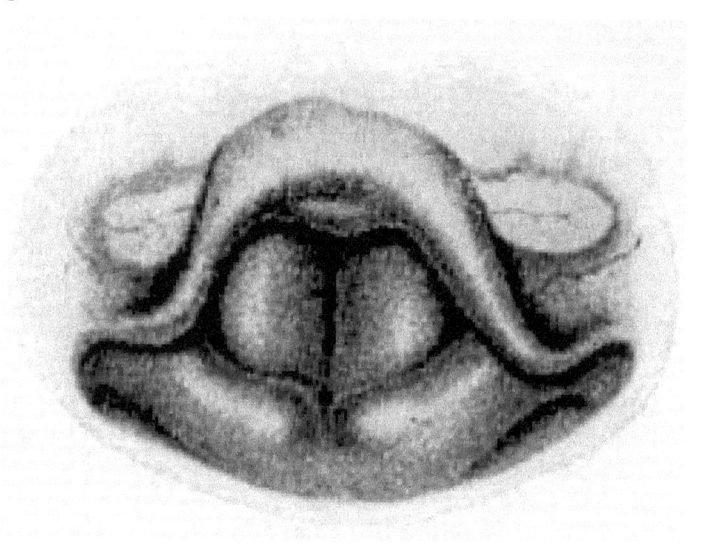

FIG. 42 (Grünwald). In this case, owing to the subject having a cold, it is with difficulty that the true can be distinguished from the false vocal bands, so reddened (dark, in the figure) were the former, with corresponding changes in the character of the voice. This view was obtained as the subject was phonating, so that the vocal bands are approximated somewhat closely.

False vocal band
True vocal band
Tracheal inner
surface
Back of the larynx

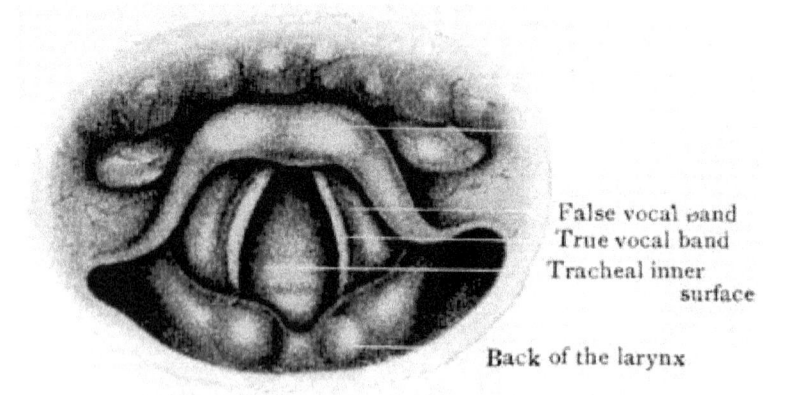

FIG. 43 (Grünwald). Shows the larynx as it may be seen only by the use of the laryngoscope. The above is an example of the appearance of the vocal bands during a deep inspiration, and in this subject, as in those

illustrated by FIGS. 40, 41, the circumstances were so favorable that the observer could see even the trachea, the rings of which are indicated in the picture. The reader will bear in mind that in this and all laryngoscopic pictures, while right remains right, front becomes back, and back front, so that the back of the larynx appears toward the observer—*i.e.*, is lowest on the page.

So far as the larynx is concerned the changes are less pronounced, usually, in the girl; nevertheless, the period is one of such change for the female that the greatest care should be exercised at this time, especially in the case of city girls. The body requires all its available resources for the growth and development which is so characteristic of this biological and psychological epoch; hence it may be ruinous for the future of the girl if at this time the same strain is put upon her as on the adult, whether in the direction of study, physical exertion, or social excitement, and of course the voice must suffer with all the rest. The farmer who would attempt to work the colt of a year or two old as he does the horse of four or five would be regarded as either grossly ignorant of his business or utterly reckless as to his own interests, if not positively cruel. Do our modern usages not show a neglect of facts of vital moment still more marked? Unfortunately, the woman all her life must live, to a greater or less extent, on a sort of periodic up-curve or down-curve of vitality; and that this fact is so generally ignored by society and educators is one of those peculiarities of our age at which, in spite of its great advancement in so many directions, a future generation must wonder.

To use the voice when the health is even slightly disordered is not without risk to the vocal organs, and it is the clear duty of every teacher of vocal culture, at all events, to allow no practice and to give no lessons that imply the actual use of the vocal organs at these times. Nor is this a great loss, rightly considered, for the intellectual side of the subject, which requires so much attention, may readily be made to take the place of the vocal for a few days.

The so-called "breaking" of the voice is largely confined to males, because the growth changes, etc., as already said, are most marked in boys. At this time, also, there is frequently an excess of blood supplied to the larynx, with possibly some degree of stagnation or congestion, which results in a thickening of the vocal bands, unequal action of muscles, etc., which must involve imperfections in the voice. In all such cases common sense and physiology alike plainly indicate that rest is desirable. All shouting, singing, etc., should be refrained from, and even ordinary speech, as much as possible, in very marked cases, especially when the individual is even slightly indisposed or weary.

In other cases the changes are so gradual and so little marked that it is not at all necessary to discontinue vocal practice, if carried out with care and under the guidance of an intelligent friend or teacher; but because of the possibility of the voice changing in quality, there is no time when the advice of an experienced and enlightened teacher or laryngologist is more necessary.

The condition present in the vocal bands and larynx generally of the boy at puberty is more or less akin to that found in fatigue, ill-health, hoarseness, etc., as well as in old age, when muscular action is very uncertain, so that in the weak larynx, as elsewhere, the old man may approach the undeveloped youth, and for much the same reason—lack of co-ordinated or harmonious control of parts.

These remarks imply, of course, that the youth has already begun studies in voice-production, and that raises another important question, viz.: When should the individual who is sufficiently endowed musically begin to sing, or study public utterance practically in some of its forms?

No faculty develops earlier than the musical, and this is a strong argument in itself for the early study of music, apart altogether from other considerations about which there is room for more difference of opinion. Should the child get his musical development through the use of his own musical instrument or another? If he shows natural ability for the use of the voice, should he be trained very early?

Against early training may be urged the facts above referred to—the liability of great changes taking place in the larynx at puberty, especially in the boy. But marked are the changes that take place in other parts of the body also, and this is not urged against exercises for general development, for the boy. It is a remarkable fact that many of the great composers sang as boys, and possibly this has had something to do with their writing music for the voice, later, when they were most of them by no means fine singers; but on this too much stress should not be laid.

The question at issue is to be sharply marked off from another—the public appearance of children as soloists, reciters, etc. In this case the question is more complicated, and cannot be settled by physiological considerations alone. Our problem is also to be kept apart from another very important question—the singing of children, or, indeed, adults, in classes, choirs, etc.

If a child shows himself a desire to sing, and especially if he has musical ability above the average and a voice that is of fair range and quality, one can scarcely see why he should not be encouraged, and placed under a wise teacher; for it is doubtful if there be any better way of developing the ear and musical nature, even if in future the child shows that he will accomplish more as an instrumentalist. Such vocal training tends to development of the larynx, and that can scarcely be wholly lost, no matter what changes puberty may bring about. At the same time, one must take care not to be too hopeful in regard to child singers. Nature gives us some surprises, and not always pleasant ones.

But as to the cultivation of the vocal organs with the view of producing a beautiful speaking voice by processes akin to those used for the singer, as the teaching of this work constantly implies, there can be no doubt. Unless the individual acquires a respect for the beautiful in the speaking voice when young, it is feared he may never get it, as the existing state of things only too clearly shows.

It is hoped that enough has been said on this subject to indicate the principles, at all events so far as physiology is concerned, on which the decisions regarding some weighty questions must be made.

The question of singing with others, as usually carried out in schools, seems to the author a very doubtful procedure, to say the least, as for those with fine throats it may prove injurious, and for those who have feeble musical endowments it does little; but of this subject and concerted singing generally again.

CHAPTER VIII.

FURTHER CONSIDERATION OF BREATHING, LARYNGEAL ADJUSTMENT, ETC.

EXPERIENCE proves that breathing, for the speaker and singer, is one of those subjects that may be very inadequately comprehended by the student, and, the author regrets to say, may be positively misrepresented by teachers and writers.

Some—indeed, a great many—teachers direct their students to employ "abdominal" or "diaphragmatic" breathing, others "clavicular" respiration. A little consideration must convince those who have read the chapters on breathing that such distinctions, in which one part of an entire process is treated as if it were the whole, cannot be justified. By "clavicular" breathing some mean upper chest breathing, and others a form of respiration in which the shoulders (clavicles, or key-bones) are raised with inspiration in an objectionable manner. The latter is, of course, to be condemned; yet, very exceptionally, a tenor of excellent training may feel that he can, under the circumstances of the hour, reach a certain tone very high in his range only by the utmost exertion. We all know how a singer's reputation may be more or less ruined should he fail to reach such a high note—one, indeed, by which he may, owing to the vitiated taste of the public, have acquired a reputation beyond his artistic merits. Under these circumstances such a singer might be justified in a momentary use of every resource of what physiologists term *forced respiration*, including clavicular breathing; but in general any raising of the shoulders should be absolutely avoided.

When "clavicular" breathing is used in the sense of upper chest breathing, it is correct as far as it goes, but the term is not a happy one to employ in this sense, and it has led to error in theory and practice.

In the same way, "diaphragmatic" breathing is perfectly correct, but its exclusive use cannot be justified, for Nature teaches us otherwise. It is true that the lower part of the chest, which always should expand with the descent of the diaphragm, is wider than the upper; it is true that by a very well-developed diaphragmatic breathing a singer or speaker is fairly well provided with breath power; but why teach this method exclusively, when thereby the voice-user is being robbed of possibly from one quarter to one third of his total breathing efficiency?

It is likely that teachers have insisted on diaphragmatic breathing, especially in the case of females, because, unfortunately, prevalent modes of dress so restrict the lower chest, etc., that individuals instinctively seek relief in upper chest or clavicular breathing, in which case it may be observed that the actual breath power of the singer is very small. It cannot be denied that few people ever adequately fill the chest—least of all, few women—and if admonitions as to diaphragmatic breathing accomplish this purpose, the practice must be commended. But another remedy should obviously precede this one: the respiratory prisoner should first be released.

No doubt, in the most vigorous singing and speaking the lower part of the chest, with the diaphragm, is of the greatest importance, but often both the speaker and the singer, as in a short, rapid passage, require to take breath, and the only way in which they can really meet the case is by a short, more or less superficial action of the respiratory apparatus, in which the upper chest must play the chief part. There is no opportunity to fill the whole chest, so that any admonition in regard to abdominal breathing is then quite out of place.

The fact is, the voice-user should have control of his whole breathing mechanism, and use one part more or less than another, or all parts equally and to the fullest extent, as the circumstances require; and if the student has not already learned such control, the author recommends his practising breathing with special attention first to filling the upper chest completely, and then the lower. It must be remembered that for a long time breathing, for the voice-user, must be a voluntary process, which, as has been pointed out, is not the usual and natural one for the individual when not phonating, which latter is essentially reflex or involuntary. The voice-user, in other words, must, with a definite purpose in view, take charge of himself. In time, breathing for him too will become reflex—*i.e.*, correct breathing for the purposes of his art will become a habit. It must be pointed out that the breathing for any particular composition, literary or musical, should be carefully studied out, for this is nothing else than determining how this part of the voice-user's mechanism can be employed with the best artistic result. This, fortunately, is now recognized by a large number of teachers, for the fact is, the artistic is at present much better understood and appreciated than the technical; were it not so, such erratic literature on the subject of breathing could never have appeared.

On another aspect of the subject there is room for much greater difference of opinion. Among even eminent singers and teachers there is lack of agreement in regard to the part the diaphragm and abdomen should play in the most vigorous (*fortissimo*) singing.

Singers of renown practise what may be termed a sort of "forced" abdominal or diaphragmatic breathing. The breath is so taken that the whole chest is filled, the diaphragm brought well down, and the abdominal walls drawn in (retracted), which gives the singer, in all parts above and below, a bellows with tense walls in all parts, with the great advantage that such breathing permits of a firmness otherwise unattainable, and he is enabled to exert his breath force with great certainty and power, and, as some maintain, with all the control necessary for even delicate effects.

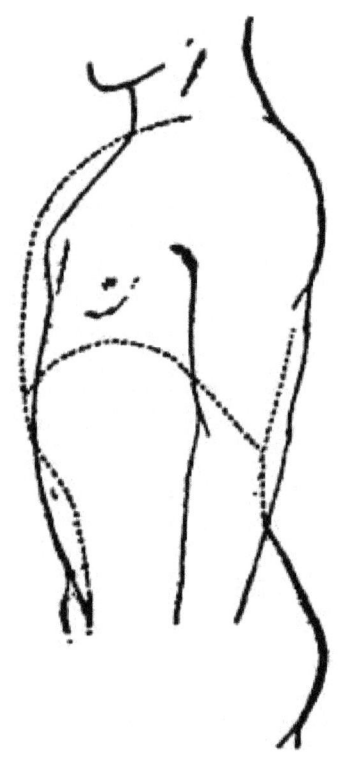

FIG. 44. Intended to express to the eye the two views of respiration discussed in the body of the work (p. 113-117). The dotted lines indicate the form of the chest and abdomen advocated by some as the best for the singing or speaking of long and vigorous passages.

Against this it has been urged that it is unnatural, not according to what is found in man and other animals in nature. It is perhaps forgotten that when we make a great effort, as in lifting, we put the breathing apparatus into just this state; we gird up our loins—or the equivalent of that process—so that this method cannot be said to be contrary to nature. The only question seems to be as to whether it is necessary and advantageous, or wasteful of energy. For ordinary efforts it does not seem to be necessary, though the chest must in singing and speaking always be *held* more or less full, not by any deliberate and painful effort, but in a quiet, unobtrusive way.

The diagram (Fig. 44) will make the difference in the theories referred to clear.

Up to the present the student has been urged to fill his chest, after days of less vigorous practice, to the fullest, retain the mechanism in this condition for a short time, and then in the slowest and most regular fashion relax it, the purpose being development and control. In actual speaking and singing such breathing is not usually either possible or desirable.

Nature herself always works with the least possible expenditure of energy and with power in reserve. These must be the voice-user's principles, to be deliberately and persistently applied. To fill the chest to the fullest on all occasions is to use up energy to no purpose and to induce fatigue. Art is ever economical. Effort, obvious effort, detracts from the listener's enjoyment. Ease in the executant corresponds with enjoyment in the listener, or, at all events, if nothing more, it puts him in such a frame of mind, that the more positive qualities of the performance find him in an undisturbed, receptive state.

The singer or speaker must breathe easily and adequately, but not so as to waste his energies. Prior to the execution of his task, he should consider what respiratory efficiency calls for in the case of any particular phrase, and meet this without waste—*i.e.*, fully, but with something to spare. For the best art, as well as the soundest technique, there should always be in the executant enough and to spare. Let the last word be so uttered or sung that the listener may feel, however vigorous the passage, that more could have been done had it been required; in other words, *speak or sing the last word feeling that several others might follow did one so choose.*

When this principle of reserve force is not observed, the voice-user may distress himself or his audience in a variety of ways, among others by a bad habit known as "pumping"—*i.e.*, endeavoring to produce sound when the breath power is really spent. It is only necessary to refer to it for a moment that its unwisdom and physiological unrighteousness may be apparent.

Another term, *coup de glotte* (blow or shock of the glottis), has led to so much confusion and misunderstanding, which unfortunately, has been followed by erroneous practice, that it would be well if its further employment were abandoned.

Breathing, so far as voice-production is concerned, is for the sole purpose of causing the vocal bands to vibrate; and at this stage we may say that the perfection of any vocal result depends wholly on the efficiency with which these vibrations are produced, so that breathing and tone are brought together, so to speak, by the mediation of these little bands, the vocal cords; and this is the justification for speaking of the larynx as *the* vocal organ. This usage, however, is objectionable, as it tends to narrowness and to divert the mind from other highly important parts of the vocal mechanism. In one sense, the respiratory organs and the resonance-chambers are each as important as the larynx.

The term *coup de glotte* has been sometimes employed as the equivalent of "attack," and again as the synonym of nearly all that is bad in voice-production. As to this latter, all depends on the sense in which the term is employed.

Before the vocal bands can be set into suitable vibrations the expiratory breath-stream must be directed against them in a special manner, and they themselves must be adapted to the blast. It is a case of complex and beautiful adaptation. The clarinet or flute player must learn to "blow," and equally must the singer learn to use his breath. The processes each employs, though not identical, are closely related; both use the breath to cause vibrations, and there can be none that are effective, in either case, except a certain relation of adaptation of breath-stream to instrument be effected—with the clarinet-player, adjustment of breath to reed, and with the voice-user, of breath to vocal bands.

Exactly what changes are made in the larynx, and by what means, have already been described, and will be again considered in more than one part of this volume. The main fact is that owing to a multitude of neuro-muscular mechanisms the different parts of the respiratory and laryngeal apparatus are brought to work in harmony for the production of tones.

The nature of the vibrations of the vocal bands, and, therefore, the character of the sounds produced, depend in no small measure on one thing, to which attention cannot be too carefully given. To a large extent the pitch, the volume, the quality, the carrying power, etc., of a tone depend on the adjustment now referred to—one of the facts which were, if not physiologically, at least practically recognized by the old Italian masters. Teachers everywhere felt the need of some technical term to express the adjustment we are considering, hence the expression *coup de glotte*, which is not in itself necessarily either incorrect or for other reason to be condemned. All depends on the sense in which it is used, as we have already said. It must, however, be admitted that it does; to most persons, convey the idea of something that is more or less violent as well as sudden, so that there seems to lurk in this term a tendency to mislead, to say the least.

There really should never be a blow or shock of the glottis; the vocal bands should never strike together violently, or, indeed, strike together at all, in the ordinary sense of the term. They should, however, be approximated with considerable rapidity and with a perfect adjustment to the breath-stream, and this must be associated with a like perfect adaptation of the breath-stream to them through the harmonious working of the many muscles (neuro-muscular mechanisms) which constitute the most important part of the respiratory mechanism. In brief, the adjustment of the breathing and laryngeal mechanisms resulting in the adequate and suitable approximation of the vocal bands for tone-production constitutes the *coup de glotte*, or, as the author prefers to term it, the "attack."

To get this perfect should be one of the aims of teachers and one of the ambitions of students. Without a good attack the singer or speaker fails to do himself justice, and the listener is left unsatisfied. The good attack suggests physiological and technical perfection, so far as it goes; artistically, it implies power and sureness, and for the listener satisfaction, a feeling that what has been attempted has been accomplished; and the best of it is that the auditor at the end of a large hall experiences this sense of satisfaction quite as fully as the persons sitting in the first row of seats. Without good attacks there can be no intellectual singing or speaking, no broad phrasing, and much more that all should aim at who come before the public, and which listeners have, indeed, a right to expect. But just because many persons feel this to be true, they make serious errors in attempting to attain the result; they substitute main force for the correct method. Impatience and eagerness may defeat the voice-user's purpose. In this and all other cases the action should be performed with but moderate force, or even, at first, softly, and with gradual increase in vigor, and always in relation to the quality of the sound produced; quality must always be the first if not also the last consideration.

If the method be correct, power can be attained with patience; if wrong, the throat and voice may be absolutely ruined. This point will be considered later, but we must at once express the opinion that a bungling attack in which main force is substituted for the proper method is one of the most dangerous, as it is one of the most serious errors in the technique of modern singing, and the same may often be charged against our public speaking.

Another of the worst faults of singing, the *tremolo*, is due to unsteadiness in attack and in maintaining the proper relations between the breathing and the laryngeal mechanism. If the voice-user fails to get a tone of good quality easily and without escape of breath to any appreciable extent, he must consider that his method is incorrect. There must be no wasted breath in the best vocal technique. This leads to ineffectiveness in the voice-producer and lack of satisfaction in the listener. Breath must, for a perfect technique, mean tone—all tone—and this must be produced so that the singer is not aware, by any unpleasant feelings, that he has vocal bands or a larynx at all; in a perfect technique one must only be distinctly aware of certain sensations in the parts above the larynx, in his mouth cavity, etc. His consciousness is concerned with tone—the result. But, to attain this, the method must be physiological—*i.e.*, natural, and not only that, but carried out with an approach to perfection in the details of the process which takes time and calls for infinite patience and care, all permeated by sound and clear ideas of what is being aimed at by the voice-user. Nothing should be attempted till the method and the end are understood thoroughly; to do otherwise is to waste time, defeat the purpose, and court failure and disappointment; and the more the student can think for himself, and the less dependent he is on his teacher, the better will it be for both and for art itself.

From all that has been hitherto said it will be inferred that one of the best tests of a good attack, or any other feature in voice-production, is the absence of escape of breath, as such, from the mouth. Many persons begin wrongly; they attempt to produce tones by forcing the breath out in such a way that all their resources in breathing are at once spent, instead of being husbanded with the care of a miser. As time is the most precious possession of man, as man, so is breath for the singer or speaker. It is his hoard. Nothing must be paid out of this always limited capital for which the best value is not obtained.

The test for perfect economy of breath known to older generations of actors still remains the best. They were accustomed to hold a candle a few inches from the mouth when speaking. If the flame did not flicker, it was clear that breath was not being uselessly expelled.

Instead of feeling that the breath passes out, the voice-producer should rather feel, when phonating, as if it passed in—an illusion, it is true, but still a safe one. It will be found that holding a mirror or the hand with the back turned toward the mouth, and a few inches (four to six) from it, will serve fairly well to indicate whether the breath is escaping or not, though in sensitiveness and convincing power this is not equal to the flame test.

We would again urge that in every instance of phonation in either speaker or singer, the breath be taken through the open mouth. Only in this way can enough breath be inhaled in the mere moment available for this purpose. Often the singer or actor must take breath with absolutely the greatest rapidity possible, and the narrow passages of the nose do not suffice to admit enough air within the time for action.

But even more important, perhaps, is the fact that when breath is taken through the nostrils the singer may find that on opening his mouth to sing the tongue and soft palate are in an unfavorable position for good tone-production; his sounds may be muffled, throaty; but if breath be inhaled through the open mouth, and not through the nose at all, the tongue tends to lie flat, and this organ and other parts assume the correct position for good intonation.

Mouth breathing, for the purposes of tone-production, is the only method which has physiological justification. Many singers especially complain of having trouble with the tongue; some believe it too large, others that it is beyond their control. These so-called large tongues have one advantage— they may exercise a great influence on the quality of the tone; and correct breathing brings them to good behavior. The author has time and again, by explaining the influence of mouth respiration, brought sudden joy to the heart of the singer who had been all his life troubled with the tongue, and worried by the consciousness that his tones lacked in clearness, carrying power, etc.

Nose breathing is of course to be used exclusively when the subject is not phonating. During the latter many opportunities occur to close the mouth; and the idea that drying of the mucous membrane of the mouth, etc., will occur by reason of mouth breathing in speaking and singing is purely imaginary.

EXERCISES.

The student, whatever his degree of advancement, will find the exercises about to be recommended, or others closely resembling them, of great value.

It cannot be too well borne in mind, obvious though it is, that all speaking and singing, whatever else they be, are tone-production; hence the first thing for every one to ascertain regarding himself is the extent to which he can form and hold tones of good quality—in other words, the success with which he can establish the essential co-ordinations or harmonious actions of the breathing and laryngeal mechanisms, and maintain them for a considerable length of time.

Many singers can produce a fairly good and powerful tone, but it is a sort of vocal explosion rather than a tone, which will continue to do the singer's bidding for as long as he will. The correctly produced and sustained tone is the foundation of all that is best in voice-production; all the rest is but a series of variations on this. Hence the author recommends the following practice to all, whatever else they may do or have done. It is to be a test of inspiration, attack, economy of breath, adjustment of the vocal bands, the resonance-chambers, etc.

1. Inhale slowly through the somewhat open mouth, filling the chest moderately full, and at once attack so as to produce a tone of but moderate force, but of the best quality possible.

2. Continue to hold this tone as long as the breath is easily sufficient, taking care that the tone be on no account sustained after there is the slightest difficulty in maintaining it of the same quality and power as before. Steadiness and perfection in quality are to be the chief considerations.

3. The student is advised, after a few days' practice in this manner, to note with a watch the time during which he can hold a tone under the restrictions above referred to, and to endeavor to increase the holding power daily by a little. It will, of course, be necessary to fill the chest more completely day by day.

4. It will also be well for the voice-producer to practise taking very deep and rapid inspirations, followed by the most prolonged expirations.

5. This method of breathing may then be put to the actual test in intonation.

Another exercise very valuable in giving breath-control is the following:

Produce a tone exactly as before, but every now and then, at regular intervals at first, then at irregular ones, cut the tone off short by suddenly arresting the breath, and, after a very short pause, continue again in exactly the same way *without* taking a fresh breath; and, as in the above and all other exercises, frequently apply the hand and, when more practised, the more exacting flame test.

The first of the above exercises may be represented to the eye by a continuous straight line; the second by straight lines with short spaces between them.

In all these exercises there must never be any sort of *push* anywhere, neither in the chest nor throat. Such methods are absolutely wrong, because so wasteful of energy. The tone should come as spontaneously and inevitably as the gas from a soda-water bottle when the cork is slightly loosened, or, if this illustration be too strong (it is employed because gas, air, is concerned in each case), let us say, as water from the pipe of a waterworks' system when the tap is turned. *The tone should come, the breath must tarry.*

If the student does not feel ease, certainty, and inevitableness in result, he has not made a good attack. If he cannot sustain the tone for a few seconds, he should conclude that his method of using his breath is wasteful. In time a tone should be easily held for at least ten seconds.

The purpose of the second exercise is to give still more fully breath-control, and to lead the voice-user to realize how important is breathing for intonation.

The student may ask: "Why not begin, as is often done, by the singing of scales?" Really useful scales are too complex; they imply the use of a series of tones formed according to the principles insisted upon above. The first thing is to get one perfect tone—to use the vocal mechanism under simple conditions; and *that tone should be chosen which the voice-user can produce of best quality and with greatest ease, with least expenditure of energy.* It should never be selected from the extremes of the subject's range. From the favorite or best tone he should work down and up the scale. After this the scale comes easy, and all actual singing is scale singing—the use of intervals—and all speaking the same thing; so that, from every point of view, this exercise should be the first in intonation, and the student will do well not to leave it till the conditions above prescribed can be fully met. Some singers have continued such exercises throughout a long artistic career.

It is to be understood always that the exercises, etc., recommended in this work are intended for all voice-users, whether they are singers or speakers. It is easy for a speaker to pass from such prolonged tones to the shorter ones required in speaking, but after such exercises he can do so with a feeling of ease, mastery of himself, improved ear, and purity of speech not otherwise attainable.

The author would also insist, in the most emphatic manner, on the great importance of making all such exercises musical. Every tone should be the best then possible to the voice-user, and power must on no account be aimed at for some time. Thus are developed and go hand in hand, as they always should, a sound technique with the artistic conscience and perceptions.

SUMMARY AND REVIEW.

The Principles of Physics, etc., Involved.

Sound (tone) is a mental result having its origin in certain changes in the ear and the brain, owing to vibrations of the air. Tones have *pitch*, depending on the number of vibrations in a second, *volume* (power), depending on the size of the waves or vibrations, and *quality* (*timbre*), determined by the shape of the waves. Pitch is determined by the vocal bands, volume by the same, in great part, and quality by the shape of the resonance-chambers above the vocal bands. The resonance-chambers influence volume also. A tone is augmented by resonance.

The larynx bears certain resemblances to both stringed and wind instruments, but it is really unique (*sui generis*). The vibrations of the vocal bands are caused solely by the expiratory current of air, which is more or less held back by the cords, owing to their approximation, so that the greater the obstruction the stronger must the blast of air be, other things being equal, and the result increase in pitch. The problem Nature had to solve is very complex.

The laryngoscope was invented in 1854 by a teacher of singing, Manuel Garcia, who soon after gave an account of it to the Royal Society of England. The instrument consists essentially of two mirrors, the external, or "head-mirror," which is concave and reflects into the larynx, and the internal, or "mouth-mirror," which reflects the picture outward to the eye. The latter mirror is plane, and set at an angle. The picture may show, under the most favorable circumstances, all the upper parts of the larynx, including the vocal bands, but sometimes, also, the windpipe as far down as its division into the two main bronchial tubes. The difficulties commonly met with in the use of the instrument are a constrained action of the throat and mouth parts of the subject, unnatural breathing, an unruly tongue, etc. The epiglottis may, also, naturally so overhang the glottis that a good view of the vocal cords is impossible. It is difficult to see more than one-half to two-thirds of the length of the vocal bands. The picture seen is that of the parts of the larynx reversed—*i.e.*, while right remains right, posterior becomes anterior. The laryngoscope shows that (1) in singing an ascending scale the vocal bands are for a certain time in action (vibration) throughout their whole length; that (2) there may be observed a rather sudden change when the vocal bands are relaxed and shortened, and that this process of shortening goes on, the bands approaching more and more, both behind and in front, till (3) in the highest tones of a soprano of great range there is only a small portion of each vocal cord toward the centre that is not approximated somewhat closely.

With certain qualifications, it may be said that the action of the vocal bands is alike for all voices. In all cases a certain degree of approximation of the vocal bands is absolutely necessary for phonation, and the mechanism is generally similar in males and females till the highest tones, above alluded to, are reached. This is in harmony with the following facts: (1) The crico-thyroids are the muscles most in use in ordinary speech and in singing the lower tones. (2) Several muscles combine in relaxing and shortening the vocal bands. (3) The peculiar mechanism of the highest tones in a soprano voice of great compass is only to be explained by a combined action of several muscles, and a very delicate and precise use of the internal thyro-arytenoids attached along the whole length of the outer surface of the vocal bands. The larynx of the male differs from that of the female chiefly in its greater size, weight, etc. The vocal bands in the male may measure from three-fifths to four-fifths of an inch when relaxed, and from four-fifths to one inch when tense; in the female, from two-fifths to three-fifths of an inch when relaxed, and from three-fifths to four-fifths of an inch when tense. There are structural differences corresponding to and determining the kind of voice, as to range and power more especially. The bass singer has, as a rule, the largest larynx and the longest and heaviest vocal bands.

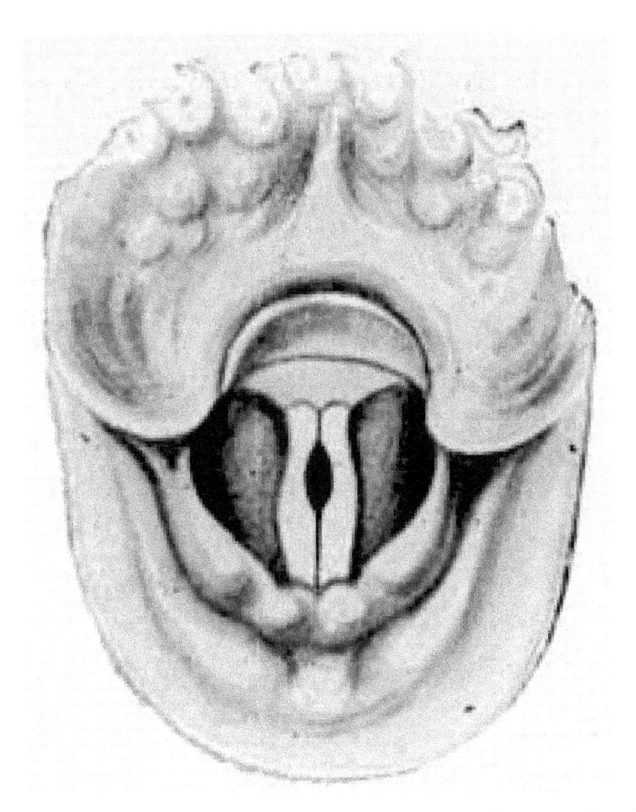

FIG. 45. Represents what the author has frequently seen, by the use of the laryngoscope, when a soprano is producing a very high head-tone, say C, D, or E in alt. It will be observed that the vocal bands approximate in front and behind ("stopped"), so that the only parts of the bands capable of vibration are those short portions which form the margins of the oval opening shown in the illustration. Only a very limited number of singers are capable of the delicate adjustments required.

At puberty the changes that take place in the body generally are associated with corresponding alterations in the larynx. The larynx grows, changes its proportions, etc., often somewhat rapidly, and the result may be a corresponding alteration in voice, as regards range, power, and quality. The voice, because of imperfect anatomical and physiological adjustment, may "break," to a greater or less extent. The same may take place, owing to similar imperfect adjustment, in old age, and temporarily, owing to disease, weakness, nervousness, fatigue, faulty production, etc. These facts indicate that under such circumstances the voice should be used with great care, not at all, or in a whisper, when the vocal bands are practically not in action.

In a singer highly endowed by nature and perfected by long training based on the soundest principles, the action of the muscles of the larynx may reach a degree of perfection only to be compared with that of the eye and ear.

Consideration of the *coup de glotte*, the attack, or adjustment of mechanisms to produce tone that begins correctly; breathing, with open mouth, with effectiveness and economy of energy; singing for children, in choirs, etc., have been discussed.

Practical exercises should be related to the principles underlying them. Musical and æsthetic principles are always to be associated with a sound technique. The artistic and technical or physiological conscience should be associated.

CHAPTER IX.

THE RESONANCE-CHAMBERS.

WHEN it is borne in mind that the vocal bands have little or nothing to do with the quality of tones, the importance of those parts of the vocal apparatus which determine quality, and the error of speaking of the larynx as if it alone were the sole vocal organ, become apparent.

It may be strictly said that the vocal bands serve the purpose of making the resonance mechanism available. What one hears may be said to be vibrations of this resonance apparatus, and not, strictly, those of the vocal bands, though this expression would also be correct, but would not indicate the final link in the series of vibrations.

The tone caused by the vibration of two such small bands as the vocal cords must, in the nature of the case, be very feeble. It becomes important for the reader to convince himself of the importance of resonance in sounding bodies and musical instruments.

When the stem of a tuning-fork so small that it can be scarcely heard when in vibration, except by, the person holding it, is laid against a solid body, as a table, its sound is at once so increased that it can be heard in the most distant part of a large room. When the same fork is held over an empty jar of suitable size and shape, a similar but much, less marked increase of its tone is to be observed.

If a cord of but moderate thickness be fastened at each end to a thin piece of wood, say a split shingle, and a little block of wood, in imitation of the bridge of a violin, be placed under the cord so as to render it tense, we have the essentials of a stringed instrument, the pitch of which can be made to vary by moving the block about and thus varying the tightness of the cord. But the sound of such an improvised instrument, produced by drawing a bow across the cord, is ridiculously feeble.

In the actual violin the volume of sound, as well as its quality, depends on the size, shape, and weight of the instrument. The strings serve the purpose of causing the body of the instrument, the air within it, and, in consequence, the air without, between it and the ear of the auditor, to vibrate or move in a specific manner.

Similarly, the imposing size of the grand piano is associated inevitably with loudness, as compared with a smaller instrument. A violoncello must produce a larger tone than a violin, though not necessarily one more intense.

These principles of resonance apply in the case of the singer and the speaker. The bass and barytone produce tones of larger volume (as well as different quality) than those of the tenor, because their resonance apparatus is different in size and shape. It is true, their vocal bands, their wind-power, and the laryngeal muscles are different—they are not of the same size, etc.—and, in a more remote sense, this is the cause of the differences in the tones they produce; but the immediate cause is to be sought in the resonance mechanism, and, above all, in the resonance-chambers.

It is true that when one speaks or sings, the chest, windpipe, and larynx may be felt to vibrate, but the essential vibrations are *supra-glottic*—above the vocal bands.

These resonance-chambers are the *mouth cavity*, in the widest sense, and the *nasal chambers*. It is highly probable that the vibrations of the chest walls and of the bones of the head may to some degree modify the vibrations of the air within the resonance-chambers, chiefly in the direction of intensification; but the idea that the hollow spaces in certain of the bones of the head have any appreciable influence on the tones of the speaker or singer, can at best not be considered as demonstrated, and it serves no practical purpose to take into account this possibility.

FIG. 46 (Tyndall). Representing water being poured into the vessel A B, till the air-space is just sufficient to respond to the vibrations of the tuning-fork. The air thus becomes a resonator of the fork.

The great facts, the facts which are so plain that they may be demonstrated to a child, are these: that the quality of any tone—*e.g.*, a vowel—is absolutely determined by the shape of these cavities, the mouth and nasal chambers. This subject will be treated further when the tones, etc., of speech are considered, but inasmuch as no one can sing, in the proper sense of the term, without the use of vowels, at least, and as we produce different vowels with ease, one may at once demonstrate to himself that this is done by altering the shape of his mouth cavity, and chiefly by the agency of the tongue and soft palate.

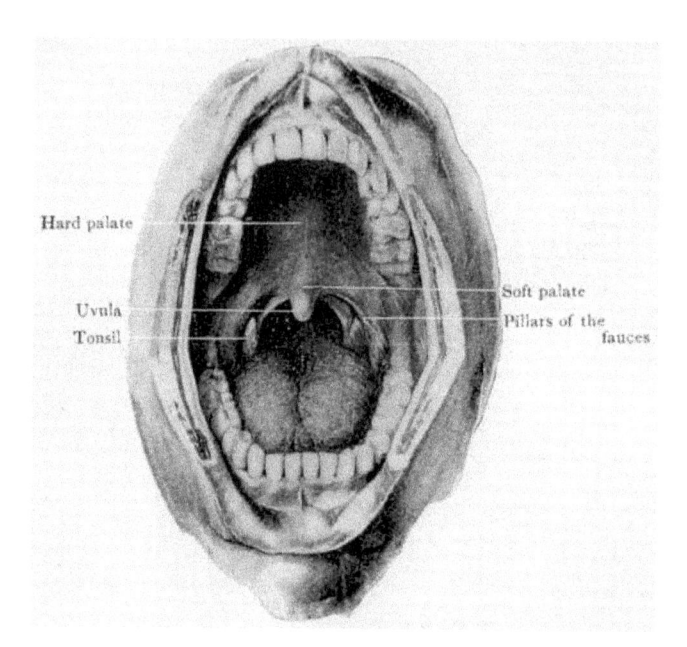

FIG. 47 (Spalteholz). The mouth is extremely widely opened. The soft palate is seen terminating in the uvula, and on each side, extending from it, are the pillars of the fauces, a pair of folds between which the tonsil is seen to lie.

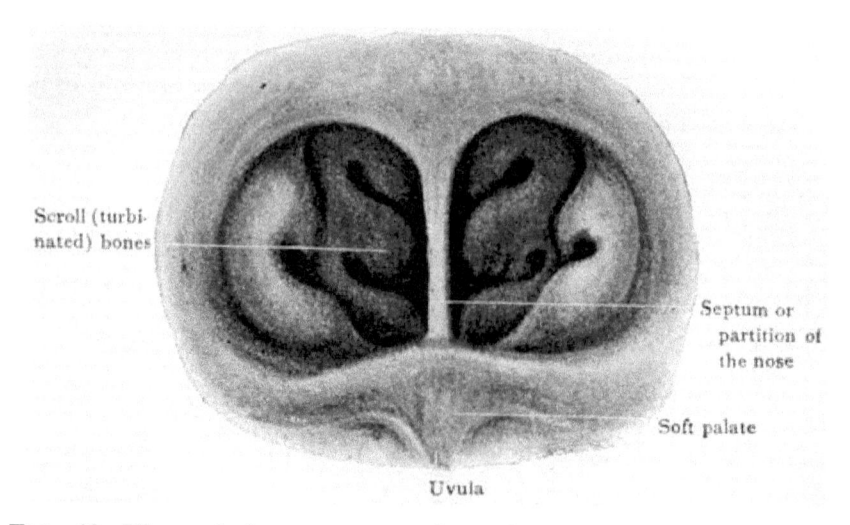

FIG. 48. View of the nose, etc., from behind, showing the parts enumerated above. It is not hard to understand that any considerable amount of swelling of the lining mucous membrane might give rise to

difficulty in breathing through the nose, and even compel mouth-breathing.

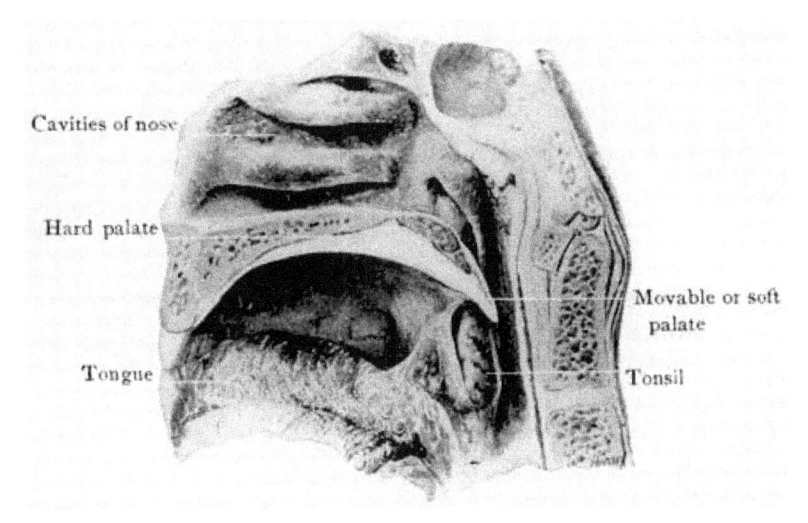

FIG. 49 (Spalteholz). Showing well the scroll (turbinated) bones of the nose, which break up the space and make it more cavernous. It can be seen that there is free communication behind, between the mouth and the nasal cavities, and that if the soft palate and the tongue approximate, the breath-stream must pass into and through the nose, giving rise to nasality in utterance.

A short description of a part to which many voice-users remain strangers all their lives will now be given. These resonance-chambers remain, for many, an apparatus used daily and absolutely essential, yet never examined. Fortunately, a few illustrations, which should be followed by an examination of the student's own resonance-chambers and their various parts as they may be seen in a mirror, will remove all difficulty in the understanding of them, and prepare for that detailed study to be recommended in a subsequent chapter.

Passing from before backward, one meets the *lips*, the *teeth* and *gums*, the *hard palate*, which is a continuation of the gums; then, suspended from the hard palate, behind, is the *soft palate*, back of which lies the *pharynx* (often termed "the throat"), and above it and constituting its continuation, the *naso-pharynx*; and lying on the floor of the mouth there is the *tongue*.

Certain of these parts, as the teeth, gums, hard palate, nasal bones, etc., constitute fixed structures, and though they determine in no small measure the shape of the resonance-chambers, and so to a degree the quality of the voice, so movable are the lips, soft palate, and, above all, the tongue, that there is the widest scope for varying the quality and even the volume of the voice; so that it is a good thing, practically, for every one to believe that so far as quality, at all events, is concerned, he is the master of his own destinies.

Though we are accustomed to believe that the mouth and nose are, though neighbors, quite separate and independent of each other, such is not the case. Indeed, in the pre-natal condition these are not two, but one; and in some instances they remain imperfectly separated, owing to the failure of the hard palate to develop to the full—a condition known as "cleft palate," and giving rise to a peculiar nasal intonation, to be explained presently.

The *nasal chambers* are divided into two by a vertical partition, as one can readily demonstrate by the use of his fingers, and are still further broken up by certain bones, the scroll-shaped or *turbinated* bones, so that the nasal chambers are of very limited size, and much divided up by bony outgrowths from their walls. The *vertical septum*, while bony above, is cartilaginous and flexible below.

Without the aid of instruments and a good light the nose can be but indifferently examined from the front, while it requires the greatest skill on the part of a laryngologist to see it well from behind. However, the whole difficulty can be got over by visiting a butcher and securing a sheep's head split through from before back. In a few moments one can learn all the essential facts, including that one of great practical importance—viz.: that every part of the resonance-chambers is lined by the same mucous membrane which is also continued downward into the larynx and the gullet.

It will be thus observed that the throat and nose communicate in the freest manner behind, and that the only way of closing off the mouth cavity from the nasal chambers is by means of the tongue and the soft palate working together. As in the proper use of the tongue and soft palate lie many of the secrets of the art of the speaker and singer, special attention must be given to these parts.

The *tongue*, which completely fills the floor of the mouth, is made up of several muscles of different attachments, which explains why this organ is so movable. To say that it can with the greatest ease and rapidity be turned toward every one of the thirty-two points marked on a mariner's compass, is but to feebly express its capacity for movements. What we are most concerned with now is its power to alter the shape of the mouth cavity in every part.

The *soft palate* is suspended like a curtain from the hard palate, behind. It is composed of muscles arranged in pairs, and is continued into a conical tip below known as the *uvula*, and on each side into folds, the *pillars of the fauces*, between which lie the *tonsils*, which are in shape like very small almond nuts. When quite normal these should not protrude much, if at all, beyond the cavity made by the folds referred to above.

Both the tonsils and the uvula may become so enlarged as to be a source of awkwardness or more serious evil to the voice-user. They may, in fact, require operative interference. So serious, however, is the decision to operate, or the reverse, for the voice-user, that the author recommends that such operations be entrusted only to laryngologists who have some knowledge of their influence on voice-production.

It is of the greatest moment to observe that the quality of tones can be made to vary in the highest degree by the joint use of the tongue and soft palate. When in vocalizing the tongue is raised behind and the soft palate made to approach it, or actually to meet it, the tone assumes a more or less nasal character. The reason of this is that the cavity of the mouth proper, or "mouth" in the narrower sense, the forward part, is shut off from the hinder part, or the pharynx, so that the breath is then directed upward and passes chiefly through the nose, producing a nasal tone or twang—always a fault, and one fearfully common in America.

When the tongue alone is raised behind, or drawn back unduly, tones become muffled—indistinct, etc. This is also a very common fault, but is found in England and Germany also. English speech is often hard and guttural, German unduly guttural, if not so hard, and American slovenly and horribly nasal.

But what may in a certain degree be disagreeable and a vocal error, is in another a positive excellence; so, in this case, the use of the tongue and soft palate in the proper degree and at the right moment gives us emotional expression. This subject will, however, be considered again later; in the meantime, the student is advised to do a little experimenting in the use of his tongue and soft palate, with a view of noting how the quality of tone may be thus made to vary. He is also advised to use a hand-glass with the object of observing the parts mentioned in this chapter, and if he can also find a friend willing to lend his mouth for observation, so much the better.

The sooner any voice-user comes to feel that his vocal destinies lie in his own hands, the better. "Know thyself" is as necessary an admonition for the speaker and singer as for any other artist, but with that must go another, "Believe in thyself"—that thou canst produce tones of beautiful and expressive quality if thou wilt; it may be only after much wisely directed work, but yet it is possible.

Allusion must be made to the danger of those engaged in mathematical and physical investigations applying their conclusions in too rigid a manner to the animal body. It was held till recently that the pitch of a vocal tone was determined solely by the number of vibrations of the vocal bands, as if they acted like the strings of a violin or the reed of a clarinet, while the resonance-chambers were thought to simply take up these vibrations and determine nothing but the quality of tone; they were believed not to have any influence on pitch. Against this view the author long ago demurred. To Prof. Scripture, however, belongs the credit of demonstrating that the resonance-chambers determine pitch also. It seems probable that the vocal bands so beat the air within the resonance-chambers as to determine the rate of vibration of the air of these cavities, and so the pitch of the tone produced. These chambers not having rigid walls, one can the better understand that the tension of these parts may not only be different in individuals, but vary in the same person from time to time, according to the condition of his health, etc. Herein we find another source of explanation of variations in the voice. All these considerations make the resonance-chambers more important than ever, so that there is greater objection to speaking of the larynx as *the* vocal organ than we were aware of before these investigations were undertaken.

SUMMARY.

Without a resonator, which may be solid or hollow, the sound made by a reed or tense string is feeble. That the mouth can act as a resonator may be proved by holding a vibrating tuning-fork of suitable pitch before this chamber when open.

The resonating chambers of importance are supra-glottic. Of these the "mouth" including all as far back as the pharynx and the nasal chambers are the principal. These two main cavities are separated from each other by the hard palate, which is a bony floor, covered with mucous membrane, as are all the parts of the resonance-chambers. The hard palate extends horizontally from the gums backward, and is continued as the soft palate. The latter is a muscular and therefore movable curtain that divides, with varying degrees of completeness, the mouth (in the narrower sense) from the pharynx and naso-pharynx—*i.e.*, the space back of the soft palate and the posterior nares (back nostrils) respectively. By the elevation of the back of the tongue and the lowering of the soft palate as when one speaks nasally, the mouth proper is largely shut off from the nasal chambers, so that the breath must be directed through the nose. "Cleft palate" also connects undesirably the mouth and nasal chambers. The tonsils lie between two folds, the pillars of the fauces, connected with the soft palate. When normal in size the tonsils should scarcely extend beyond these folds. The uvula is the central lower tip of the soft palate. The nasal chambers are divided by a central bony and cartilaginous partition, the septum nasi, but are further encroached upon, on each side, by three scroll-like (turbinated) bones. The tongue is composed of several muscles, which explains why its movements may be so complicated and delicate. The mouth cavity is bounded in front by the gums, teeth, and lips.

The form and, to some extent, possibly; the size of the resonance-chambers determine the quality of the tone produced in speaking and singing. The shape and size of the mouth can be made to vary by the soft palate and lips, but chiefly by the tongue, so that the movements of the latter, especially, cannot be too well studied.

It was formerly considered that pitch was determined solely by the rate of vibration of the vocal bands; though the author opposed this view as rigidly applied. Very recently Prof. Scripture, by the use of new methods, has shown that the supra-glottic chambers cannot be correctly likened to a resonator with rigid walls. It is held that the vocal bands give a number of sudden shocks to the air in the resonators, so that, in a sense, the resonance-chambers determine both the pitch and the quality of the tone; and as the tension of the resonators varies with both the physical and psychical condition of the individual, variations in tone-production, more especially as to quality, can now be the better understood. According to this view these chambers are not properly resonators but sounding cavities.

The reader's attention is particularly drawn to the new views of the method of action of the vocal bands, etc., referred to on this page. Since the above was written, such views have become more widely known, and it is hoped that as they are very radical they may be established by other methods.

CHAPTER X.

THE REGISTERS OF THE SINGING VOICE.[1]

ABOUT no subject in the whole range of voice-production has there been so much confusion, difference of opinion, and controversy as that of registers; so that it is important at the very outset to define register, and throughout to aim at the utmost precision and clearness.

"A register is a series of consecutive and homogeneous sounds rising from the grave to the acute, produced by the development of the same mechanical principle, the nature of which essentially differs from any other series of sounds equally consecutive and homogeneous, produced by another mechanical principle" (Manuel Garcia).

"A register consists of a series of tones which are produced by the same mechanism" (Behnke).

"A register is the series of tones of like quality producible by a particular adjustment of the vocal cords" (Mackenzie).

From a consideration of the above proposed definitions it will be seen that for the successful or, at all events, complete or ideal investigation of a subject so many-sided and difficult, many qualifications are desirable, if not absolutely essential. It is not too much to say that the ideal investigator of the registers should have a practical knowledge of general anatomy and physiology, together with a detailed and exact knowledge of the vocal organs; be versed in the laws of sound; have an adequate knowledge of music; be capable of examining himself with the laryngoscope (auto-laryngoscopy) as well as others (laryngoscopy); possess an acute ear for the pitch and quality of tones; be himself able to use his voice at least fairly well in singing and speaking; be provided with the all-important ballast of common sense, and an impartial mind longing above all things to learn the truth.

As few can hope to unite all these qualities in themselves in even a moderate degree, openness of mind, temperance in the expression of opinion, and common sense with experience, must be largely relied on to furnish working conclusions.

A discussion of a subject so difficult and complicated is not easy to follow. It is but just to other investigators, and fair to the reader, to present the views of those who have possessed special qualifications for dealing with the questions involved. The author will endeavor to present the grounds on which others have taken their stand, in a few words and clearly, if the reader will patiently follow. There will at first seem, possibly, to be little agreement, but it will be shown that on some of the most essential points there is substantial unity of opinion; and the subject is of such vital moment, as the author will endeavor to make clear, that it is hoped that the most patient examination will be given to the questions that arise, from the beginning to the end of the discussion. For the author to express a dogmatic opinion, and simply state his disagreement or agreement with others, would be contrary to the whole spirit of this work, and leave the subject where it once was—in the realm of hopeless disagreement and controversy. If the problem of the registers is to be solved to the satisfaction of the rational thinker, it must be by evidence, and not the mere opinions of any teacher or writer, however eminent. To lay this evidence before the reader is now the author's task.

One of those most eminently equipped, by a great variety of qualities, for the investigation of this subject, or any other question of the voice, was Madame Seiler. Whenever the author is obliged to differ from this really great investigator, he does so with the sense of the highest respect for her opinions generally, because she always sought for scientific grounds for such opinions. Her views may be thus briefly presented:

She recognized three registers, chest, falsetto, and head, with their subdivisions.

(1) The first chest register extends to [notation] in men, and to [notation] in women.

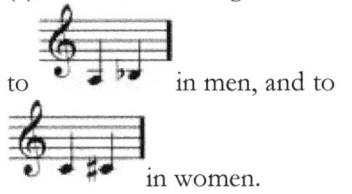

(1) The whole glottis (vocal bands) is moved in loose vibrations.

(2) The second chest register extends to [notation] in both sexes.

(2) The vocal ligaments (or ligamentous glottis) alone are in action.

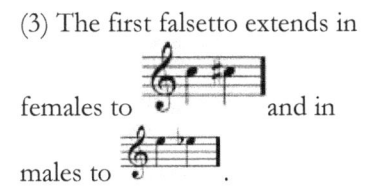

(3) The first falsetto extends in females to [notation] and in males to [notation].

(3) The edges alone of the vocal bands vibrate, but the whole glottis is in action.

(4) The second falsetto in the female extends to [musical notation] and to [musical notation] in women.

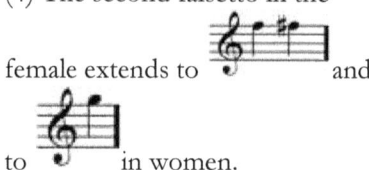

(4) The edges only of the vocal bands are used, and the vocal ligaments alone are in action.

(5) Above this point head tones begin.

(5) Edges only of the vocal bands in vibration; partial closure of the ligaments posteriorly (behind).

It will be noted that Madame Seiler spoke of the vocal bands (cords) proper as the "ligamentous glottis," and included in the "glottis" the arytenoid cartilages themselves, or, at all events, that part of them, their lower anterior angles, known as the vocal processes (or extensions), to which the vocal bands proper are attached.

The above tabular statement shows (1) that Madame Seiler recognized five registers for both male and female voices; (2) that she used the term "falsetto" in a sense different from its ordinary one. Usually this term is not applied at all to the female voice, but only to that special modification of the male voice seldom employed now, and almost never except by tenors. With this writer, "falsetto" as applied to female voices replaces "middle," in the commoner usage.

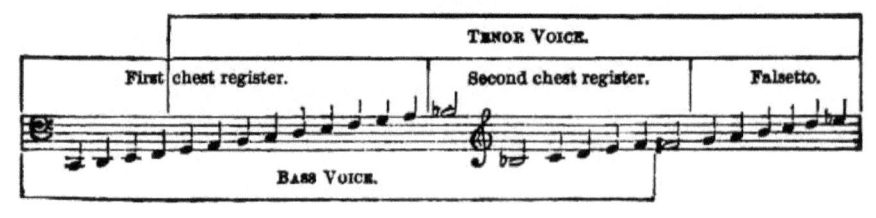

FIG. 50. Tabular representation of Madame Seiler's division of the register.

Garcia, also, recognized five registers. Behnke, a teacher of singing, who practised laryngoscopy and auto-laryngoscopy in the investigation of the registers, used "lower thick," "upper thick," "lower thin," "upper thin," and "small," as answering to the "first chest," "second chest," etc., of Madame Seiler and others.

Nearly all writers have used the term "break" to indicate the point at which a new register begins. Behnke held that the break between the thick and the thin register occurred in *both* sexes at about [musical notation]. The vocal bands in this part of the scale vibrate in their entire breadth, and the series of tones above the point just referred to is produced by a new mechanism, but one which is the same for all voices and both sexes—*i.e.*, only the inner edges of the vocal bands vibrate.

According to Behnke, the male voice has but two registers, the thick and the thin, but the female voice three, the thick, the thin, and the small. These terms were not original with Behnke, but had been used earlier by Curwen.

Behnke was emphatic on one point, to which we would call special attention, in his own words: "If there is *straining* anywhere, it is during the attempt to carry the mechanism of the upper thick beyond its natural limit."

Mackenzie (afterwards Sir Morell Mackenzie) held that "It is certain that however over-refined musicians may multiply the 'registers' of the voice, physiologically there are but two—*i.e.*, 'chest' and 'head,' the falsetto of the man answering to the head production of women."

According to the same author, "The essential factor in chest production is the long reed, whilst the essential factor in head delivery is the short reed." The terms "long reed" and "short reed" were the equivalents of Madame Seiler's "glottis" and "ligamentous glottis" respectively. Mackenzie held that the cartilaginous (inter-arytenoid) glottis is generally open in the lower and gently closed in the upper tones of the chest register, while a segment of the ligamentous glottis (vocal bands proper) is tightly closed in the head voice.

As the result of the examination of 50 persons gifted with fine voices, 42 of whom were "trained" singers and 8 "natural" singers, Mackenzie formulated his conclusions as follows:

1. In tenor voices the whole glottis may be open to [♪] and not unfrequently to [♪]. Beyond this point there is closure of the cartilaginous glottis. Sometimes the whole glottis is open throughout.

2. In barytone voices the whole glottis is often open to [♪], and occasionally to [♪]. Beyond this point the cartilaginous glottis is closed, except in rare cases.

3. In bass voices the whole glottis is sometimes open to [♪]. Beyond this point, except in a few instances, the cartilaginous glottis is gradually closed.

4. In sopranos and mezzo-sopranos the whole glottis is sometimes open to [♪], often to [♪], beyond which the cartilaginous glottis is usually closed. The glottis is sometimes closed throughout the scale, and in one case it was open throughout.

5. In contralto voices the whole of the glottis is often open to [♪], beyond which the cartilaginous portion is closed.

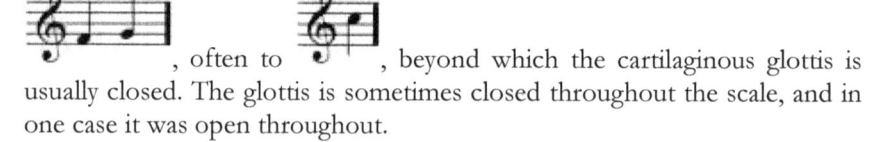

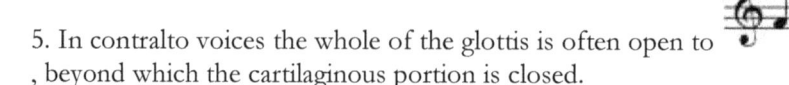

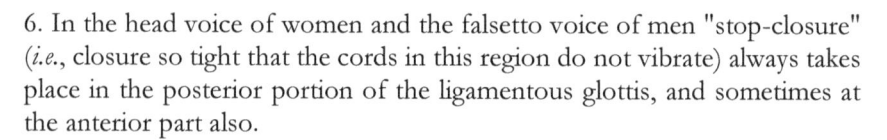

6. In the head voice of women and the falsetto voice of men "stop-closure" (*i.e.*, closure so tight that the cords in this region do not vibrate) always takes place in the posterior portion of the ligamentous glottis, and sometimes at the anterior part also.

This writer also held that "Boys who sing alto always use the chest register." He was of opinion that "The quality of the voice generally, but not always, indicates which mechanism is being used."

The views of the author, published at a former period, and based on the special examination of a large number of persons with the laryngoscope, etc., and on auto-laryngoscopy, may be briefly stated as follows:

A nomenclature for the registers involving no theory would be best, such, for example, as *lower*, *middle*, and *upper* registers. Mandl, who recognized only two registers, spoke of them as "lower" and "upper," equivalent to "chest" and "head," as commonly used.

The author examined with the laryngoscope 50 persons, who might (with Grützner) be divided into "trained singers," "natural singers," and "non-singers." The whole glottis was found to be open in all voices in the lowest tones of the chest register, and this condition obtained up to about [♪], beyond which another mechanism came into play, except in rare cases.

The high falsetto of men and the head voice of women are produced by a similar mechanism and method.

In the investigation of registers more attention should be given to the use of the breathing organs than has hitherto been done by those writing on this subject.

As Madame Marchesi, of Paris, has taught with preëminent success, and with the greatest practical consideration for the preservation of the voice and the vocal organs in an unimpaired condition, and as the author has had, through her kindness, the opportunity to become acquainted with her methods by observation, her views on the registers are here presented. It is to be understood that as she teaches only ladies, her views are considered, so far as she is concerned, as applying only to female voices. These views are further presented because Madame Marchesi was herself taught by Garcia, who was in the direct line of the old Italian masters, though it will be observed that the pupil has retained only the essentials of the master's views on the registers.

1. There are three registers in female voices: chest, middle, and head.

2. While there are small differences in voices and individuals as regards the registers, the following principles apply to all of them:

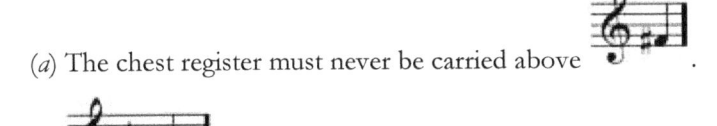

(*a*) The chest register must never be carried above [♪].

(*b*) [♪] should be "covered" or modified chest tones.

(*c*) In all cases [♪] must be a head tone.

(*d*) In quick passages chest should not be carried beyond [music: treble clef notes] —*i.e.*, [music: treble clef notes] are middle in quick passages.

CHAPTER XI.

FURTHER CONSIDERATION OF THE REGISTERS OF THE SINGING VOICE.

IT will, it is hoped, be apparent to the reader that the subject now under treatment may be considered either theoretically or practically. If science be exact, systematized, and, when complete, unified knowledge, then every source of information must be employed in the investigation of so difficult a subject as the registers. There may be differences of opinion as to the relative importance of some of these means of investigation—*e.g.*, auto-laryngoscopy, but that it should be utilized, there can be no question. The value of photography of the larynx, as carried out up to the present, may be questioned; but there can be no doubt that if this method of studying the action of the vocal bands could be pushed to a certain point, much light might be thrown on the questions at issue.

Merely to assume that a method of treating the registers which has given, apparently, good practical results in the hands of one teacher is sound, and rests on a scientific basis, is unwarranted. It may be simply a little better or a little worse than some other. How is the student to distinguish, in his choice, between Mr. A and Mr. B, in the case of two successful teachers, both of whom recognize registers? A physiologist may be sound as far as he goes, yet lack that practical knowledge of the voice which the vocal teacher properly considers requisite in determining how a pupil shall use the registers. Among those who are most dogmatic on this and other questions there is often a plentiful lack of knowledge of the vocal organs; and some clever laryngologists must have learned, when they were carried into the discussion of this subject, that some knowledge of music and singing is absolutely indispensable, and that enough cannot be picked up, even by an able man, in a few minutes devoted to interrogating singers, especially when these vocalists have been trained by widely different methods, and have, as is too often the case, given but little real *thought* to the scientific, or, indeed, any other side of their art.

We find "break" confounded with "register," and the meaning attached to the latter, at best, one-sided or inadequate in some respects. The truth is, such a subject cannot be settled by the physiologist, even when a laryngologist, as such; nor can the solution to a scientific question of this kind be given by a singer, as a singer. Such a problem can only be settled, as we have throughout insisted, by those possessing many qualifications, and even when the investigator unites in himself every intellectual qualification, something will depend on his temperament and spirit. An atmosphere of controversy is not favorable to scientific investigation, and among the dangers that ever lie in the path of the teacher are pride and prejudice. The assumption that one is prepared to teach is too often associated with views and feelings that prevent the guide from remaining himself a student and being ready to learn even from the very beginner, as he must if he have the true spirit. Unfortunately, several of the most highly qualified writers on this subject have formulated their views under conditions unfavorable to the attainment of the whole truth.

It is to be borne in mind always that a register implies (1) a series of tones of a characteristic clang, *timbre*, color, or quality; (2) that this is due to the employment of a special mechanism of the larynx in a particular manner. It follows that in thinking of registers scientifically, one must take into account both the tones and the mechanisms by which they are produced.

Naturally, with most untrained people the passage from one register to another is associated with a suddenness of change which is unpleasant, and which is termed the *break*. It is often suggestive of weakness, uncertainty, etc., and to an ear at once sensitive and exacting through training is intolerable when very pronounced. Often this break is very marked in contraltos, and is invariably so pronounced in the male voice when it passes to the upper falsetto that even the dullest ear does not fail to notice the change.

It is, therefore, not surprising that teachers should have sought to lessen the unpleasant surprise for the listener caused by the break. Some have looked on registers as almost an invention of the Evil One, and forbidden the use of the term to their students; but such ostrich-like treatment of the subject—such burying of the head in the sand—does not do away with a difficulty, much less can such a plain fact as the existence of registers be ignored without the most detrimental results, as we shall endeavor to make plain. Some, feeling that the break was an artistic abomination, have proceeded to teach the student to reduce all tones to the same quality, which is about as rational as asking a painter to give us pictures, by the use of but one pigment.

To attempt to abolish registers would be like leaving but one string to the violin; which instrument, in its present form, has a register for each string; and the player endeavors to avoid the breaks that naturally occur in passing from string to string, and to get a smooth series of tones just as the intelligent vocalist does.

The registers may be represented to the eye by the method illustrated in figure 52.

The wise instructor recognizes registers; they are a fact in nature, and one to be valued. The more colors, the greater the range of the artist's powers, other things being equal, whether the artist paint with pigments or tones; but just as the painter uses intermediate tones of color to prevent rude transitions or breaks, so must the singer modify or "cover" the tones between the registers—*i.e.*, use to some extent the mechanism of both neighboring registers.

The reader who has perused the previous chapter thoughtfully may naturally ask: "With such difference of opinion among eminent authors like those quoted, how am I to know which one to follow, and what to believe on this subject?"

The answer to that question we propose now to give. It will be wise to endeavor to show just wherein the writers quoted differ and on what they agree. A careful examination will show that there is substantial agreement on the most important points:

1. All agree that there are registers, or natural changes of quality of tone, corresponding to changes of mechanism or method.

2. All, with the exception of Madame Seiler, agree that the most important changes take place at or near $\begin{smallmatrix}\text{♪}\end{smallmatrix}$ in female voices, and the majority consider that this applies to both sexes equally.

3. Often in males there is some laryngeal change lower than this.

4. All agree that the high falsetto of tenors is of a special quality, and produced by a mechanism of its own—*i.e.*, all consider it a separate register— and often, at least, it begins naturally about $\begin{smallmatrix}\text{♪}\end{smallmatrix}$, which is usually, however, written an octave higher, though really sung as given above.

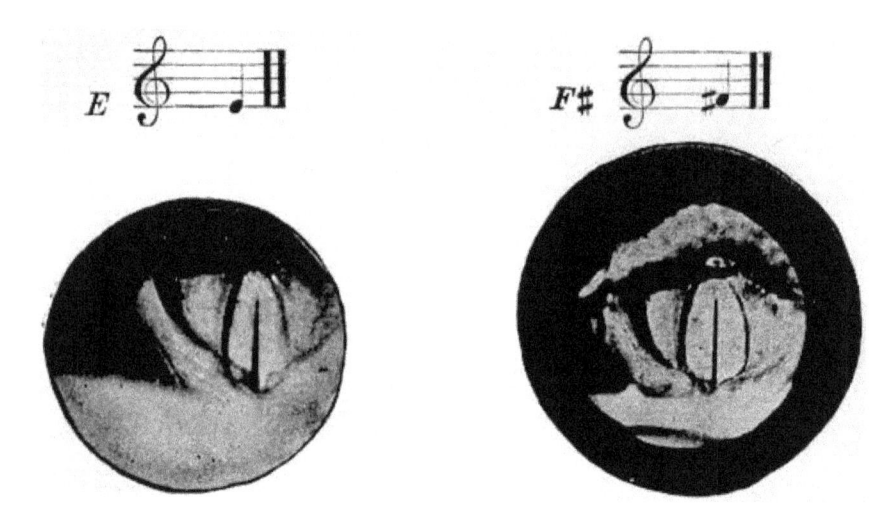

FIG. 51. A photographic representation of the appearances of the vocal bands when the subject is sounding first E and then F sharp, in which latter case "the vibratory portions of the vocal bands are shortened about one-sixteenth inch," according to Dr. French, who has been eminently successful in photographing the larynx. It will be noted that this is the point in the scale at which the change of register usually takes place—*i.e.*, there is a change of mechanism corresponding to the change in quality. (French-Raymond.)

The point of greatest strain is generally, for both sexes, about this point, and many persons cannot sing higher than this—*i.e.*, about for males, and its octave for females.

It is to be remembered, as Madame Seiler has pointed out, that at the period of greatest perfection in vocal training, some hundred and fifty years or more ago, concert pitch was very much lower than it is to-day; so that to teach tenors to sing in one register up to then, was quite a different matter from what that would be to-day. The old Italian masters were accustomed to train singers to the use of the falsetto, and whatever views may be held as to the desirability of the tenor using this register, so far as art is concerned, there can be no question whatever that physiologically it is easy, and one of the means by which relief may be sought from the high tension caused by carrying up the lower register.

The author, after a special investigation of this and other questions connected with the registers, came to the conclusion that the falsetto in males and the head voice in females are produced by a similar mechanism. In the high falsetto the vocal bands do not vibrate throughout their whole breadth, and there must be, for a successful result, in every case a feeling of ease, due to the relaxation of certain mechanisms in use up to that point and the employment of new ones.

FIGS. 52. These figures are meant to convey through the eye some of the main truths regarding the nature of registers and breaks. The figure on the left applies to the case of one with three registers in the voice, and with the breaks only very moderately marked; the illustration on the right applies to the same person after training, when the breaks have become indistinct, almost imperceptible. For teaching purposes the author is accustomed to use a similar diagram, but in shades of the same color, the difference being rendered less obvious by intermediate shades *between* the register shades in the right-hand figure.

The author now offers, with all respect, but confidence, a few criticisms on the eminent investigators whose conclusions and methods he has been discussing.

Madame Seiler was the writer who, as has been already said, brought more numerous and higher qualifications of a scientific and practical kind to the investigation of this subject than any other person. However, the study of physics, involving as it does the use of methods of extreme precision, tends to beget habits of mind which are not in all respects the best for the consideration of biological problems. Madame Seiler and her master, the physicist Helmholtz, regarded the vocal mechanism very much in the same light as they did their laboratory apparatus. Only in this way can the author explain some of Madame Seiler's positions; but on this assumption one can understand why she should make five registers, and consider them all, apparently, of equal importance. This latter, together with the tendency generally to present her views in too rigid a form, was, we think, her great error.

Behnke admitted that all five registers might be heard, especially in contraltos, but he did not attach equal importance to each of these registers.

Mackenzie the author conceives to have been misled by the very method that he considered a special virtue in his investigations—the examination of trained singers. Surely, if one would learn what is Nature's teaching on this subject, he must not draw conclusions from trained vocalists alone! By training one may learn to walk well on his hands, but this does not prove such a method the natural one, nor would it be good reasoning to draw this conclusion, even if a few individuals were found who could thus walk more rapidly than in the usual way.

The diversity that Mackenzie found in singers does not, in the author's opinion, exist in nature; much if not most of it was due to training, and all that can be said is that several people may sing in different ways with not greatly different æsthetic results; but such methods of investigation may, as in this case, lead to conclusions that are dangerously liberal.

The author holds to-day, as he did when he published his results many years ago, that "Impressions from general laryngoscopic observations or conclusions drawn from single cases will not settle these questions. Very likely differences such as these writers allude to may exist to a slight degree; but if they do, I question whether they are sufficiently open to observation ever to be capable of definition; nor is it likely that they interfere with methods of voice-production which are alike operative in all persons."

Holding these views, not only can the author not agree with those who believe that the change in a register occurs in different persons of the same voice (*e.g.*, soprano) at appreciably different levels in the scale, and even varies naturally from day to day, but he holds that to believe this in theory and embody it in practice is to pursue a course not only detrimental to the best artistic results, but contrary to the plain teachings of physiology in general and that of the vocal organs in particular.

The change in a register should be placed *low* enough in the scale to suit all of the same sex. *It is safe to carry a higher register down, but it is always risky, and may be injurious to the throat, to carry a lower up beyond a certain point.* The latter leads not only to a limitation of resources in tone coloring, but also to straining, to which we have before alluded. Though this process may not be at once obviously injurious, it *invariably* becomes so as time passes, and no vocalist who hopes to sing much and to last can ignore registers, much less make the change at a point to any appreciable extent removed from those that scientific investigation and equally sound practice teach us are the correct ones at which to make the changes.

Why is it that some artists of world-wide reputation sing as well to-day as twenty years ago, while others have broken down or have become hopelessly defective in their vocal results in a few years? There is but one answer in a large proportion of these cases: correct methods in the former and wrong methods in the latter class of singers—and "correct" in no small degree refers to a strict observance of registers.

The author has known a professional soprano to sing every tone in the trying "Hear, O Israel" (*Elijah*) in the chest register. How can such a singer hope to retain either voice or a sound throat? But so long as audiences will applaud exhibitions of mere lung-power and brute force the teachings of physiology and healthy art will be violated. But, surely, all artists themselves and all enlightened teachers should unite in condemning such violations of Nature's plain teachings!

The question of the registers is generally considered now a somewhat simpler one for males than for females. Basses and barytones sing in the chest register only; tenors are usually taught to sing in the chest register; but few teachers believe that the high falsetto is worth the expenditure of the time and energy necessary to attain facility in its use.

Probably in many male voices there are the distinctions of register Madame Seiler alludes to—*i.e.*, first chest and second chest, or some change analogous to the middle of females; but, from one cause and another, this seems to readily disappear. Whether it would not be worth maintaining is a question that the author suggests as at least worth consideration. Certain it is that, speaking generally, there is no change in males equally pronounced with the passage from the lowest to the next higher (chest to middle) register in females.

What, then, are the views that the author believes so well grounded, in regard to the registers, that they may be made, in all confidence, the basis of teaching?

Without hesitation, he recommends that arrangement of the registers set forth in the last chapter. It is not the exclusive invention nor the basis of practice of any one person, but it may fittingly enough be associated with the name of a woman who for over fifty years has taught singing with so much regard for true art and for Nature's teachings—*i.e.*, for physiological as well as artistic principles.

Such a method for female voices is wholly consistent with the best scientific teaching known to the author; it is in harmony with the laws of vocal hygiene; it gives the singer beautiful tones, and leaves her with improved, and not injured, vocal organs. Such an arrangement of the registers is not marred by the rigidity of Madame Seiler's nor the laxity of Mackenzie's, but combines flexibility with sufficiently definite limitations.

As to just how much a teacher of singing should say to the pupil on the subject of registers, and especially in a physiological way, must depend on circumstances. About the wisdom of teachers of singing (and elocution) understanding the vocal mechanism, and carefully weighing the matter of registers from every point of view, the reader of this book will have no doubt, by this time, the author ventures to hope.

Of course, one may object that for every tone, as it differs slightly in quality from its neighbor in the scale, there should be a new register—a new mechanism. Such an objection, though theoretically sound, is of no practical weight. What students wish to know and instructors to teach is how to attain to good singing—the kind that gives genuinely artistic results, and leaves the throat and entire body of the vocalist the better for his effort. The teaching of this work in regard to the registers and other subjects is intended to accomplish this, and not to occupy the attention of readers with vocal or physiological refinements of no practical importance.

The author has always been of opinion that those who have investigated and written on this subject have devoted insufficient attention to one point— viz., the manner of using the breath. The breathing in the use of the high falsetto, for example, is as different as are the laryngeal processes; and this is a point of practical importance, for the voice-user must ever consider economy in breathing. It is expenditure in this direction that most taxes all singers, even the best trained and the most highly endowed.

But the student, deeply impressed with the importance of the subject of registers, may ask: "How am I to distinguish between one register and another? How am I to know when I am singing with chest, middle, or head voice?" The answer is: "By sensations"—chiefly by hearing, but also by certain sensations (less properly termed "feelings") in the resonance-chambers and to a certain extent in the larynx. Of course, before one can thus identify any register, he must have heard a singer of fairly good voice form the tones of this particular register. One who has never heard sounds of a particular color or quality cannot, of course, learn to recognize them from mere description, though by this means he is often *prepared* to hear, and to associate clear ideas with that hearing.

As the registers are of such great practical importance, especially for the female voice, there is no period when it is of so much value to have a lady teacher as just when the voice is being "placed"—which should mean the recognition of its main quality, and the teaching of registers by imitation as well as description. The student should be made to understand, by practical examples, the subject of "covering," or modification. Certainly, the training of a vocalist cannot be adequately undertaken by even the most learned musician, however good an instrumentalist, if he has paid no attention to the voice practically. Much of the teaching done by those ignorant of voice-production, however well meant, may be a positive drawback, and leave the would-be singer with faults that may never be wholly eradicated.

The author would recommend all students who have begun a serious practical study of the registers to hear, if possible, some singer of eminence who observes register formation strictly. In this way more can often be done in getting a clear notion of their characteristic qualities, in a single evening, than by listening to an ordinary amateur, or to such a voice as an otherwise excellent vocal teacher can bring to her work, on many occasions; better one hour listening to a Melba, with her observance of registers, covering, etc., as set forth by the author in this chapter, than a score of vocalists of indifferent, even if not incorrect production. One then has before her an individual who, after long and careful training, attains results not, indeed, within the reach of all, but such as may be approached if the same methods are pursued long enough; and in Madame Melba, and others that might be named, the student has examples of how those using correct methods, and not worshipping at the shrine of mere vocal power, may retain the vocal organs uninjured and the voice unimpaired after the lapse of well-nigh a score of years of exacting public singing. Teachers will do well to encourage their pupils to hear the best singers; for do not students need inspiration as well as discipline?

Granted that the ear can at once determine what register the pupil herself or another singer may be using, what other guide has she?

There are certain sensations, as already said, felt within the resonance-chambers and larynx, which are sure guides. In a person who had learned to recognize the correct register formation by the help of the ear and those sensations now referred to, the latter would suffice to be a partial guide, at least, even had he become deaf. While these sensations are absolutely characteristic, it is difficult to describe them; they must be experienced to be understood. To attempt to describe the taste of a peach to one who knew that of an apple but had never eaten a peach would be, perhaps, not absolutely useless, but would certainly serve little purpose. The sensation must accompany the correct formation of the tone. The term "straining" carries with it the idea of unpleasant sensations; all understand practically what this term means; yet the sensation of strain in a tenor carrying his chest register too high is no more marked than the sensation of relief when he changes to the falsetto.

When once the voice has been well placed, little attention need be, or is usually, paid *consciously* to the sensations associated of necessity with all changes in the vocal organs. When one becomes unduly conscious of any of the normal sensations of the body, he is no longer a perfectly healthy person. At the same time, as we have pointed out in Chapter II., and shall do more at length shortly, sensations are absolutely essential guides for all muscular and other processes of the body; but they should enter just so much into consciousness, and no more.

It is practically helpful to the voice-producer and the teacher to think of the resonance-chambers and the ear as bearing a close relationship to the movements essential to tone-production. The sensations from these parts are of importance above all others in voice-production. They are the chief guides, and the attention may to advantage be concentrated on them.

No doubt the question of registers for the speaker must be considered, but this can be done to greater advantage in a later chapter.

SUMMARY.

All good definitions of a register must recognize two things: change of quality in the voice, and change of mechanism in the vocal apparatus. A break is not a register, but occurs because of the existence of registers. The abrupt transition, or break, is to be avoided by covering, or modification of the upper tones of the lower (at least) register.

For an adequate scientific examination of the question of registers, many qualifications are required in the investigator; and the student, when not an investigator, should endeavor to weigh the evidence presented so as to choose with caution from among conflicting opinions. He should be suspicious of those who scout the value of scientific study of this or any other subject, and also of those who claim that experience is of no importance in settling such a question.

Though several well-qualified persons who have written on the subject differ in some respects, they are in agreement as to many of the more important points. They are practically all convinced that there is commonly a change of register for all voices, at or near one point in the scale (F), and that if this be practically disregarded, dangerous straining may result.

Conclusions drawn from trained singers, alone, may be misleading. All classes of persons should be examined with the laryngoscope, if correct and far-reaching generalizations are to be safely made.

The precision and rigidity of physics and mathematics cannot be introduced with safety into a subject of this character; otherwise the division and limits of registers will be fixed with a narrowness of margin that does not comport with Nature's methods.

In all questions of register, the method of breathing—*i.e.*, the nature of the application of the expiratory blast—must be duly considered.

With male voices, the subject is usually considered much simpler than in the case of female voices. Men sing mostly in the chest register; basses and barytones wholly so, with the rarest exceptions. Tenors are taught to do so. Whether there might not be a subdivision of this register made to advantage in training, the author leaves as an open question; but about straining, in the case of tenors and all others, and as to the importance of recognizing three registers for female voices, there is in his mind no question. The fact that some may not be able to produce head tones does not justify carrying up the chest register to any appreciable extent, even by altos.

Now, as in past times, the high falsetto for males, if good, the result of proper training, has the warrant of both art and sound physiology.

In the use of registers, sensations are infallible guides. Of these, the most important are those associated with the organs of hearing, but those arising in the vocal organs are also valuable.

Those only should expect to sing artistically, and to preserve their voices unimpaired for a long period, who wisely observe Nature's teachings in regard to registers.

CHAPTER XII.

FUNDAMENTAL PRINCIPLES UNDERLYING VOICE-PRODUCTION.

IT is highly important for the speaker or singer to realize early in his career that all forms of artistic expression can be carried out only through movements—muscular movements; in other words, technique or execution implies the use of neuro-muscular mechanisms. However beautiful the conception in the mind of the painter, it can only become an artistic thing when it assumes material form—when it is put on canvas. The most beautiful melody is no possession of the world while it is in the mind of the composer alone; till it is *expressed*, it is as good as non-existent.

Even poetry can only affect us when it exists in the form of words produced by lip or pen. Between the glowing thought of the poet and the corresponding emotion produced in ourselves there must intervene some form of technique—*i.e.*, some application of neuro-muscular action. This latter term is a convenient one, and has been already explained. It is a condensed expression for that use of the nervous and muscular systems that results in movements, simple or complex.

Without nerve-cells and muscles movements are impossible, speaking generally, and for a willed or voluntary movement there must be something more, an idea or concept. Before one can make a movement resulting in a simple line or even dot on a piece of paper, he must have the idea of that line or dot in mind. In like manner, before one plays or sings a single note, he must have the idea of that note in mind; in other words, the idea is the antecedent to the movement, and absolutely essential. To have such an idea, memory is necessary. It is impossible to sing a tone after another, as an imitative effort, unless one has the power to retain that tone in memory for at least a brief period of time; and before this same tone can be reproduced on sight of it as represented by a written note, the memory of the sound to which it answers must first be recalled; and not only so, but other memories—indeed, memories of all the sensations associated with the bodily mechanism used in producing it.

This applies to all movements, of whatever kind, that we at any time execute. Without the past—*i.e.*, without memories—no present. Some of the memories associated with an act may be lost, and others, sufficient for its performance in some fashion, remain. A man may forget, after the lapse of months or years, how to tie his necktie in a certain way, as he stands before a mirror; yet on turning away he may succeed at once. In this case the visual memories, those that come through the eyes, were lost, but others, those associated with muscular movements, remain. The muscular sense may prove an adequate guide when the visual is ineffective.

In the same way, one may call up a melody by moving the fingers over the piano keys, when it cannot otherwise be recovered, or one rescues an air from oblivion by humming a few of its tones; all of which is explained by the revival of muscular and similar memories.

All voluntary movements are at first accomplished relatively slowly and with difficulty. They soon weary us. A child learns to walk with the greatest difficulty, and only after numberless failures or errors. The first tones of the would-be pianist or violinist are produced but slowly and with great difficulty, in spite of the most determined effort. If the attempts to vocalize are any more successful, it is because one has already learned to talk—a process that in the first instance (in infancy) was even more laborious than that of walking.

The degree to which any one succeeds in his earliest efforts to sing a scale will depend on the readiness with which he can use a variety of neuro-muscular mechanisms—indeed, all those associated with the respiratory, laryngeal, and resonance apparatus. Fortunately for the voice-user, this apparatus has all been in use in ordinary speaking. But when this latter process is analyzed, it is found that it is not essentially different from singing. In each the same mechanism is used, and in much the same way; but every one knows that not all who can talk are able to sing, and it is usual to say that those who cannot have no "ear" for music; and this expresses a part of the truth, though not in a scientific way. What is really the truth is found to be, on analysis, that certain guiding sensations, chiefly those from the hearing apparatus (ear, nerves, brain), are insufficient, owing either to natural defect or lack of training; but that this is not the only explanation is plain from the fact that many composers with the most vivid musical imagination, the most perfect auditory memory, and the most acute ear, cannot sing in any but the most imperfect manner. As we have said before, the speaker of great power to affect his fellows through tones, or the artistic singer, must be a sort of vocal athlete. In the athlete there is a very perfect association into one whole of certain sensations from eye, skin, muscles, etc., and certain movements. These exist in all men, but in very unequal degree. The singer is a tone specialist in whom the perception of the pitch and the quality of sounds may not be more acute than in the composer, possibly less so, but he can do what the composer of music often cannot—viz., associate these sensations with muscular movements of a highly perfect character; in different words, he has the technique which others have not in an equal degree.

In the singer and speaker there is a very close association between the sensations of the resonance-chambers, the larynx, and other parts of the vocal mechanism, and those from the ear. So perfect does this become from training that the necessary technique at last becomes easy. But it is of the greatest importance that the exact nature of this process be realized by both students and teachers, for weighty considerations grow out of it.

We wish to impress the fact that the nature of all neuro-muscular processes is essentially the same. Learning to sing is like learning to talk, and the latter is not radically different from learning to walk. This last is at first slow, imperfect, laborious, and largely a voluntary or willed process, or, more strictly, a series of processes. As progress is made, there is less of the voluntary and more that is involuntary, or what physiologists term reflex. When ideas, feelings, etc., enter into a process which is carried out reflexly, a *habit* is formed.

One may say that talking implies a series of associated reflexes, the parts associated being the respiratory, the laryngeal, and the resonance apparatus. Singing only approaches this condition of reflex action and habit after practice, and yet no air is perfectly sung except when the result is the outcome of a sort of new habit. Every song involves, the learning of new vocal habits. One forms a new habit of an athletic character all the more readily because of previous ones. A man learns to play one game of ball the better, usually, if he have already played at another, the reason being that he has only to modify the action of neuro-muscular mechanisms, not associate new mechanisms together to the same extent as in the formation of a habit of a widely different kind, as rowing a boat. At the same time, one must always unlearn something—break up old habits, to some extent. An opera singer often makes a failure of oratorio at first. The sets of reflexes or the habits, bodily and mental, which he has found valuable for the one form of art do not suit the other perfectly; nevertheless, the same materials are used, the reflexes are in the main the same. He must use preventions, or *inhibitions*, as the physiologists term them. Rather is it that he must avoid doing certain things—*i.e.*, modify his neuro-muscular processes or reflexes, than form wholly new ones.

Were it not for reflexes and habits, learning would be so slow one lifetime would not suffice to make an artist. It must be apparent that habits and reflexes are Nature's ways of economizing energy. As the best have but a limited amount of energy, it should be the aim of every one who will not be a mere reckless spendthrift to economize, to make the most of what Nature has given him; hence the purpose of practice is not only to render success more certain and more perfect, but to make efforts tell to the fullest extent with as little expenditure of energy to the speaker or singer as possible. *He sings or speaks best who attains the end with the least expenditure of energy.*

It may with scientific accuracy be said that the object of the student should be to attain to the formation of correct habits in singing and speaking, and of the teacher to guide in this process. It follows that all practice by the beginner should be carried out only in the presence of one who knows the correct methods and can teach the student how to form his habits wisely. Practice alone may not only do little good, but, by the formation of wrong habits of production, be positively mischievous; yet a trainer of athletes often lays more restrictions on his ward as to when and how he shall practise, and exercises more supervision over it, than do some teachers of singing, in spite of the fact that the apparatus the singer or speaker uses is much more delicate, and wrong habits much more injurious.

The admonition "Practise, practise," is greatly overdone. The best results cannot be obtained in either singing, speaking, or playing, with the lengthy and necessarily more or less imperfect if not careless practice in which many students of music indulge. Better ten minutes with the whole attention of a fresh and interested mind given intelligently to a subject than ten hours of mere mechanical movement. It is a mistake to suppose that the acquirement of a sound technique is a purely mechanical process. We have shown that for all successful effort there must be the idea, and as soon as that fades, from weariness, etc., the practice should be discontinued. Students are not treated fairly when given exercises the meaning or purpose of which is not explained to them.

There is now more need than ever that the teacher of music or elocution should be intellectual and not mechanical in his methods. Technique is mechanism, but it should be mechanism subordinated to ideas. Technique is essential to art, but it is not art. Art is the soul, technique the body. The soul will be unknown to the world without technique; hence the author strives in this book to teach the principles on which a sound vocal technique rests, but only that what is best in the soul be not hidden, that the one noble or poetic thought shall be multiplied a thousand times—indeed, that if it be sufficiently worthy, it shall, like Tennyson's Brook, "go on forever." To believe, on the one hand, that the highest art can be attained with a very mediocre technique, and, on the other, that a perfect technique is the main object of musical training, are alike great and mischievous errors.

The author has been asked frequently such questions as the following: "When is the best time to practise? How long should a singer practise at one time, and for how long during a single day? Should one practise softly (*piano*) or vigorously (*forte*)?"—etc.

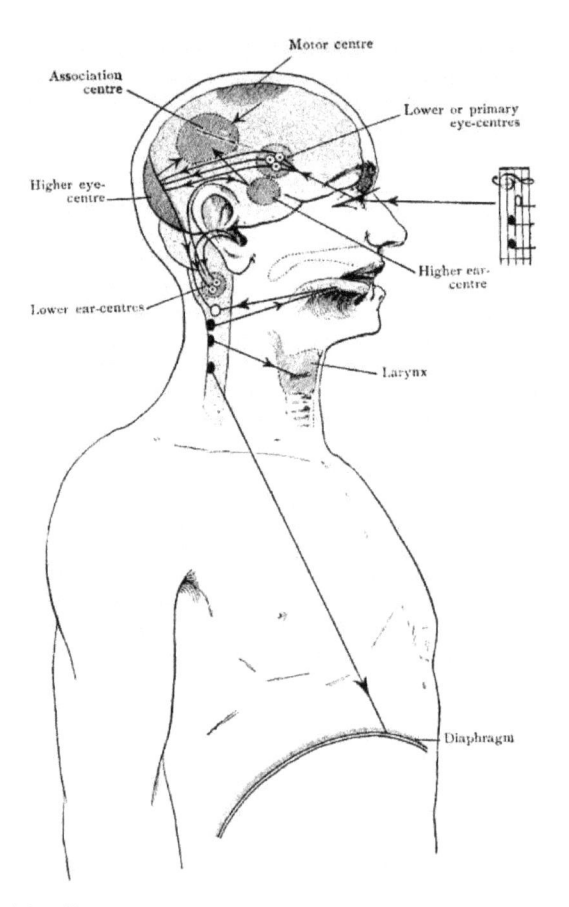

FIG. 53. By this diagram the author has attempted to give the reader some idea of the nature of the chain of processes involved in singing a single tone, from the time the eye looks on the note till the muscles concerned have given it utterance as a tone. The various nervous centres concerned are all in the brain (though the spinal cord supplies some subordinate centres). There are sensory centres, or those for the eye and the ear, and motor centres, or those sending the commands to the muscles involved. Further, these must be *connected* by paths not shown in detail, but represented by one centre spoken of as an "association" centre, which may also, possibly, have much to do with emotions, etc. But, at all events, the dependence of movements on ingoing messages or sensations is emphasized. The deaf cannot speak or sing, and the blind cannot read (ordinary) music. The defect may not be in either senses or muscles, but in the relating nervous mechanism between them. As explained in the body of the work, execution depends on at least two factors, sensations, or ingoing messages, and movements determined by these. Now the *connection*

between the ingoing and the outgoing impulses is the most important and the least understood part, but the above diagram will at least serve to emphasize the fact that such connections exist, and that in a general way the result, performance, can be explained. No attempt has been made to trace the path of other sensory impulses than those from eye and ear, as this would make the diagram too complicated.

Often the student is puzzled by contradictory opinions on this subject. One celebrated prima donna states that she never practises more than one hour a day; another, equally distinguished, that she has often spent several hours in almost continuous strenuous practice. What is the student to believe, and whom to follow? No one, for no two persons are alike. All the above questions can be safely and surely answered in the light of science and experience combined, but such questions cannot be settled by the dictum of any singer, teacher, or writer, nor does the experience, in itself, of any one person furnish an adequate guide for others.

Investigation has shown that the use of muscles tends to the accumulation of the waste products of vital activity; that such accumulation is associated with the experience in consciousness of what we term "fatigue," and which is preceded by "weariness." The latter is a warning that the more serious condition is approaching, but is to be distinguished from another feeling not necessary to name, often present in unwilling youthful students, and for which various forms of treatment are sometimes tried so unsuccessfully that it is as well to discontinue study altogether.

1. The time at which, as a rule, any work can best be carried out is during the early hours of the day, so that if it is possible, practice should be begun early, and after some preliminary exercise for the good of the body generally—*e.g.*, a short walk, during which the lungs may be filled with pure air. As the muscles of the chest, etc., are to be used in voice-production, such a walk or other form of general exercise should not be lengthy. Energy should be reserved for the muscular activities involved in vocal practice.

2. The principle that guides in all use of the muscles, all exercise, is that it be taken under the most favorable circumstances and short of fatigue, even of weariness; hence the question whether the student should practise five minutes or one hour is one that he himself, and he alone, can determine, provided he is old enough and observant enough to know when he begins to feel weary in his vocal mechanism, whether it be in the respiratory organs, the larynx, or the resonance-chambers. With some there is a weak spot, and this settles the question for all other parts. As a rule, beginners will do well not to practice, at first, for longer at one time than five minutes, not only

because of the possible weariness, but because at the outset it is difficult to keep the attention fixed. The ear and brain tire as well as the muscles.

Naturally, the condition of the student at the time has much to do with the length of a practice, but all things are determined by the sensible application of that principle which science and experience alike show to be a safe guide.

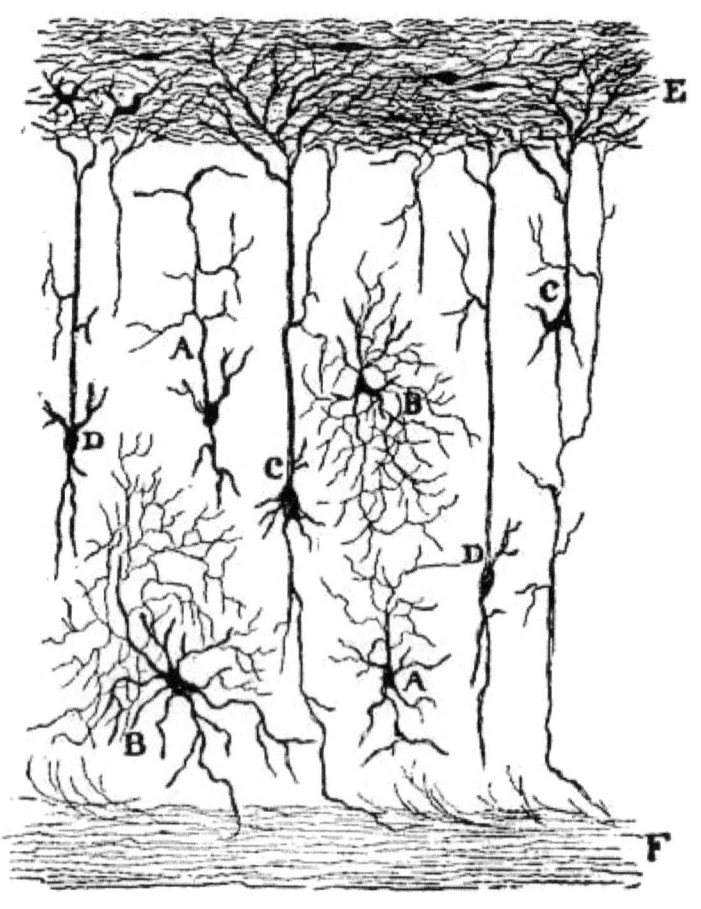

FIG. 54. The above is a diagrammatic representation of a highly magnified section (or very thin slice) through the outermost or most superficial part of the great brain (cortex cerebri), and is inserted to help the reader to form some idea of the complexity of structure of the most important part of the brain so far as the highest mental processes are concerned. This complexity is greater in man than in other animals.

Naturally, as in other exercises, the duration of an exercise may be gradually lengthened with experience. One singer may find an hour a day sufficient, if she be already perfectly trained in every respect—be "in good form," or "fit," as the athletes say—and have only light or *coloratura* parts to sing; but would this suffice to form a singer to sustain the heaviest dramatic parts for hours together before a large public audience? The training of a hundred-yards sprinter should not be the same as that prescribed for a long-distance runner or a wrestler.

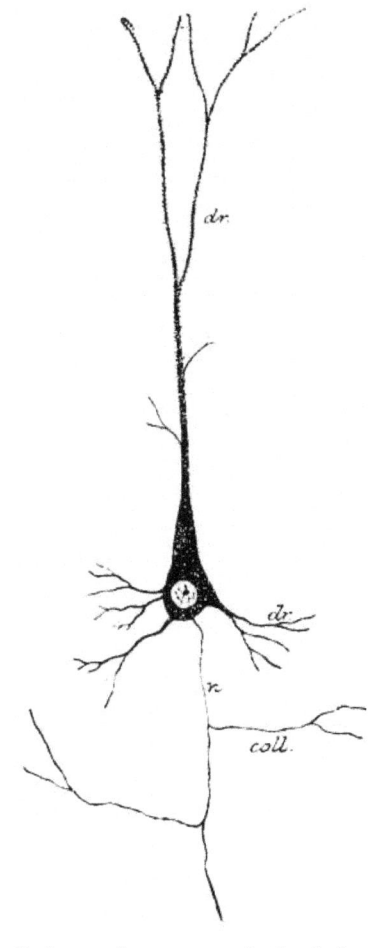

FIG. 55. A nerve-cell from the outer rind of the great brain (cortex cerebri), much magnified. (Schäfer.)

3. In all practice it is ever to be borne in mind that the end, even in an exercise, is artistic. Tones of that quality only which is the best possible to the singer at the time are to be produced, and everything else must yield to this.

4. No wise trainer ever allows his charges to go on a racing track and at once run a hundred yards at the highest possible speed. Such a course would be against all sound knowledge and all the best experience. Hence the question of *piano* and *forte* practice answers itself; the singer should never begin any exercise *forte*, but either *piano* or *moderato*—as to which depends on the individual. Some persons can only after long study produce really good tones *piano*; such if not most persons should, of course, begin practising with moderate force.

Certainly, the voice-user should, in order to gain volume, gradually increase the vigor of his practice, but exactly how to do this, and to what extent daily, are questions in which the advice of a sensible and experienced teacher is of great value, though the principle on which that opinion should be founded is clear enough.

5. The questions as to the total amount of time to be devoted to practice in a single day, and as to whether practice should be continued day after day for weeks and months without interruption, must be decided by the condition of the student, and not by any arbitrary opinion. Some individuals and some racers have a capacity for steady work not possessed by others, and happy are they; but there are others who go on by spurts, and such natures are often capable of reaching lofty artistic heights, if they be wisely managed. They need much the same sort of care as a very fleet but uncertain race-horse, and they are often a source of disgust to themselves and of worry to their teachers; but they in some cases get far beyond what the more steady ones can attain to, while others are so unsteady without being talented that they are a trial, and a trial only, to all concerned. Such people should, even when clever, not be encouraged in their vagaries, but brought gradually and tactfully under a stricter discipline.

6. "Hasten slowly" applies to all musical practice, that of the voice included, and there never was a time in the history of the world, unfortunately, when people believed in it less. The author would especially warn the student against attempting to force progress by violent or unduly long-continued practices, for if the vocal apparatus be strained, it may remain impaired for months or even for life. "Little and often" is a good maxim for vocal practice, all the more as the discontinuation, for the time, of voice-production need not imply that the mind must cease to act. An artist is not formed by vocalization alone, but by processes of education that are many and

complicated, into which we might be tempted to enter did they not lie beyond the range of the present work.

If the principles set forth in this chapter are scientifically reliable, and we believe they will not be questioned, certain practical considerations are well worthy of special attention. If practice, repetition, leads to the formation of habits more or less fixed, then there can be no surer way to ruin a speaker or vocalist than to permit him to practise by a wrong method; the more he practises, the more he stamps in what is bad. It follows that the most hopeless cases eminent teachers have to deal with are to be found among those vocalists who come to them after years of professional life before the public. One must look on some of these people as on a building spoiled by a bad architectural design. In some cases there is nothing to do but to take the whole structure apart and put it together afresh. It may be humiliating to the vocalist, and it is a severe condemnation of certain methods of teaching, but there is often no other course open, the only question being as to whether the material is good enough to warrant such a radical proceeding. Every eminent teacher can recall such cases, and might fill volumes with their histories. If more of these were published as warnings to students and teachers, a good purpose would be served. It is truly sad to find that the prospects of one who might have been formed into a fine artist have been hopelessly ruined by years of practice based on principles that are radically unsound.

In the next chapter some specific applications of the principles discussed in the foregoing pages will be considered.

SUMMARY.

All forms of artistic and other expression imply movements. For a willed or voluntary movement there are required (1) an idea, (2) a neuro-muscular mechanism. Such movements may be relatively simple or highly complex. They all tend, when frequently carried out, to become reflex, and to some extent unconscious or subconscious. Combinations of reflexes when associated with consciousness become habits. Movements only attain their highest perfection when they reach this stage. It follows that the purpose of all musical practice should be to establish those reflexes which attain the end, the ideal, and to form correct habits. A poem properly recited or a song satisfactorily sung implies a combination of certain reflexes or habits. Some of these are in their main features common to all speech and song, but many are peculiar to each example.

As phonation implies the use of the muscles (neuro-muscular mechanisms) of the (1) respiratory organs, (2) vocal bands, (3) resonance-chambers, and as these must all work in harmony, or be "co-ordinated," it will be seen that speaking and singing are physiologically highly complex. When, in addition, ideas and feelings are associated, and determine the exact form of these co-ordinations, the whole matter is seen to be still more complex. The emission of a single tone implies (1) an idea—the nature of the sound as to pitch and quality, (2) such an arrangement of all the parts of the mechanism as will produce it. The former involves memory of the tone; the latter, memories of former movements. Then, partly as a series of voluntary acts and partly reflexly, according as the student is more or less advanced, or the particular tone new or old in experience, do the various neuro-muscular arrangements pass into orderly action. In this process the ear is the chief guide, always in relation to memories. When one uses the printed page, the eyes also guide—*i.e.*, the nervous impulses that pass in through these avenues determine the outgoing ones that bring the muscles into action. In doing so they rouse many others (associated nervous connections) which are highly important when an artistic result is to be reached.

To consider a single case: Assume that the note is to be sung. The following are required: (1) Memory of this tone. (2) Adaptation through eye and ear of all the neuro-muscular mechanisms required for (*a*) bringing the vocal bands into the correct position and degree of tension; (*b*) the proper shape, tension, etc., of the resonance-chambers; (*c*) that use of the breathing apparatus suitable to cause the proper vibrations of the vocal bands. All use of the voice implies this much, but in most instances there are *associated* nervous mechanisms and ideas that are highly important in determining the exact volume, quality, etc., of the tone as related to expression of ideas and feelings according to conventional usage.

The breath-stream must in all cases be so employed that there shall be economy of energy—no waste. Waste occurs whenever air escapes to any appreciable extent through the glottis chink, as that implies an imperfect adjustment of the vocal bands and the expiratory current. From this and other points of view it may be said that *he is the best singer who gets the most perfect result with the least expenditure of energy.*

It is of the highest importance that during every practice, and every moment of each practice, attention be given to as perfect a result as possible, and that the same method be invariably employed.

All questions as to methods of practising can be decided on well-known scientific principles which harmonize with experience, and need not be left in that loose and unsatisfactory condition when the dictum of some individual is substituted for principles capable of actual experimental demonstration.

CHAPTER XIII.

CHIEFLY AN APPLICATION TO VOICE PRODUCTION OF FACTS AND PRINCIPLES PREVIOUSLY CONSIDERED.

CERTAIN sounds may be made without the use of words or syllables, even without the employment of vowels or consonants, but intonation proper cannot be carried out without vowels, at least.

The exact nature of vowels and consonants will be considered in the next chapter, but in the meantime it may be pointed out that a vowel is a free and open sound requiring for its production a certain form of the resonance-chambers. Neither vowels nor consonants are absolutely pure—that is, entirely free from foreign elements, from noise; but for all practical purposes a vowel is a pure sound, a consonant a sound accompanied inevitably by much noise. This noise is largely due to the difficulties of sounding consonants, the breath breaking against the vocal organs, especially the teeth, lips, etc., much as the waves of the sea against a rocky beach. So far then as musical quality is concerned, a consonant is an unmitigated nuisance. On the other hand, none but the most elemental communication by sounds could be carried out by the use of vowels alone. The consonants stop the breath-current, separate the vowels, and thus lay the foundation for the expression of ideas. Ideas imply differences; a new idea is conveyed by a new word, which in its simplest form is a syllable.

When a consonant is introduced after a vowel sound, a momentary arrest is produced in the breath-flow, and this has its corresponding effect on the mind. It is, in fact, equivalent to a pause—say a comma or a period. If introduced before a vowel, it is marked off in a more definite way. The effect of this is to enable the ear the better to grasp the sounds. There is the principle of differentiation and the principle of rest, both highly important in all sensory and other psychic or mental processes.

Consider the sentence "He is a man"—composed purely of monosyllables. Remove the consonants, and we have the following: "e i a a." Their ineffectiveness in conveying ideas is at once plain, for though "a man" conveys two ideas, such are not expressed by the vowels, which are identical, while "e" and "i" are common to too many words of one syllable to serve any useful purpose, alone, in the conveyance of *definite* ideas. The consonants at once mark off the limitations; they fence around the ideas, so to speak. For the communication of ideas they are indispensable; nevertheless, being largely noises, they are musically abominable.

It follows that voice-production should begin with vowel sounds, and not words—not even syllables. For successful intonation, the first steps should be made as simple as possible, as we have already endeavored to show, hence no such complication as a consonantal noise should be introduced. Upon this point there is room for no difference of opinion, though as to which vowel sound is best suited for the beginner, and for more advanced voice-production, there has been great diversity in teaching—a diversity which we propose to show, in the next chapter, need not exist to any appreciable extent.

Certain vowel sounds may be said to be common to most of the languages used by civilized peoples. These are u (*oo*), $\bar{o}$, a (*ah*), $\bar{a}$, i (*ei*), and $\bar{e}$. There is, fortunately, among teachers considerable agreement as to the question of the best vowel sound with which to begin intonation, or the process of forming musical tones. There can be no question that a (ah) is for general purposes the best, the reason for which will appear later. Unfortunately, there is not in the minds of students or teachers generally a sufficiently deep conviction of the importance of forming the voice by long-continued practice with vowels only, for which lack the spirit of the times is largely responsible. Until a student of either speaking or singing can form every vowel perfectly, which implies the recognition of these sounds as pure and perfect, and the ability to sing them as the tones of a musical scale, he should not take a single step in any other direction. To do so is to waste tune and to lower artistic ideals.

When words are to be used, the question as to which language should be employed is for the singer, at least, a very important one. The ideal vocalist who will bring before the ideal public the best in vocal music must sing in Italian, French, German, and English, at least. Each of these languages produces its own effects through the voice, and each presents its own advantages and difficulties; but all competent to judge are agreed that Italian, because of the abundance of vowels in its words, is the best language in which to sing, or, at all events, to begin with as a training. Because of the prevalence of consonants, the German and the English languages are relatively unmusical. The English abounds in hissing sounds, which are a trial to the singer with an exacting ear and perfect taste, and produce most unwelcome effects on the refined listener who really puts music first and the conveyance of ideas second in a vocal composition. It should, of course, be the aim of the student to overcome these difficulties, as German and English, the languages of Goethe, Schiller, and Shakespeare, are for dramatic and some other purposes not equalled by any other languages.

But the artist, and above all the musical artist, must be a citizen of the world. He deals with those forms of emotion common to all mankind, and not with the peculiar little combinations of ideas that grow up in a province, city, or village; though of course he will not neglect local coloring, so well illustrated in the folk-songs or popular melodies that have survived for ages in different countries.

Though a vowel can be produced pure only when the resonance-chambers assume a certain form, this is, of course, only one link in the chain of production. The breathing apparatus and the larynx are also concerned, and we are again brought back, as ever, to the triple combination of the three sets of mechanisms so often alluded to, yet, we venture to think, very inadequately linked in the minds of learners, if not also of teachers.

In producing a vowel sound the end aimed at is, on the one hand, purity, on the other, as a result, the easy and effective use of mechanisms—*i.e.*, the technique. In every case the breath must be used without waste—just enough, and no more; the laryngeal apparatus, the vocal bands, must be so adapted as to set the air of the resonance-chambers into perfect vibration, which only occurs when the expiratory blast is applied in the correct way and at the right moment to the properly adjusted vocal bands. This latter we have defined as the attack. It implies giving a good start to the tone. It is not all, but it is a large half, in the artist and for the auditor.

RECONSIDERATION OF THE RESONANCE-CHAMBERS

We shall now give further attention to some of the more important parts of the resonance-chambers, in so far as they bear directly on voice-production.

In singing and speaking, the larynx should be *steadied*, but not held rigidly fixed in any one position. It will be remembered that to this part of the vocal mechanism are attached, below, the trachea, and above, the tongue, indirectly through the hyoid bone and the thyro-hyoid membrane, as well as certain muscles which influence the relative position of these various parts, so that to maintain the larynx in the same position, absolutely, must be against Nature's methods. The tongue alone must in its movements tend to alter the position of the larynx, as we have before pointed out. At the same time, the laxness and lack of control which some singers permit in their vocal organs, under the mistaken idea that all the parts of the "throat" cannot be too free, prevents them from getting the effects they desire, with that vigor and certainty the public so much admires, and rightly so. The golden mean should be observed; between undue tension, which implies inability to control, whether it be in the larynx or the breathing apparatus, and a looseness inconsistent with neat and certain results, the voice-producer must choose, with that common sense so indispensable to success in all undertakings, but which will never be adequately encouraged till students look more frequently for the reasons of the procedures recommended to them, and teachers strive to gain influence with their pupils by showing them that what they recommend lies beyond their own minds—that it, in fact, has its foundation in the laws of Nature.

Of the tongue, soft palate, and lips, which are the principal modifiers of the shape of the mouth cavity, the tongue has by far the most influence. When the tongue lies flat in the mouth, it may be considered to be in its primary position, and it is important that in singing and speaking the student learn to begin his voice-production with this organ in that position, or a slight modification of it, for it is only when it is thus placed that a tone at once round, full, and pure can be produced.

In order to secure this result, the vocalist or speaker must begin by taking breath through the mouth, as we have already insisted, and at once, before there is time for any stiffening of parts, commence to intonate—*i.e.*, as soon as enough air has been inhaled for the purpose intended. The correct position is facilitated when one taking breath through the mouth acts as if about to *yawn*. If this act be well imitated, the student will find, on looking into a hand-glass, that the tongue is more or less furrowed behind in the middle—in other words, it forms a sort of trough; and the deeper the trough the student learns to form at will, the better, for there are times in actual singing and speaking when this must be as deep as possible. It is clear that in this way the central convexity above, formed by the hard palate, forms with the corresponding concavity in the tongue a sort of trumpet-shaped organ admirably adapted for the production of the desired tone.

The tongue is important in the highest degree not only in the formation of vowels, as will be shown more fully in the next chapter, but also in shaping consonants.

It is sometimes important to move the tongue from one position to another with great rapidity. Such a composition as Figaro's song (cavatina) in Rossini's "Barber of Seville" could not be properly sung by any one not possessing great control over the tongue. Indeed, this composition may be considered a perfect test of the extent to which the singer is a master of mouth gymnastics; and this is only one of many such works. In like manner, many passages in Shakespeare and others of the best writers in all languages can only be spoken with effect by those with a mastery over the tongue, lips, soft palate, etc., but above all, the tongue.

Important as are the lips, many persons tend to use them too much, and the tongue too little, in speaking and singing. They attempt to make up for a mouth almost closed in front by the teeth, by excessive movements of the lips.

Special tongue and lip practice should be carried out before a mirror. The lips should be kept rather close to the gums, and moved away as little as possible (*i.e.*, the lips), as to do so serves no good purpose, and is unpleasant to the eye of the observer. Teeth and lips must be regarded, so far as musical sounds are concerned, as danger regions—rocks on the shore, against which the singer or speaker may shipwreck his tones. His object should be to use them adequately to form vowels and consonants—in other words, in the formation, not the spoiling, of words, as is so often the case.

We cannot too much insist on both speaker and singer attending to forming a connection between his ear and his mouth cavity. He is to hear, that he may produce good tones, and the tones cannot be correctly formed if they be not well observed. To listen to one's self carefully and constantly is a most valuable but little practised art. The student should listen as an inexorable critic, accepting only the best from himself.

This leads to the consideration of the question of the open mouth. The expression "open mouth" means, no doubt, to most people, the open lips rather than the open mouth cavity—*i.e.*, open in front, the teeth well separated. In voice-production, by "open mouth" both open cavity and open lips must be understood.

There is a special tendency in many, perhaps in most persons, to close the mouth cavity unduly in singing a descending scale. This is often accompanied by a bad use of the breath, and a general relaxation of the vocal apparatus, which is possibly more frequent in sopranos and tenors, whose chief effects are often produced by their high tones. But to-day, more than ever, when refined intellectual and emotional effects are demanded, is it important that the lower tones, so effective in producing emotional states, should not be neglected by any singer of whatever voice; while for speakers high tones are really comparatively little used.

Much more attention is paid by teachers and students to the open mouth at the present time than formerly; in fact, like some other good things, it is often overdone. The individuality of the singer and speaker must always be borne in mind. If some are obliged to open the mouth as much as others, the result will not be happy. Any one may demonstrate to himself that the quality of a tone may be at once changed by unduly opening or closing the mouth. One may say that *the mouth should be sufficiently opened to produce the best possible effect.* We have never seen the mouth opened to such an extent that it was positively unsightly—reminding one of the rhinoceros at a zoo—without feeling that the tone had suffered thereby.

If all would remember that the mouth is best opened by simply *dropping the lower jaw*, passively, in the easiest manner possible, the difficulties some students experience would disappear. Many act as if the process were chiefly an active one, while the reverse is the case, as one may observe in the sleeper when the muscles become unduly relaxed—a condition that is often accompanied by snoring, which is produced by a mouth-breathing that gives rise to vibrations of the soft palate. We mean to say that the lower jaw drops when muscles relax, and that opening the mouth is largely a passive thing, while closing the mouth is an active process.

The position of the head in its influence on tone-production is an insufficiently considered subject. It is impossible that the head be much raised or lowered without changes being produced in the vocal apparatus, especially the larynx, and if the tone is not to suffer in consequence, special care must be taken to make compensatory changes in the parts affected. It is only necessary to sing any vowel, and then raise the chin greatly, to observe a distinct change in the quality of the tone, with corresponding sensations in the vocal organs.

To speak or sing with the head turned to one side is plainly unfavorable to the well-being of the parts used, because it leads to compression, which gives rise to that congestion before referred to as the source of so many evils in voice-users. To sit at a piano and sing is an unphysiological proceeding, because it implies that the head is bent in reading the music on a page much lower than the eyes, and when, with this, the head is turned to one side to allow of reading the music on the distant side of the page, furthest from the middle line of the head, the case is still worse. If all who thus use the vocal organs do not give evidence of the truth of the above by hoarseness, etc., it is simply because in young and vigorous organs there may be considerable power of resisting unfavorable influences. The student is recommended to use his voice in the standing position only, when possible, as all others are more or less unnatural.

One often has the opportunity to observe how the effect is lost when a reader bends his head downward to look at his book or manuscript; and he himself, if the process is long-continued, will almost certainly feel the injurious influence of this acting on his vocal organs.

CHAPTER XIV.

SOME SPECIFIC APPLICATIONS OF PRINCIPLES IN TONE PRODUCTION.

IT is no doubt valuable, indeed for most singers essential, to employ a series of elaborate exercises, or *vocalises*, which in some cases differ from each other only by slight gradations; but it is to be borne in mind that all the actual principles involved can be expressed practically in a very few exercises. These are: (1) The single sustained tone; (2) the tones of a scale sung so as to be smoothly linked together; (3) the same, sung somewhat more independently of each other; (4) the same, but each tone beginning and ending very suddenly. If the execution of any vocal musical composition be analyzed, it will be found that these four methods cover substantially the whole ground. As one other is very extensively used in giving expression in the form of shading, it is worthy of special mention—viz., (5) the swell. All others are modifications of the above.

As these methods of tone-production are of so much importance, it will be worth while to analyze them. It will be found that in each there is a characteristic use of the breathing mechanism. The larynx and the resonance-chambers are of course intermediate, as usual, between the breath-stream and the result, the tone; without them there could be no tones. But if the student have clearly in mind the memory of the tone he wishes to produce, including its various properties of pitch, volume, quality, etc., it will be found that the point requiring strict attention, in production, is the breathing, especially the manner of using the expiratory current.

1. The sustained tone requires an amount of breath proportional to its length, and the great aim in its production should be to convert, so to speak, all the breath into tone, as we explained in a previous chapter. This sustained tone, which may be practised with advantage on every one of the notes of a scale, is, in the nature of things, the very foundation of all good singing and speaking.

2. In the second and third exercises the differences in the method lie in the attack and the manner of using the breath. The smoothly linked tones are the more difficult for most people, since they require special control over the laryngeal mechanism and the breathing apparatus. Between the singing of a scale in this manner (*legato*), and as it is frequently done, there is the same difference as in walking up-stairs as does a perfectly trained ballet-dancer, and this act as carried out by a rough countryman, used only to ploughed fields, etc. For a perfect execution, the attack, while decisive enough, must be most carefully regulated, and the breathing, which is always to be considered in a good attack, must be of the most even character; the outflow

requires the most perfectly controlled movements of the respiratory apparatus. In the other form of exercise (detached tones) there is often, at least, a little more emphasis on the attack, and the breathing is perhaps not always so even, but in some passages, in actual singing, the method employed for these less closely linked tones is in most respects the same as the last.

3. Very different from all the preceding is the mode of production usually designated by musicians *staccato*, *marcato*, etc. The tone is attacked suddenly, and as suddenly dropped, which, expressed physiologically, means that the entire vocal mechanism is rapidly adjusted, one part to another, and as suddenly relaxed; and the one seems to be about as difficult as the other. In this a certain sudden tension of the vocal apparatus is essential. The whole respiratory apparatus, after the breath is taken, is held more or less tense. In executing these abrupt (staccato) effects the diaphragm is the chief agent, and operates against the column of air in the lungs, the chest and abdominal walls being kept more or less tense.

Though this is the case, the voice-producer will succeed best if he gives attention to the resonance-chambers, after having put the breathing mechanism into the right condition. There should be as little movement of the chest walls, diaphragm, larynx, etc., as possible. The whole is a question of tension, but not rigidity, and the reason the staccato effect is so difficult for most persons is that they attempt to accomplish it by *excessive movements* of the breathing apparatus or larynx.

The *mind* must be relieved of any feeling of undue tension, and the result attained by the establishment of a close connection between the ear and the resonance-chambers. The first interrupted effects should be of very brief duration and as *piano* as possible, but the attempt to produce the real staccato may to great advantage be preceded by an exercise recommended in Chapter VIII.,—viz., singing a tone of some duration, then suddenly interrupting it, and, with the same breath, beginning the tone again as suddenly as it was interrupted. In fact, till this can be done with ease the staccato proper should not be attempted, for though the principles involved are the same, the execution requires far more skill than the exercise recommended for an earlier stage, and which it is well to continue throughout.

Simple as these exercises seem from mere description, or as carried out with a certain degree of success, perfection in them is not to be attained short of years of the most diligent study. How many singers living can sing an ascending and a descending scale, in succession, with a perfect staccato, to mention no other effect? Yet among all the resources of dramatic singing and speaking none is more important than this one. What so eloquent as the silence after a perfect stop—a complete and satisfactory arrest of the tone? How many modern actors are capable of it? How many singers? Instead of the perfect arrest, the listener is conscious, not of the rounded and complete tone, but of an edge more or less ragged. There is some noise with the actual tone.

The above exercises, when carried out to a perfect result, give us *bel canto* singing, for which the old Italian school was so noted, and which is now largely a lost art, not so much because the methods are not known to teachers, as because students will not do the work necessary to attain to this *bel canto*. We seek for short cuts, and we get corresponding results.

The *bel canto* is, simply, beautiful singing, the result of perfect technique, and is opposed to effects which are not truly artistic, though no doubt often highly expressive to the unmusical and the inartistic. They may appeal to us as feats, but they are not artistic results, and, as we have before insisted, they are injurious in many cases to the vocal organs, while good voice-production strengthens them.

5. The swell is simply a modification of the sustained tone. When a tone is perfectly sustained, without any change in volume, etc., we have a most valuable effect, and one very difficult to achieve, because it implies such a steady application of the breath power and such nice adjustments of all the parts concerned. To produce a tone with variations in it is easy enough, and that is what is usually given us instead of the perfectly even tone, reminding us of a straight line.

In the swell, as the name suggests, the tone should rise gradually in volume or loudness, and as gradually decline. If this can be done readily, and continued for several seconds, it will be easy to produce other effects, as the sudden swell, but such effects should come after, not before, the slower ones. A critical observer soon realizes the defects of modern technique when he listens to a singer's tones when attempting slow effects, as in a softly sustained melody. Only the well-trained vocalist can hope to sing such a melody, especially if long sustained, in a way to meet the demands of an exacting ear and advanced musical taste. It will be apparent that the swell is the basis of shading, a quality that is so highly appreciated in this refined age. He who can manage the swell perfectly has the secret of this effect in his possession as have none others.

Although we have referred more to the singer than to the speaker, in this chapter, it is to be understood that these and all other exercises suggested are of great value in forming the voice for public speaking. It is not so important, it must be admitted, for the speaker as for the singer that his tones be musically perfect, as he relies more on ideas than on tones, still, with every idea employed by the public speaker there is the inseparable feeling, or "feeling-tone;" so that the speaker, as well as the singer, is to some extent dependent on tone painting—indeed, must be, if he will be no mere man of wood, a "dry stick," to some extent, in spite of the use of appropriate language, gestures, etc. There are many avenues to the heart, and that by tones cannot with impunity be neglected by the speaker, though for his purpose the singing of tones need occupy only weeks or months, while for singers, in the case of all who would attain to a high degree of excellence, it must extend over years.

"FORWARD," "BACKWARD," ETC., PRODUCTION.

Certain expressions are in common use by teachers and singers, such as "to direct the breath forward," "forward production," "backward production," etc. No doubt such terms may serve a practical purpose, though they are often used with lamentable vagueness, but it must be understood that they do not answer to any clearly demonstrated physiological principles. There is, for example, no clear evidence that the breath can be directed toward the hard palate in the neighborhood of the teeth, as the drawings sometimes published would indicate.

It has already been many times urged that when breathing is satisfactory, breath does not escape to any considerable extent into the mouth cavity, but that the expiratory blast is used to set the air of the resonance-chambers into vibration. The changes that must be made in these cavities, to lead to certain effects, are accompanied by characteristic sensations, and these, and not the direction of the breath, are largely responsible for the ideas on which the above expressions rest.

As before shown, the soft palate is constantly being used more or less, and when it and the tongue unite in action so as to cut off the mouth cavity, or, more strictly, the anterior portion of it, from the nasal chambers, a very pronounced modification in the tone results, and, of necessity, such actual escape of breath as occurs takes place through the nose. In reality, there is a special modification of the shape of the resonance-chambers for every tone produced, and especially when the color or quality is changed, as well as the pitch. There is, therefore, not only "forward" and "backward" but also middle production, though, in reality, these terms at best but imperfectly describe, even for practical purposes, what happens.

It is to be feared that with some teachers of both singing and speaking "forward production" has become a sort of panacea for all vocal ills; but it is not, and just the reverse teaching is required in certain cases. If a voice be brilliant, yet hard, it will be improved by a more backward production, judiciously employed, and in this way the French language is often to be recommended to such singers, as it favors this backward production, with such use of the nasal resonance as mellows the tones. The tenor who has not learned the use of the nasal resonance, to give richness to the tones of his middle and upper range, has missed a valuable principle. On the other hand, for voices that are too soft, lack brightness, and fail in carrying-power, a more forward production will often improve the quality of the voice greatly. But a little consideration must convince the student that if he is to be master of his voice-production throughout, if he is to produce tones of every shade of quality, he must be able to shift that voice about in every quarter as occasion demands; in other words, *all the changes possible in the resonance-chambers must be at his command.* Such is the case in the very greatest singers of both sexes; and, of course, this applies equally, if not still more, to speakers.

When the voice-producer has learned to intonate surely, when the voice is "placed," and the secrets of the registers are known to him, he will do well to experiment a little, cautiously, with his own resonance-chambers, so as to widen his practical knowledge of the principles underlying the modification of tones. Why should the student of the voice remain a mere imitator, when the one who works in any other direction is, or should be, encouraged to be an original investigator? The inability of students to judge of either the grounds for or the value of the exercises and methods recommended to them by their teachers seems to the author to indicate a regrettable state of things, which teachers of every form of vocal culture should endeavor to remedy. Some teachers do not use the terms "backward" and "forward," but "darkening" and "brightening" the voice; and, of course, the result of a certain use of the tongue and soft palate is to darken or veil the quality of the voice. But the attentive reader will scarcely mistake the author's meaning in the above and other references to this subject.

It is scarcely necessary to point out that in what has been said no encouragement is intended to be given to the nasal twang, or any thing resembling it—and it is easy to so use the nasal resonance that it becomes a defect; but the value of a judicious use of the nose in singing and speaking is, we are convinced, not as well known in vocal teaching as it deserves to be.

SUMMARY.

The relation of vowels and consonants to singing and speaking. Intonation should be by vowels only, at first. Consonants are a necessary evil in singing, but all-important in the formation of words—*i.e.,* in imparting ideas.

Every language has its own special merits and defects for the purposes of song and speech. That language which abounds in vowels is the best adapted for vocal exercises, etc.

It is a cardinal error to begin a course in speaking and especially singing with exercises based on words. Vowel sounds should be exclusively employed at first. In the formation of vowels and consonants the resonance-chambers are especially involved.

The tongue, soft palate, and lips are the most movable parts, and so have the largest share in giving color and meaning to sounds—*i.e.*, they are the organs most important in the formation of the elements of words.

The "open mouth" should mean open mouth cavity and duly separated lips.

It is important that there be control of all parts of the resonance-chambers, and always in relation to other parts of the vocal apparatus.

CHAPTER XV.

THE ELEMENTS OF SPEECH AND SONG.

THE subject treated in this chapter may be made dry enough; but if the student will, while reading the descriptions given, endeavor to form the sounds described, observing at the same time his own resonance-chambers (mouth parts) carefully in a hand-glass, and then follow up the applications made, the reader's experience will be, in all probability, like the author's: the more the subject is studied the more interesting does it become, especially if one experiments with his own resonance apparatus.

Vowels and consonants are the elements of syllables, and words are composed of the latter. However pure a vowel is, it is accompanied in its utterance by some noise; a consonant, by relatively a great deal of noise.

A *noise*, in distinction to a musical tone, is characterized by irregularity as regards the vibrations that reach the ear, while in the case of a tone a definite number of vibrations strikes against the drum-head of the ear within a given time; so that so far as syllables and words, even vowels, are concerned, we are not dealing with pure tones.

For the formation of each vowel a definite form of the resonance-chambers is essential. In uttering, either for the purposes of speech or song, the vowel *u* (*oo*), the mouth cavity has the form of a large flask such as chemists use for their manipulations, but the neck in this case is short. The whole resonance cavity is elongated, and the lips are protruded; the larynx is depressed, and the root of the tongue and the fauces (folds from the soft palate, usually spoken of as the "pillars of the fauces") approach. The pitch of this vowel is very low.

Hard palate

Wide flask-like cavity

Soft palate ending in the uvula

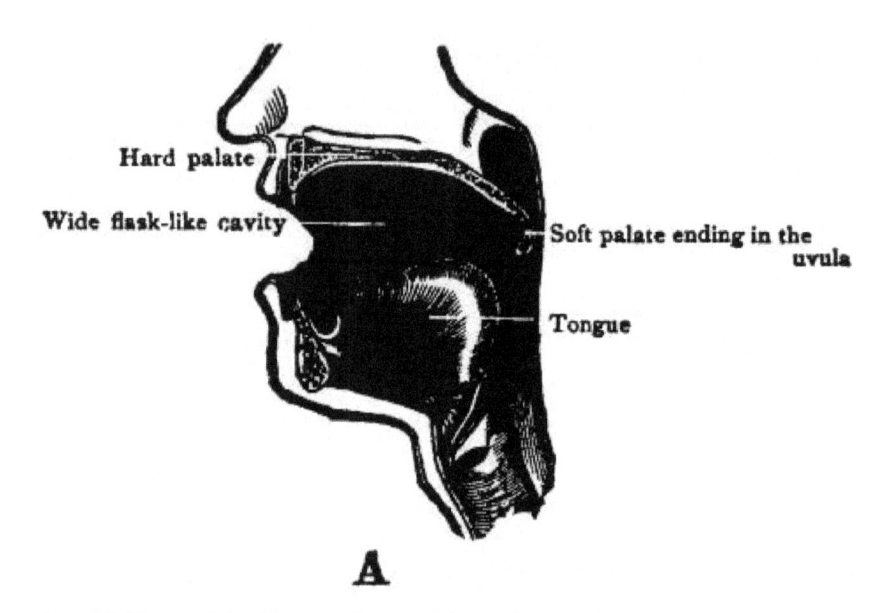

Tongue

A

FIG. 56 (Beaunis). Shows the position of parts in sounding the vowel *a*. By comparing this illustration with those following, the relatively greater size of the cavity of the mouth in this case will be evident. The reader is recommended to at once test the correctness of these representations by sounding the vowels, and observing the parts of his own vocal mechanism with a hand-mirror.

In *ō* the lips are nearer to the teeth, and the neck of the flask is shorter and wider; the larynx is somewhat more elevated than in the last case, and the pitch of the sound is higher.

When sounding *a* (as in *father*) the mouth cavity has the shape of a funnel, wide in front; the tongue lies rather flat on the floor of the mouth, the lips are wide apart, and the soft palate is somewhat raised.

In *ā* (as in *fate*) there is some modification of the last, the tongue and larynx being more raised. The pitch of this vowel is higher than is that of the more open *a*.

In the case of *ē* (as in *me*) the flask is relatively small, and the neck is long and narrow, the larynx much raised, the lips drawn back against the teeth, and the tongue greatly elevated, so as to form the narrow neck of the flask. The pitch of this vowel is high.

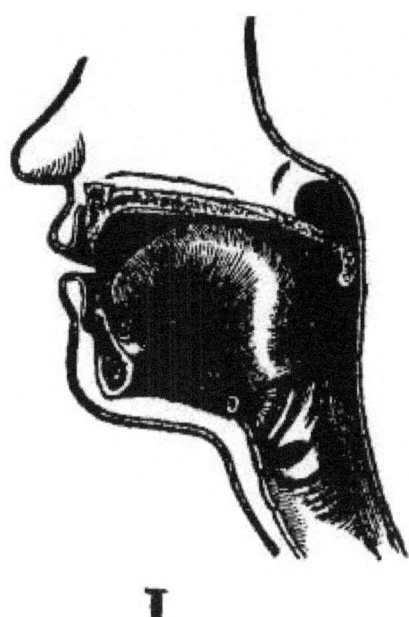

FIG. 57 (Beaunis). Shows the relative position of parts in sounding *I*. In sounding *E* the position is a good deal like that for *I*.

When sounding *ī* (as in *mine*) the cavity of the mouth behind resembles a small-bellied flask with a long, narrow neck, the larynx is at its highest, and the lips assume a position much as in the case of *ē*; between the hard palate and the back of the tongue there is only a narrow passage—a mere furrow. The pitch of this vowel is also high.

It is thus seen that every vowel has its characteristic quality and pitch, the order as regards the latter being from below upward, *u, o, a, ā, e, i*.

That the mouth cavity really can act as a resonance-chamber can be easily demonstrated by holding a small vibrating tuning-fork before the open mouth, and varying the shape and size of the cavity till the sound of the fork is observed to be suddenly increased in volume. The cavity then is a resonance-chamber for the fork, and thus intensifies its sound; in other words, the air in the mouth cavity vibrates in harmony with the tuning-fork.

To demonstrate in a simple manner that each vowel has its own pitch, the mouth cavity is put into the form usual in sounding the vowel, and the finger is filliped against the cheek, when a tone answering in pitch to that of the vowel in question results. The demonstration is easier with the lower-pitched, broader vowels, but the correctness of the order of the pitch mentioned above can thus be shown to be established.

Some very important principles for the speaker and singer hinge upon the above-mentioned facts. It follows, for example, that it is impossible to give a vowel its *perfect* sound in any but one position of the mouth parts, so that for a singer to utter a word containing the vowel *ŭ* (*oo*) at a high pitch is a practical impossibility. The listener may know what syllable is meant, and overlook the defect either from habit or from an uncritical attitude, but composers of vocal music should bear such facts in mind and not impose impossibilities on singers. At the same time, the vocalist, in order to satisfy a modern audience, is obliged to sound every word and every syllable as correctly as possible, even if the tone suffer somewhat thereby. It is wonderful how fully the best poets have, with the insight of genius, adapted their words (vowels) to the ideas they wish to convey, and had all composers of vocal music done the same, the path of the singer would not have been strewn with so many thorns. The difficulties in the case of the speaker are similar, but less marked, as his range is so much more limited as regards pitch.

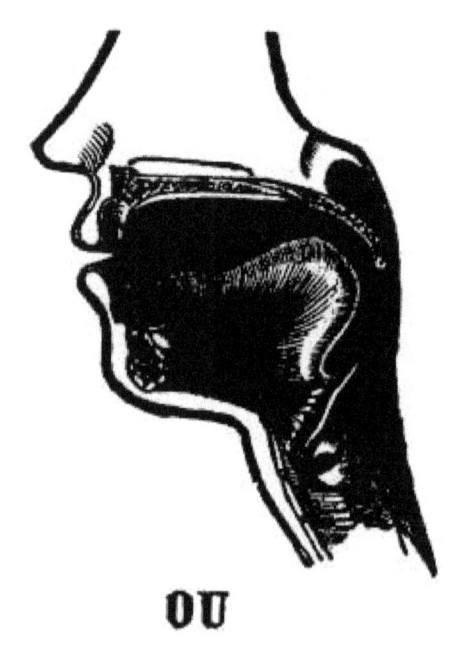

FIG. 58 (Beaunis). Shows the relative position of the parts in sounding *OU*.

This subject has also most important bearings on the learning of languages. One is born with tendencies toward certain mouth positions, etc., and from infancy he is constantly using the resonance-chambers in certain characteristic ways. In the course of years these positions, etc., become such fixed habits that it is difficult to change them, so that for this as well as many other reasons the learning of languages by persons beyond a certain age is a difficult matter. But to all students of a foreign tongue it is really essential to explain the physical mechanism by which the various sounds are made. The author has known an adult to struggle for months with French and German pronunciation, and get into a state of discouragement, fearing that he never would be able to learn the languages in which he wished to speak and sing, when a few moments spent in explaining just what we have written above for vowels, and what we have earlier and shall now more fully set forth in this chapter as regards consonants, have been followed by the lifting of the cloud from the mind and of a load of heaviness from the heart.

The learner should (1) hear the sound (elemental—a vowel, say) from the lips of the teacher, and actually perceive just what that sound is—*i.e.*, he must really hear it; (2) observe the shape of the resonance-chambers; (3) try to produce the same shape of his own, and under the guidance of his ear and his eye (watching the mouth of the teacher) so utter the sound correctly. This sound should be fixed in the mind, and the ear trained by comparing it with other sounds, as the wise teacher will do, and require imitations. Any language can be pronounced correctly in a short time, if this method be followed. It is, indeed, the only one that rests on science and common sense. The student when away from the teacher, after he has once learned to form the vowels correctly, should practise with a hand-glass before him for some time, at least.

The learning of a new language is the acquiring of a new mouth, or, at all events, entirely new methods of using the old one. In reality, however, this is not so fully the case as it at first seems. In all the languages one wishes to acquire, the same vowels occur, and for the learner it is often a question of lower or higher pitch, or greater or less breadth, though all this involves the formation of new habits and the fighting of old ones, and often in the case of the adult the struggle is a long-continued and severe one. Some nations speak at a lower pitch than others, and if a foreigner enunciate ever so well, yet at the pitch of his own and not that of the new language, his utterance may seem foreign. The Germans speak at a much lower pitch than Americans, and their tongue, even when grammatically spoken by the latter, is apt to have a sort of foreign flavor. It slightly disturbs the listener, who is not accustomed to hear his mother-tongue transposed into another key, so to speak.

We have known a learner to derive great benefit from having it pointed out to him that certain of his vowel sounds would at once cease to be incorrect if their pitch were altered. Of course, in doing this, there were at once many changes made in the resonance-chambers, in order to get the changed pitch. Pitch, accent, and duration of the sound throw much light on the subject of dialect, as a little analysis of Irish or Scotch will show.

Consonants are, as we have already said, noisy nuisances for the singer, but indispensable for word-formation, and so for human intercourse. Each has also its own pitch, and investigators have come to a measurable degree of agreement on this subject.

To illustrate: Madame Seiler found that *r* and *s* are separated from each other by an interval of many octaves: , *r*; , *s*. The latter, *s*, cannot be sounded without more or less of a hissing sound, suggesting escape of air, which is very unpleasant to the ear, and, unfortunately, these hissing sounds are very common in English, so that the speaker or singer is called upon to use all his art to overcome this disagreeable effect. This is also prominent in *whispering*—i.e., the escape of breath, with its corresponding effect on the ear. Whispering is effected chiefly, if not solely, by the resonance-chambers, the vocal bands taking only the slightest part, if any at all.

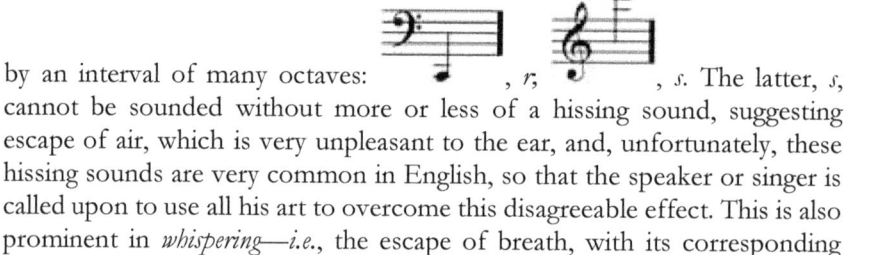

The physiologist Brücke, treating of the utterance of consonants, considered that they were formed by the more or less complete closure of certain doors in the course of the outgoing blast of air, and we have already referred to a consonant as an unpleasant interrupter, musically considered. Perhaps we should be disposed to compare them to the people that talk during the performance at a concert, did we not wish to avoid bringing such useful members of the speech community into undeserved disrepute.

Consonants, like vowels, have their own mouth positions. This follows from their having pitch, but, in addition, they require the use of the tongue, lips, etc., in a special way. The principal articulation positions are the following: (1) Between the lips; (2) between the tongue and the hard palate; (3) between the tongue and the soft palate; (4) between the vocal bands.

To indicate this, certain terms have been employed, and as they are in common use by those who treat of this subject, it will be well to explain them.

Explosives are consonants in uttering which there is complete closure with a sudden opening of the resonance-chambers in front, as in *b* and *p*.

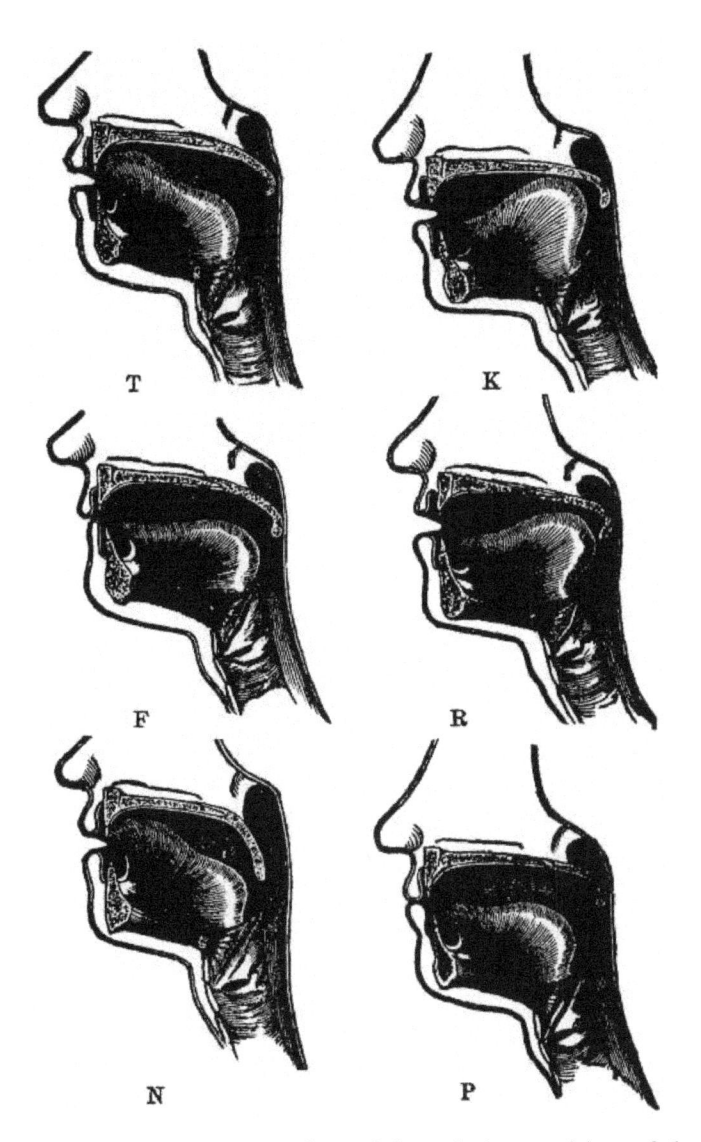

FIG. 59 (Beaunis). Representation of the relative position of the parts and the resulting shape of the sounding chamber when the consonants indicated are formed vocally. Verification of the truthfulness of the illustrations will prove profitable.

Vibratives call for an almost complete closure of the door and a vibration of its margin, as in *r*.

Aspirates partly close the opening, which is at once suddenly opened again, as in *f, v*, etc.

Resonants close the mouth, so the sound must find its way out through the nose, as in *m, n, ng*.

The above may be put in tabular form as follows:

Articulation Positions.	Explosives.	Aspirates.	Vibrates.	Resonants.
1	*b, p*	*f, v, w*		*m*
2	*t, d*	*s, z, l, sch, th*		*n*
3	*k, g*	*j, ch*	Palatal *r*	*ng*
4		*h*		

Of course the above is only one of many possible classifications, and expresses only a part of the whole truth, for the formation of a single consonant is a very complicated process, the exact nature of which can only be very imperfectly analyzed and expressed in words.

In complexity of action the resonance-chambers are wonderful beyond any instrument devised by man, and the more one studies the subject, the greater the wonder becomes at the amount and complexity of the work done in a single day's speaking. It is also easy to understand how difficult it is to attain to absolutely perfect results. To enable one's fellow-creatures to understand him in even his mother-tongue involves an amount of effort and energy, a complexity and facility in function, that can only be reached after months of practice in infancy; but to attain to that degree of perfection that makes an artist in speaking, how much greater is the expenditure in vital capital! Is not the result when attained worth the best efforts of the most talented individual?

CHAPTER XVI.

FURTHER THEORETICAL AND PRACTICAL CONSIDERATION OF VOWELS AND CONSONANTS.

THE reader will now be prepared to consider the answer to be given to the question as to the *vowels* most suitable for practice in intonation. Plainly, *a* (*ah*) puts the resonance-chambers into the easiest and best position to form a good pure tone. The pitch of the vowel is intermediate—not very low and not high in the scale. For the higher tones, evidently, *ā*, *e*, and *i* are better than *a* (*ah*), much less *o* and *u*, which are quite out of the question, comparatively speaking.

However, as music must be sung with vowels in every position, it is plainly necessary to learn to sound all the vowels well throughout the scale. In fact, one might wisely, after preliminary practice on *a*, begin a scale below with *u*, then go on to *o*, *a*, *ā*, *e*, and *i*.

Some have recommended that the vocalist begin his scale practices with *a*, and when the higher middle tones are reached, that he use *ā*, and for head tones *ā* and *e*, an advice which is obviously sound, as it is based on scientific principles.

Sounds that are very expressive in public utterance, whether in speech or song, are *l* and especially *r*. In ordinary speech most persons use only the guttural *r*, in the formation of which the soft palate takes a prominent part; but for the speaker and the singer the lingual *r* is often much more effective. It is produced by the vibration of the tip of the tongue, and can only be formed well, in most cases, after long-continued and persevering practice.

Certain consonants tend to nasality. These are *m*, *n*, *ng*, and of these all persons who are disposed to this production to the point of excess must especially beware. These letters, with such people, should be given a rapid and forward production, while singers with hard and metallic voices will do well to sing syllables beginning with these consonants, such as *maw, naw, ang, eng*, etc.

According to the teachings of physics, the quality of a tone is determined largely by the number and variety of the *overtones* accompanying the fundamental tone. Practically all musical tones, whether vocal or instrumental, are made up of the ground tone and certain others less loud and prominent, and the latter are the overtones. These may be very numerous, and some are favorable and others unfavorable to excellence in quality. It has been thought, as the result of scientific investigation, that when the first octave of the fundamental tone and its fifth interval are prominent, the voice is soft, and with the fifth and seventh well in evidence, the voice is bright and clear.

It might be said that the voice-user should endeavor to keep out of his voice certain overtones, especially those which are not within the range of our modern harmonies. A harsh voice is one in which such unharmonic intervals preponderate.

The most beautiful quality of tone is produced by keeping intensity within limits, and by a sudden, elastic attack, a point on which we dwelt at some length before; but this only emphasizes the importance of all who use the voice employing, not only when beginners, but throughout their career, exercises with vowels alone. Only in this way will the association between the hearing of pure tones and their production be established.

Such exercises are also necessary to give good carrying power to the voice. If more attention were given to this point, and less to the production of mere volume of sound, it would be well for the best musical art. Naturally, the higher the pitch of tones, within certain limits, the greater their carrying power, and the reverse, of course, with the lower tones; so that it is very important that the speaker and singer use all reasonable means to produce these lower tones well, else they are muffled, and the words associated with them are not heard. This principle should be borne in mind especially by tenors and light sopranos, in whom the lower tones are not usually the best, or the easiest to produce; so that a good attack and careful and neat syllable-formation, with all attention to both vowels and consonants, should be especially studied, and, above all, in tones below about G on the treble clef. The tendency to close the mouth, especially in a descending scale, below this point, and to confound blurring with soft (*piano*) singing, is common. A *piano* tone should be formed with especial care as to attack, open mouth, etc., and all words associated with the duller, lower-pitched vowels be spoken with the greatest distinctness, both in singing and speaking. At the same time, the barytone and contralto should not boast themselves over the tenor or soprano, if they are more successful with lower tones and the words associated with them, for the latter class of singers can often revel like birds in regions not approachable by the deeper-voiced singers. Each in its own order!

It follows that if the organs of speech are used so as to produce vowels, consonants, and their combinations, with unusual and, for practical purposes, unnecessary distinctness, the actual performance, as demanded by a critical ear, will be easier. One that can run two hundred yards as readily as another can one hundred is in a better position for the shorter sprint than the other man; hence the wisdom of the singer and speaker practising first with unusual and indeed unnecessary distinctness, so far as the listener is concerned, in order that he may satisfy even the critical with *ease*—that all-important principle in art.

All persons must, of necessity, speak in some register, and even an ear but little cultivated can recognize that the pitch and quality of the tones of adult males, adult females, and children differ greatly from each other.

Madame Seiler has thus expressed herself on this subject:

"Women use mostly tones of the second chest and first falsetto registers, sometimes also those of the first chest register. Men speak an octave lower than women, and use mostly the upper half of the chest register. In public speaking, as well as on the stage, the second chest register is used by men, and sometimes also the lowest tones of the voice. The second falsetto and head registers are used only by little children."

It will be remembered that Madame Seiler's "second chest" corresponds to the upper chest tones of some writers, and that "falsetto" is equivalent to "middle," as generally employed.

Ordinary speech is economical, and a range of very few tones, usually not more than two to four intervals of the scale, suffices, but on the stage, and by some of our best public speakers, twice this range may be exceeded. In nature, the cat, under the excitement of a heated interview with a fellow-vocalist, may pass through an entire octave.

SUMMARY.

The shape of the resonance-chambers varies in the formation of vowels and consonants, which may be classified accordingly, or according to their pitch.

Practical implications for singing and speaking, the learning of foreign languages, the study of dialects, etc.

The importance of special attention to those words containing the low-pitched and dark vowels, especially when low in the scale, and when sung *piano*.

Overtones, and their bearing on the quality of the voice.

The carrying power of the voice, determined by the method of its production, is more important than its volume.

The value of practice with the use of a mirror, and of the formation of the sounds in practice with a distinctness in excess of the actual needs of the listener. Ease is essential to art.

CHAPTER XVII.

THE HEARING APPARATUS AND HEARING IN MUSIC.

SO important are the ingoing sensory messages (impulses) that originate in the ear, as a guide not only in the appreciation of musical sounds but in those movements on which all musical execution, all vocal effects, whether of song or speech, depend, that we think the reader will welcome a chapter on the ear, even though it be no part of the vocal apparatus proper.

The essential mechanism used by Nature to give us the sensation of sound consists of (1) a complicated form of nerve-ending; (2) an auditory nerve leading from, and a continuation, in a certain sense, of, the latter; (3) nerve tracts and hearing centres in the brain. The whole constitutes a very complicated mechanism, but the principles on which it is constructed may be reduced to a few. Mechanical or physical principles, as well as physiological ones, are involved.

The entire apparatus has for its purpose the conversion of the vibrations of the air into the vibrations of a fluid, which thus stimulates the end-organ, and brings about those changes in the nerve which result in corresponding changes in the brain, that are associated, in some way we cannot explain, to that state of consciousness we term hearing. Complicated as is the auditory apparatus, it can be readily enough comprehended, if the reader accompany the perusal of the text by an examination of the figures introduced.

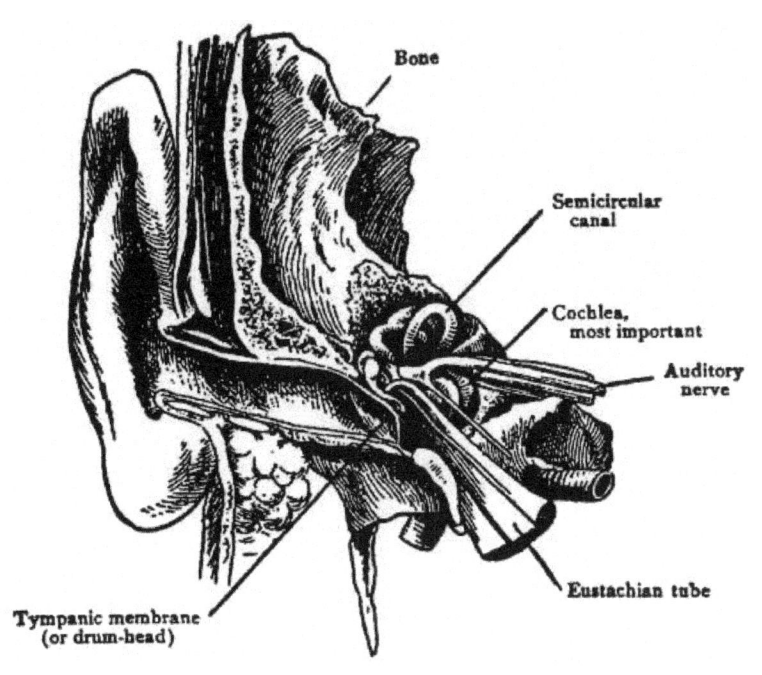

FIG. 60. (Beaunis). In this illustration parts are exposed to view by the removal of others. The whole of the inner ear lies within bone, which in this figure is cut away. The drum-head (membrana tympani); the Eustachian tube, extending from the back of the throat, and opening into the middle ear; the semicircular canals (which are not concerned with hearing, but with the maintenance of equilibrium); the cochlea, (snail-shell), which contains the various parts most essential to hearing, as the "hair-cells," the terminals of the auditory nerve, the latter nerve itself, and several other parts—are well shown. Should the Eustachian tube be closed owing to swelling of its lining mucous membrane, a certain amount of temporary deafness may result, because, the air within the middle ear (drum) being absorbed, and fresh air not being admitted, the outer air presses against the drum-head uncounteracted, and renders the conducting mechanism too rigid.

Anatomists speak of (1) an outer or external ear, (2) a middle ear, drum, or tympanum, and (3) an inner ear, or labyrinth.

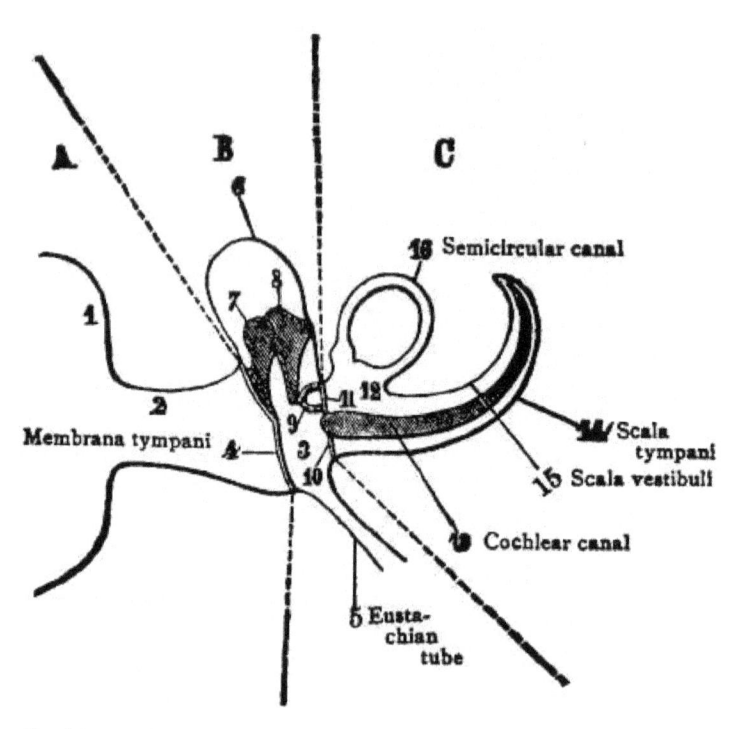

FIG. 61 (Beaunis). Diagrammatic representation of the auditory apparatus. The external, middle, and internal ear are separated by dotted lines. A, the external; B, the middle; C, the internal ear; 1, auricle; 2, external auditory meatus; 3, tympanum (middle ear), with its chain of bones, 7, 8, 9. Into it opens 5, Eustachian tube, leading from back of throat; 4, membrana tympani or drum-head, closing the middle ear off from the external ear. The most important part of the inner ear is 13, the cochlear canal, in which the "hair-cells" are found, around which latter the final branches of the auditory nerve end. Above it is the scala vestibuli and below it the scala tympani, passages filled with fluid. The openings to these canals are closed with membrane. Attached to the membrane of the oval opening is the stapes (stirrup). It is thus seen that vibrations communicated to the chain of bones from the tympanic membrane are passed on to the fluid filling the passages (scalæ) of the cochlea, and thus affect the hair-cells, and so the nerve of hearing, and through it the brain. The parts indicated by 12 and 16 are important in the maintenance of equilibrium, but are not concerned in hearing.

The purpose of the *outer ear* is to collect the air vibrations and convey them to the middle ear, which passes them on to the inner ear, where they produce the vibrations in the fluid therein contained and which affect the end-organ and nerve-endings, and thus initiate the essential physiological processes in the nerve of hearing. It follows that we have an instance of the conversion of one kind of vibrations, those of the air, into another kind, those of fluid, which latter furnish a sufficiently delicate stimulus or excitation of the fine hair-like extensions (*processes*) of the cells known as *hair-cells*, about which the nerves in their final smallest branches wrap themselves.

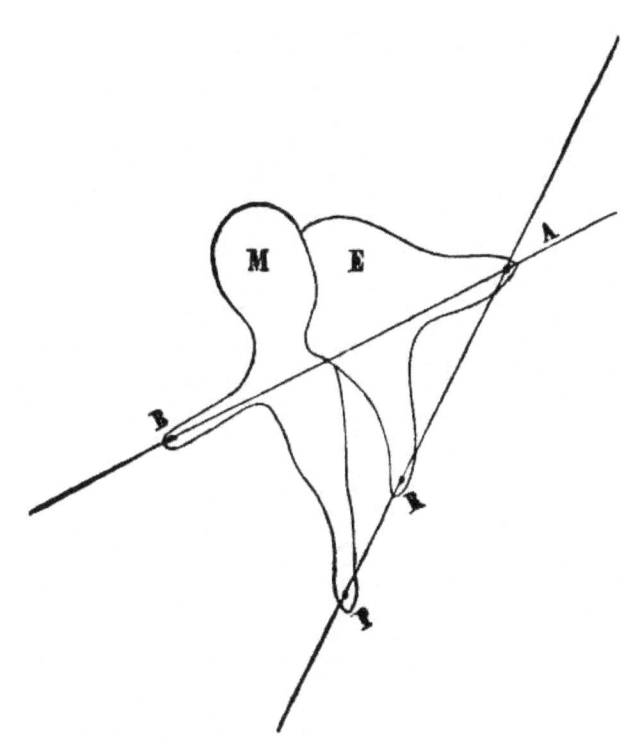

FIG. 62 (Beaunis). Two of the bones of the ear (the malleus or hammer and the incus or anvil) enlarged. These small ear-bones have joints like larger ones. The line of conveyance of vibrations is indicated by B A.

When we ourselves hear sounds when under water, we are affected directly by the vibrations of that water; in this case we, in our whole body, represent the hair-cells which are stimulated by the fluid (*endolymph*) which surrounds them.

FIG. 63 (Beaunis). The complete chain of bones. The arrows indicate in a general way the direction of the line of transmission of vibrations from the tympanic membrane on to the fluid within the passages of the inner ear.

The external ear, well developed in many of the lower animals, being often highly movable, is practically immovable in man, and is wholly wanting in some animals, as the frog. The circular plate one sees behind the eye of the frog is the drum-head of the middle ear.

From the *drum-head*, or *tympanic membrane*, the vibrations, which are now those of a solid, are communicated by a series of very small bones, most beautifully linked together by perfect joints, to another membrane, which closes a small hole in the outer wall of the inner ear.

The *middle ear*, it will be seen, is a drum with its stretched membrane like any other drum, and it too has a communication with the exterior air through a tube, the *Eustachian tube*, which leads from the drum into the back part of the throat. When one has a cold, the mucous membrane which lines this tube may become swollen or even catarrhal, and be so closed that no air can enter from the throat; the air already within the drum being absorbed, the outer air presses unduly against the drum-head, with the result that the whole conducting apparatus is put more or less out of condition, and a certain degree of deafness naturally results. The tension of the drum-head is regulated by a muscle attached to the bone which is connected with the inner part of this membrane.

It is now easy to understand how any unfavorable condition of the throat may affect the ear, or that of the ear influence the throat.

In the hearing mechanism of man, the *inner ear*, or *labyrinth*, well so named because of its complexity, is really situated in the inner hardest portion of the "temporal" bone. It consists of a membrane and a bony portion, the former containing the essential mechanism of hearing, the latter being chiefly protective to it. The membranous portion consists of a series of canals communicating with some similarly membranous sacs, the whole being surrounded by and filled with fluid. These latter communicate with an extension termed the *cochlea*, which contains a central canal in which that collection of cells is found which constitutes the *end-organ*, among them the hair-cells, about which the nerve ends.

This end-organ in the cochlea may be compared very fitly to the telephone which receives the message, and that portion of the brain where the auditory tract ends, to the telephone at the distant end of the path, the listener there representing consciousness. The auditory path within the brain is long and complicated, there being, in fact, many way-stations through which the message passes before it reaches the final one.

The auditory nerve proceeds first to the lowest or hindermost portion of the brain, known as the *bulb*, or *medulla oblongata*; thence a continuation of the nerve tract passes forward to a central region, the *posterior corpora quadrigemina*, then, by a new relay of nerve-fibres, to the highest and most important part of the brain, that most closely associated with consciousness, the *cortex of the temporal lobe*, where there is situated the most important of all the centres of hearing.

It will be apparent, on consideration, that "hearing" is a very elaborate result, the outcome of many physiological processes (initiated by physical ones), the initial and final being better understood than the intermediate ones.

One asks, with natural curiosity and interest, "Is the auditory apparatus of the highly endowed musician different from and superior to that of the individual with little talent for music?"

It is not easy to give a short and definite answer to this question. No special examinations of the essential parts of the ears of eminent musicians have been made, so far as we are aware, and as yet few of the brains of this class of men. It is, however, practically certain that there is a brain development peculiar to the born musician, and that this, whatever else it may be, involves a special excellence of the auditory path within the brain, rather than any unusual development of the essential parts of the ear. The individual who is a musical prodigy has, without question, *a more perfect connection* established between his auditory apparatus, in the widest sense of the word, and those muscular mechanisms employed in the execution of music, whether vocal or instrumental, than is the case with the average man. Usually, with this goes a wide series of brain associations or connections, we may presume, between the auditory tracts and other regions, for without this it is difficult to explain temperament and artistic perception. That they are not necessarily associated, however, is clear from the fact that some have a high degree of executive ability and little real artistic development.

It must never be forgotten, however, that whatever else music may be, it is essentially and primarily a sensuous experience. The one who enjoys music must feel its sensuous charm, and the artist who furnishes that which is enjoyed addresses himself primarily to our auditory mechanism. Executing music is hearing music, and enjoying music is hearing music, though both may involve much more than this, and herein individuals must differ greatly, owing to education, past experience, etc.; but all who have the power to really appreciate music must be capable of the sensuous enjoyment of tones. In this all everywhere find something in common; often that which we enjoy is of the most varied nature.

One thing is certain: those connections between the hearing and the motor processes we term singing or playing should be made early in life, if they are to reach that degree of facility and general excellence essential to success. We think there is good reason to begin voice-production early, as well as the practice of an instrument, though we do not maintain that the argument is as strong in the one case as in the other.

That the "ear for music" may be well developed, in the sense that one may know perfectly what is correct in time and tune, without the power to execute well, there can be no doubt, as witness the case of many composers, but the reverse does not hold. There can be no doubt that *the nervous impulses that pass from the ear to the brain are of all sensory messages the most important guides for the outgoing ones that determine the necessary movements.*

The author would advise every serious student of music to believe in the unlimited capacity of his own ear for improvement. The lack of "ear" of many people is due largely, if not solely, to inattention. Indeed, an excess of temperament may be a positive hindrance to musical development, both as regards appreciation and execution, for it may be accompanied by inattentive listening and consequent inadequate hearing. On the other hand, no one should, because he has a good faculty for time and tune and the memorizing of airs, conclude that he is an artist. The one faculty may exist altogether apart from the capacity for the highest art. It is a matter of history that several vocalists now before the public, and who rank in the highest class of musical artists, displayed at one period of their career a lack of perception as to pitch or rhythm that was, to say the least, very discouraging, and which, but for their force of character, would have kept them from ever being eminent.

If one have neither ear, temperament, nor artistic perception, he should not waste his energies on musical study—at least, not extended efforts; but if he have the two last, and but a moderate ear, he will do well to try to improve the lower for the sake of the higher qualities.

In children the difficulty often is due wholly to inattention.

Those who would cultivate the speaking voice are frequently discouraged from lack of "ear," and when urged to follow such exercises as have been recommended in this work, complain that they have not the "ear" to do so. To such the author would say, "Persevere; believe in your ear; learn to listen—*i.e.*, to attend to sounds having musical qualities."

Besides, it must not be forgotten that in addition to the "ear"—*i.e.*, the ability to appreciate relative pitch, tune, and rhythm—there is also the entirely distinct faculty that appreciates the *quality* of sounds. The latter is really more important for the speaker, who can succeed with a very moderate development of the faculty for time and tune, but to whom the power to appreciate the *quality* of sounds is essential.

No doubt the first and fundamental qualities in the make-up of a musician are the capacities to appreciate pitch and rhythm, but no result worthy the term "artistic" can be produced in which attention is not given to the quality of sounds, hence the technical and artistic should be developed together. The lack of attention on the part of a certain class of vocal teachers to the quality of the tones produced is one of the special defects in the instruction of the day.

In the early weeks of vocal training, when the student should intone only before his teacher, the former need not be left without musical culture, and it is for each teacher to give the pupil that training, at this time, which will forestall disgust and impatience at the apparent slowness of his progress. At this time much can be done to cultivate the ear in all its various powers.

And the author would like to put in a plea for the development of the *appreciation of music*. Whatever difference of opinion there may be as to choral singing, singing in schools, etc., there can be no question that time spent in developing the appreciation of musical art is well spent, and makes for the development and provides for the innocent and elevating sources of enjoyment of a people. If some of the time spent in bad piano-playing were devoted to the development of the power to appreciate and delight in really good music, including the sweet sounds of speech and song, the world would thereby be greatly the gainer.

The author would impress on all students of music, and of the voice as used in both singing and speaking, the paramount importance of learning early to listen most attentively to others when executing music; and, above all, to listen with the greatest care to themselves, and never to accept any musical tone that does not fully satisfy the ear. When one considers how much harshness is passed as singing or speaking, by the student, even by those who pose as public singers and speakers, one must often wonder where they keep their ears. As a matter of fact, the ideal listeners are rare, and the critical ear, like a sentinel on guard, is among students, really seldom to be met with, if one extend the term "listening" to mean giving attention equally and in the most critical way, not only to pitch and rhythm, but also to the quality of sounds, the effects of pauses, shading, etc., all of which are perceived through the ear.

If such listening requires, as it does, the closest attention, it must give rise to fatigue, so that it is clear that the lengthy practices some undertake are against the plainest laws of physiology and psychology, even if the hearing processes alone be considered; but as we have before shown, there are other reasons why such long-continued exercises as some attempt are in every way unwise; in fact, in the author's opinion, they are in the musical world a great evil under the sun.

SUMMARY.

Hearing is finally a psychological or mental condition, a state of consciousness, but is always associated with certain physiological processes, which are initiated by a physical stimulus in the form of waves in a fluid surrounding the hair-cells of the auditory end-organ; which waves may again be traced to the movements of the bones of the middle ear, caused by the swinging to and fro of the drum-head, owing to vibrations of the air produced by a sounding body.

The ear is anatomically divisible into external, middle (tympanum or drum), and internal (labyrinth). The outer ear collects the vibrations, the middle ear conducts them, and the internal converts them into a special physiological condition of the hair-cells and the auditory nerve. This condition is communicated to the other links in the anatomical hearing chain, until the highest part of the brain, or cortex, is reached. Hearing, from the physiological point of view, is the outcome of a series of processes having their development in a corresponding series of centres, or collections of nerve-cells.

The perceptions associated with the ear, in the mind of the musician, are those of the pitch, rhythm (and time), and quality of tones. The loudness of a tone is, of course, recognized by the ear also, but this is hardly a musical quality proper. In reality, like all that belongs to hearing, these perceptions are the result of a series of physiological processes, in which the ear takes an important but not the sole or even the chief part, which is to be referred to the brain.

It is practically important to recognize that these various qualities are distinct perceptions, and that the "ear" for relative pitch may exist well developed and the color, clang, or quality of a tone be imperfectly recognized, and the reverse.

The most comprehensive ear-training involves attention to each of the above characters of tones, and then uniting them in a musically perfect result. Lack of "ear" is often simply want of attention to the characters of sounds.

The auditory messages are the most important of all the nervous impulses that reach the brain, for the musician, whether appreciation or execution be considered. They are the chief guides for the outgoing nervous impulses to the muscles.

The good executant must, above all, be a good listener.

CHAPTER XVIII.

CONSIDERATION OF GENERAL AND SPECIAL HYGIENE AND RELATED SUBJECTS.

HYGIENE deals with the laws by the observance of which health is to be maintained and disease prevented; but as such laws must be based on physiological principles, hygiene follows from physiology. Accordingly, throughout this work our method has been to point out the correct way as soon as the physiological principle has been laid down, so that the reason for the recommendation made would be obvious. However, it may be well if now some of the more important tendencies, errors, bad habits, and dangers to be guarded against by the singer and speaker be pointed out afresh, briefly, with some additional observations that experience has shown to be of practical importance.

Hygiene, for all persons, should, in the widest sense, refer to the whole man, his body, intellect, feelings, and will, though the term has usually been restricted to the preservation of bodily health. But, fortunately, it is being more and more recognized that man is a whole, and that one part of him cannot suffer without the others participating, so we shall pursue the broader course, and consider the general welfare of the voice-user as properly coming under consideration.

He, being a human being like his fellows, must, of course, observe the same laws for the preservation of his general health as they, but just because he comes before the public, his case is peculiar, and he must, in addition, take special precautions to avoid every form of temporary or permanent disability.

There is, of course, much in the life of a public speaker or singer that conduces to health of body and mind, such as the vigorous use of the breathing apparatus, the favorable effect of praise expressed in one way and another, etc., but even with the most successful, all this may be more than counter-balanced by other unfavorable factors. When one considers the necessary travelling, often including night journeys, the late hours, the concentrated efforts essential to success, the uncertainty of the public taste, the rivalries, jealousies, exhaustion, etc., often associated with a public career, it must be clear that no one should embark upon it without counting well the cost. For one with mediocre ability, imperfect training, voice of very limited range, power, and quality, feeble will, an imperfectly developed body, and indifferent health, to enter on a public career is practically to court failure and to ensure disappointment and unhappiness.

It is to be remembered that never was the world so exacting of the artist, and never were there so many aspirants to popular favor, so that the competition in the ranks of the actors and singers, at least, is very keen. At the same time, there is room for a certain class of persons—viz., those with good health, excellent physique, first-rate ability, self-control, sound moral principles, perseverance, industry, musical feeling, and artistic insight, with vocal organs trained like the muscles of the athlete, and, in the case of singers, sound musical knowledge and an exacting and reliable ear.

Considering that the actor, often the public speaker, and the singer are constantly being put under excessive strain, it follows that (1) such persons should begin with an unusually good physical organization—others can scarcely hope to get into the first class, even with the best abilities; and (2) because there is a tendency to exhaustion of the body and mind through emotional and other expenditure, the public voice-user must take precautions, on the one hand, to prevent this, and, on the other, to make good his outlay by special means. He needs more sleep and rest generally than others, and he should counteract the influence of unhealthy conditions on the stage or platform by some quiet hours in the open air, all the better if with some congenial friend, sympathetic with his aims, yet belonging, preferably perhaps, to another profession, and who will speak of topics other than those that are ever recurring in the life of an artist. The uninterrupted pursuit of one thing, without the mind and spirit being fed from other springs, can be good for no human being. The specialist who is only a specialist will never reach the very highest point. The artist must seek sources of inspiration and mental nutriment outside of his own line of thought, or he will suffer professionally and in his own spirit.

The reader will by this time understand why the author considers that for one who would be an artist to enter on his public career without the fullest mental equipment and vocal training is an exceedingly unwise course. Technique should be acquired before an aspirant to success steps on a public stage or platform, and this is exactly what is so seldom done in these days, and why we have so few singers, actors, and public speakers of the highest rank. Many, very many, know what they wish to express, and, in a sense, how to express it, but they have neither the formed voice nor the control of that voice by which their ideas are to be embodied. Let no one delude himself into the belief that technique will be learned in public; such is rarely, if ever, the case. Expression, style, etc., may come to the vocalist or speaker all the more readily if he occasionally goes before the public; but that such may be so, he must first have voice and technique. It is because of the neglect of this training for the acquirement of technique that so many naturally good voices are of little practical use for the public, and this explains why the ranks of the professions are crowded with inferior artists, if, indeed, artists they may be called.

The *isolation* of the dramatic and musical artist from his fellows generally is a great evil. Much that society complains of in the lives of artists would never exist but for this isolation, in spite of the fact that the artistic temperament is so moody and so impulsive, so little regardful of ordinary conventionalities. That it is so is partly the fault of society. It is quite true that because of journeying, rehearsals, etc., the travelling artist has little time to meet the members of the community in private life; but this state of things could be mitigated were society and the artists themselves convinced that for any class of people to live in little hives, wholly separated from their fellows, must be unfortunate for them and society. Artists as men and women are practically unknown to the world, though their false selves as represented by sensational paragraphs in newspapers are only too familiar to us. It may truly be said of the artist: "Be thou as chaste as ice, as pure as snow, thou shalt not escape calumny." It is within the power of society to alter this, and it should do so.

Why is it that actors and singers do not prepare themselves by as prolonged and thorough a vocal training as in a past time?

Considering that there never was a period when there was the same scope for art, never a time when the public was so eager to hear and so able to pay for art, as now, never a period of such widespread intelligence on all subjects, music included, the question is a very pertinent one. We believe there are many factors underlying the technical decadence we must regret. The orchestra has greatly developed, choral singing is common in all countries, and the spirit of the times has changed. So analytical, so refined is our age, that singing sometimes becomes a sort of musical declamation, but, unfortunately, without that power to declaim possessed by the actors and often the opera-singers of a former period. A singer often attempts now to make up by an expressive reading of a song, for technical defects. We must all commend every evidence of intellectuality in music, but this does not imply that we should accept good intentions for execution—performance. Let us have every possible development of orchestral music; let every village have, if possible, its choral society, but let none enter it who have not been trained vocally.

Out of the author's own experience he could a tale unfold of the evil done to the vocal organs by those who have sung in choirs without adequate vocal training. Choristers are tempted to reach high tones by a process of their own, without any regard to registers, and with corresponding effects on their throats, some of which imply also lasting injury to the voice itself.

In choral singing there is the tendency to lean on certain singers who are natural leaders, with the result that there is little independent listening and individual culture, even if the singer could hear his own voice well, which is not usually the case. The same objections and others apply to class singing in schools, which does little for music, and tends to make slovenly singers. If some of the time given to school singing were taken up in illustrating why certain musical selections are good, and others mere rubbish—in other words, in forming the taste of the nation in the children—a valuable work would be done; but school class singing, as commonly carried out, tends rather to injure than develop voices and good musical taste.

We cannot honestly pass by the subject of Wagner's music and some of its tendencies. Wagner was an intellectual giant among men, and his works are amazingly grand, yet they unfortunately are, in a certain sense, responsible for much bad singing and not a little injury to fine voices.

First of all, Wagner's operas are, in their present form, too long. To sing these compositions night after night is beyond human powers, even in the case of those of the most perfect musical and technical training. If they were divided into two, and one half sung on one evening and the other on the next, it would be a gain for the public and the artists. It is impossible for even the musically cultivated to absorb and assimilate the whole of such an opera as "Siegfried" or "Tristan and Isolde" in one evening, and it is too much to expect any artist to sing them through without a rest.

Again, they call for such strong accents, such deep and strenuous breathing, that the artist impersonating a hero or a god or goddess is put to a degree of exertion that is too great for human powers when continued for more than a very moderate period; besides, there is a temptation to a wrong use of the larynx—a forcible *coup de glotte*, or attack—that is exceedingly dangerous, and has injured many voices and ruined others. The man or woman who would sing Wagner's greater music dramas should, in addition to a strong physique, be master of a wonderfully perfect technique. These operas should never be attempted by very young singers of either sex, and especially not by very young women. They are for the powerful, the mature, the perfectly trained, the experienced.

Turning to some special faults, we would warn against the "scoop," the excessive use of the *portamento*, or glide, so common a fault at the present time, and the *vibrato* and *tremolo*.

The two former are musical faults, so we pass them by without further consideration. Otherwise is it with the last two faults; they both result from a wrong use of the vocal organs. They are both due to some unsteadiness and lack of control, and, unfortunately, when once acquired, are very difficult to remedy. The unsteadiness may be almost anywhere in the vocal organs, but is usually referable to the respiratory apparatus or to the larynx.

A *vibrato* is the milder form of the evil, and is encouraged, we regret to say, by some teachers, while the *tremolo* is due to an extreme unsteadiness, and, so far as we are aware, is universally condemned. It is about the worst fault any singer can have. It is evident in some cases only when the vocalist sings *piano*, but mostly in vigorous singing, and often arises from straining, disregard of registers, etc. It may be due to the singer trying to control too large a supply of air, or from bringing a blast to bear on the vocal bands too strong for them. In every case there is lack of adjustment between the vocal bands and the respiratory organs. The remedy must be adapted to the case, but usually the singer must for a time give up the use of the voice in *forte* singing altogether, and gradually again learn to control his vocal mechanism.

Associated sometimes with this fault is another, which, indeed, often gives rise to the former—viz., "pumping," or attempting to vocalize after the breath power is exhausted. One should always have enough air in reserve to sing at least two tones more than what is required.

It will be observed that good singing and speaking are always physiological—*i.e.*, they depend on the observance of well-known physiological principles; we wish we could add, principles clearly recognized by singers and teachers generally. It is to those who do that we would recommend the student of the vocal art to go at the outset of his career, otherwise much time may be lost and possibly much injury done. We distinguish, of course, between the teacher who recognizes physiological principles only practically and the one who does so consciously. The former may be an excellent and safe teacher, though, we think, not so good, other things being equal, as one of the latter type,—as yet somewhat rare.

At an earlier period we referred to the important matter of classifying the voice. It often happens that one who is a tenor is trained as a barytone, or a contralto as a soprano, and the reverse, only to discover later that a mistake has been made. If it could become the custom to have vocal consultations among teachers, as medical ones among doctors, the author is convinced it would be well. Often a patient is sent a long distance to consult a medical man, and to return to his own physician for treatment based on the diagnosis made. In these instances the doctor consulted is expected to write his views privately to the patient's doctor, and to recommend treatment. Why should the same not occur in the vocal teacher's profession? It is considered scandalous in the medical profession to "steal" another physician's patient, and why should not a similar etiquette prevail in the profession now under consideration? The teacher in doubt about a voice might thus obtain the views of another member of his profession, of longer experience, on such a vital point as the classification of a voice, and with satisfaction alike to himself and to his pupil. If the teacher or pupil were not satisfied with the diagnosis, another eminent vocal teacher might be consulted, which would only be following custom in the medical profession.

We would again remind the reader that voices are to be *classified by quality*, and not by range, at least not to any appreciable extent.

Of all persons, the singer should know himself. He must learn his limitations, and the sooner the better. At the outset of his career he may be able to take certain liberties with himself with apparent impunity, but sooner or later he will pay the penalty; so that we recommend him to live with all the care of an athlete in training. However it may be with other men, spirits in every form, tobacco, etc., are not for him. Both tend to irritate and relax if not to inflame the throat, not to mention their bad effects on the general health, both psychical and physical. This advice is all the more necessary when one considers the exacting nature of the professional life of the artist. Strenuous exertion tends to fatigue and exhaustion, with a natural desire to relieve them by some special means, such as alcohol. To do so is often but to make a beginning of the end. How many bright lights in the dramatic and musical professions have been prematurely quenched through indulgence in the delusive draught! If tonics, sedatives, etc., are to be taken, which should not be a habitual practice, they should be used only under the direction of a medical man, and not self-prescribed.

As the speaker and singer must often practise their art in an atmosphere that is far from pure, they will do well to carry out in a routine way some sort of mouth toilet on their return home and the next morning. Various simple mouth and throat washes may be used, such as (1) water with a little common salt dissolved in it; (2) water containing a few drops of carbolic acid—just enough to be distinctly tasted; (3) water containing listerine; (4) either of the last two with the addition of a pinch of bicarbonate of sodium to a teacupful of the fluid, when there is a tendency to catarrh.

The use of lozenges in a routine way is not to be commended, and those containing morphia, cocaine, etc., should be employed only under the supervision of a medical practitioner. Sometimes, especially in the case of nervousness, a licorice pellet or a particle of gum arabic serves a good purpose in aiding in keeping the mouth moist.

For one with a healthy throat the sipping of water is unnecessary, and the habit is one on no account to be learned, for the most admirable effect may be spoiled through the speaker stopping to sip water; there is the fatal and rapid descent from the lofty to the little.

It is much more important to avoid eating certain things which interfere with the voice than to take anything to improve it before singing or speaking. Each individual should learn just what he can or cannot with safety eat. Certain kinds of fruit, cheese, fat meat, pastry, nuts, occasionally even butter, not to mention puddings, etc., must be put on the list of what singers and speakers had better not partake of before a public appearance. But the quantity is quite as important as the quality of the food taken. About one half the usual quantity, at most, and of very simple but nourishing food, is enough for any one who would do himself justice before the public. If blood and energy be drawn off to the stomach by a large meal, it cannot be available for the uses of the artist. Moreover, a full stomach pressing up under the diaphragm greatly hampers the movements of this, the most important of all the muscles of breathing. Of course, the public singer or speaker should eat after his work is done, of what and how much he can best learn by experience.

As the author has felt called upon to condemn the use of alcohol in every form, he should, perhaps, point out that to take a cup of such a mild stimulant as tea or coffee during an interval, in the case of those who feel weary, is generally an unobjectionable, indeed, often a useful, procedure; but the less the artist coddles himself, especially while still young, the better.

We would again call attention to one anatomical fact of great importance for the explanation of certain facts of experience—viz.: that the whole respiratory tract, the larynx included, is lined with a *mucous membrane*, which is continuous with that covering the inner surface of the digestive organs. That is to say, the nose, the mouth, the back of the throat, the larynx, the windpipe, the bronchial tubes, the gullet, the stomach and intestines are all brought into structural connection by this common lining membrane. Moreover, these parts have to some extent the same nerve supply, and are, in fact, so related that derangement in one region must affect sooner or later, and to a variable degree according to the resisting power of each individual, other related parts. Thus it is that a disordered stomach affects the voice, that a cold may affect digestion, that a catarrh of the nose will eventually reach the vocal bands, etc.

Another principle of wide-reaching importance is that all sorts of *compression* must, of necessity, be attended by functional disorders, which, if long continued, will result in organic or structural changes implying deterioration of a kind that must be more or less permanent. Whatever the cause of compression of the chest or neck, the result is the same: a retention of blood in parts for too long a period—a condition of things which must inevitably be injurious.

The tissues are made up of cells, which are the individuals of the bodily community. Around these cells are found the smallest of the blood-vessels, the capillaries, between which and the tissues a sort of physiological barter is continually going on, the capillaries handing over oxygen and food supplies from the blood, and receiving waste materials in return, as the blood creeps along at a very slow rate. If, however, in consequence of pressure on a part, the blood be kept back in these minute vessels too long, there is naturally a double evil: first, the food and oxygen supplies fail—they have been used up already—and, secondly, the waste products accumulate in the tissue cells, so that there is a combination of starvation and poisoning—a sort of physiological slum life, with corresponding degradation; so that it is not at all difficult to understand why tight collars, neckbands, corsets, etc., must be unmixed evils, apart altogether from the fact that they so greatly hamper the very movements the voice-user most requires for the successful execution of his task.

All sorts of straining or forcing also involve this same evil, known to medical men as *congestion*. The sore throats so common with those who force, owing to methods essentially wrong, or simply to the too vigorous use of methods correct in themselves, are to be traced to the above—*i.e.*, to this congestion, which is bad, and bad only.

If one who had a naturally sound throat at the outset finds that after vocal exercise he experiences either a soreness or an undue weariness of parts, he should conclude, if he is living under healthy conditions, that the methods he is employing are incorrect, and seek the natural remedy. Proper vocal exercise should, in those with healthy vocal organs, always improve them and the condition of the whole man. The author has met those who have been ruined vocally for life by the use of certain methods recommended by would-be professional guides. Why should not all who assume the responsibility of guiding speakers and especially singers be required by the state to show that they have not only a knowledge of music and vocal technique, but also at least a moderate amount of practical knowledge of the anatomy and physiology of the vocal organs, with some elementary information on general physiology? If the injury done by incompetent teachers were realized, we feel certain that the above proposition would not be questioned.

A common cause of congestion of the digestive organs, with which, of course, other parts sympathize physiologically, is *constipation*, very often the result of insufficient exercise, and injurious in many ways. Speakers and singers very generally ride to and from their engagements, so that there is special reason why they should see to it that some time is set aside for general exercise, as walking in the open air, which would of itself work against that tendency to grow fat which is the physical curse that seems to fall on artists above most others.

It seems scarcely necessary to point out how important it is for those who propose to take up the life of the stage or the platform to look to hardening themselves against catching cold, by friction of the skin, cold bathing, etc. The use of a sponge-bath of cold salt and water to the upper parts of the body, especially the neck and chest, will prove valuable in many cases, but the enervating effects of hot water should be avoided by all.

The remarks made in regard to Wagner's music on page 257 have been among the very few to which exception has been taken by my reviewers.

To those who disagree with me on the merits of the case I have nothing to say, but some have assumed that the writer was speaking out of pure theory, in real ignorance of Wagner's works. I wish to set that class of critics right.

I have spent a great many seasons in Germany, and have heard Wagner's works under a great variety of circumstances, and have heard them also in several other countries. I have also had the opportunity of getting behind the scenes in a way that falls to the lot of few, so I think I am entitled to speak with rather more than the usual authority.

My convictions as expressed in the foregoing chapter have in the interval rather strengthened than weakened. I am firmly convinced that it would be in the interests of art, the singer, and the auditor alike, either to shorten these operas, or to produce them in some way which will relieve the continuous strain. It must not be forgotten, either, that the poor overworked and greatly underpaid orchestral player often suffers severely in his nervous system from long continued Wagner playing.

CHAPTER XIX.

FURTHER TREATMENT OF PHYSICAL AND MENTAL HYGIENE.

Stammering and *stuttering* are allied but not identical defects. They require special treatment, the earlier the better. Much can be done by the exercise of a little patience and kind consideration, to make the subject of these infirmities feel at ease, and so manifest the defects as little as possible. It is, of course, as a general rule, very unwise to take any notice whatever of such imperfections, as they are thereby made worse. As a rule, they are best treated practically by those who have made this branch a specialty.

Those who have been badly taught, or who have overworked the vocal organs and, in consequence, may have broken down, are among the most discouraging if they be not the very worst cases that come under the treatment of the physician or vocal teacher. If the throat be out of order, a specialist should be consulted. He will likely enjoin complete rest of the vocal organs, and his advice should be implicitly followed. But usually the time comes when some sort of vocal exercises may be resumed. When this is the case, the choice of a teacher becomes of the utmost importance, more so than in ordinary cases, for further injudicious treatment may lead to the utter ruin of the voice. Assuming that medical treatment is no longer or not at all required, we recommend: (1) That all practices be only *piano*, or, at most, *moderato*, for some time; (2) that they be of very brief duration at any one period, so as to avoid fatigue; (3) that they be well within the range of the singer. The same principles apply to speakers who have broken down, whether owing to bad methods or to over-use of the voice. It is most important that strength and facility be gradually gained, and that weariness, not to say fatigue, be strictly avoided. If the general health be good, time, patience, and the utmost care in the application of the above principles, under the direction of an enlightened teacher, will in a large proportion of cases restore the voice for efficient use in at least moderate efforts. Of course, much depends on the age, general health, intelligence, etc., of the subject.

On the question of the extent to which a singer's range can be safely increased, the greatest difference of opinion exists, and very extreme views have been held. On the one hand are those who almost ridicule the idea of "making" tones, and on the other, those who maintain that the range of all young singers can be increased by proper training.

As a matter of fact, there are many singers before the public to-day whose range, either upward or downward, has been increased by many tones, in some cases almost an octave, and these singers are successful artists and sound vocalists; while others have sought to add but two or three tones to their range, and in vain. This is quite intelligible. As a rule, those of the former class have fallen into the hands of very good teachers, while yet young, have had excellent health and well-formed vocal organs, and been patient and attentive students. The acquisition has been gradual, and never forced. We have before said that if a pupil felt his throat the worse for a lesson in vocal culture, there was something wrong: either the method was incorrect in itself, or the practice was continued too long or carried out too vigorously. Of course, it is always assumed that the vocal organs are in a normal condition, and the student's health good not only generally but on the day of the practice.

It is in every case for the student himself to determine, from his own feelings, whether the attempt to reach a certain tone produces straining, and for the teacher to judge whether this be so, from the appearance of the face of the pupil, the character of the tone, etc. One thing is certain: harm, and harm only, is done by any form of forcing or straining. At the same time, as the athlete increases the height to which he can jump, or the speed with which he can run, even during a single season, it seems illogical to conclude that in no case can a singer safely reach tones that are not originally in his voice— meaning thereby that he is unable to sing them at the outset of his career. This is one of those subjects on which common sense and science unite in admonishing us to test cautiously and to progress gradually, if the purpose is to be achieved with good results for the individual and for art.

It is also unwise for a singer to attempt those selections in public the range of which taxes him to the very utmost. They lead to undue anxiety as to success, violate the principle of reserve force, to which reference has several times been made, and may lead to vocal failure, if not to injury to the throat. Though it is true that occasionally a song suffers by transposition to a lower key, if the vocalist is determined to sing a composition even slightly beyond his easy range, it is better to resort to it than to risk the possibilities mentioned above and other undesirable ones.

Everyone who purposes to follow the arduous career of the vocal or dramatic artist would do well to realize early the importance of learning the art of conserving energy, or making the most of all that Nature has given him. When a man or woman is small, and has less breath power than some others, it becomes more important that they observe the laws of contrast, rest, etc., in their public efforts. A *forte* has much the same effect, if it be preceded by darker, quieter tones, as if it were really louder. In like manner, a pause may often serve a very good purpose in preparing the ear of the listener for an effect that should be telling, yet a difficult one for a person of limited physical powers.

In reality, all the best art recognizes, mostly unconsciously, the peculiarities of our physical and mental nature. A continuous *forte*, for example, ceases to be a *forte*, in reality, since the ear and the mind weary under it, and all the effect of contrast is lost. As we have more than once said, good art is physiological—in harmony with the laws of the body, as well as of the mind. It follows that each one should study especially how to make the wisest, the most effective, use of his powers, for what is best for one may not be so for another.

A singer or speaker, by reason of a voice somewhat small in volume, may seem to be shut out from certain buildings. This need rarely be the case. The artist must simply the more carefully consider how he shall vary his effects, how so use his powers that they shall suffice. A loud voice may be a very bad one for the hearer, and may annoy and weary rather than please. When a building is large, nearly all effects should be increased—*e.g.*, all pauses lengthened, the *tempo* taken a little slower, the contrasts made stronger, etc.,—rather than the volume of tone increased. The method of attack becomes of the utmost importance; all low or soft passages should be sung or uttered with the greatest distinctness, all final letters most perfectly finished. It is especially important for a speaker to be aware of his favorite—*i.e.*, most easy and natural—pitch, and also that pitch which best adapts his voice to a certain building. Many forget that sound does not, in reality, travel very rapidly, and that allowance must be made for this, so that one tone shall not break on the ear before another has had time to be attended to—one idea to be grasped before another is presented.

Of all things pauses are of the greatest importance, to the listener, that he may apprehend the ideas presented, and to the speaker, that he may have time to take breath and a brief rest, and also seize the opportunity to readdress himself, so to speak, to his auditors, by the use of another accent, pitch of tone, or whatever he deems most apt to his purpose. Speakers who make suitable pauses with intention (not from lack of ideas), or from an artistic instinct, give pleasure, as well as effect their intellectual purpose, for the listener also gets his moments for rest, perceives readily what is meant, and enjoys the purely sensuous in the art far more than when the speaker's utterance rushes on like a torrent. All this applies to a certain extent to the singer, though it is but very inadequately observed—we must say, however, much better than at a former period, when "ranting," on the stage especially, was a very common fault.

In an earlier chapter attention was given to the precautions to be taken before a public appearance, especially by those who are inexperienced; and we would again emphasize the fact that those who have the best training, and have made the most perfect special preparation for the coming event, are least likely to suffer from that great disturber, nervousness; and when they are somewhat tense, the well-disciplined often recover rapidly, and frequently astonish their friends by the success of their first appearance. We strongly recommend all who can to take rest on the day preceding and following a hard evening's work, and preferably, in summer, in the open air. A quiet walk in a park, where one may think or observe or not, as he feels inclined, is an excellent thing to do, either before or after a strenuous artistic effort. If the battery is to be well charged, it must not be discharged even partially before the right moment. Amateurs and the inexperienced are particularly apt to neglect such precaution for success, and to fritter away their energies by attention to details, possibly trivial ones, up to the last moment.

Happy is he who, well prepared for his task, free from worries, unmoved by envy, jealousy, or undue ambition, can step before the public resolved to do his best for art, and who, having done it, can rest in the satisfaction that he has contributed something to the innocent and ennobling enjoyment of his fellows, and so has helped to advance those of his own generation; caring little for either the flatteries of admirers or a criticism that may be ignorant, unjust, or malignant, but feeling that the best reward is the approval of his own conscience, knowing that "Art is long, and life short."

CHAPTER XX.

REVIEW AND REVISION.

ALL the most important truths of any subject may be stated in a brief space. The Author proposes to make this final chapter one of a restatement of the essentials of the subject in the light of our present-day knowledge, and with a distinct relation to practice.

The object of the speaker or singer is to produce certain sounds which shall as easily as possible convey to the listener his own state of mind. It follows that he must have a clear idea of these sounds, that he must hear them mentally prior to their utterance; in other words, the psychological must precede the physiological. Voice production for the purpose of speaking and singing implies a coöperation of the psychic and the physiological, a co-ordination of processes that are psychic, and physical, somatic or physiological.

It is well to regard the subject from as many points of view as possible, and to consider the various ways in which the same truth may be stated.

Stress must be laid on the idea of co-ordination, for processes may be independently satisfactory yet fail to lead to the desired result if they are not connected, harmonised or co-ordinated. The latter is the better term because it suggests a certain order of progress. As a matter of fact, first the psychic, then the physiological. The idea may be clear, yet from a physical defect, as in stammering, the result does not follow, though this physiological imperfection in movement may itself be the result of a psychic condition and generally is so. A clearer case is that of paralysis of the vocal organs. The ideas to be expressed may be perfectly clear in the mind yet impossible of expression. The defect is at the distal end of the combination—*i.e.*, in the physical, somatic or bodily part of the process to express the same idea by the use of different terms. The consideration of conditions of defect or pathological states may make normal psychological and physiological ones clearer, as has been shown by the above illustrations. The practical importance of the co-ordination of processes is very great. It is not possible for one born deaf to speak because the necessary mental or psychic conditions for co-ordination do not exist—*i.e.*, there is no sound in the mind to be expressed—not because there is any serious anatomical defect. In like manner the student of singing will produce no better tone than he has in mind no matter how much he practices vocalization. It follows, therefore, that the psychic state of the student should be kept in advance of his actual powers of execution. This he will most successfully do by listening to the best artists either directly or if this be impossible by hearing their gramophone records—all this in addition to the best the teacher can do for him by the correction of faults, giving him illustrations of better tone by his own efforts, etc. If the student has the opportunity of hearing himself by means of a phonographic record, he should not fail to do so. No one ever hears himself as others hear him.

As the mind and the brain are always associated in thought and feeling; in other words, in psychic processes, and these latter find expression chiefly through movements, in one sense a study of vocalization may be considered a study of movements. These are always brought about by the use of several muscles which act together for a definite end—*i.e.*, they are co-ordinated. As such movements generally involve many muscles and to be effective must be exact and under perfect control, much practice is necessary, though "much" should have reference rather to the clearness of the mind in reference to what is to be attained and the means of accomplishing it, rather than to the amount of time spent over the actual performance. We may confidently assert that technique or the physical side of putting the ideas into execution, which is simply making certain movements, is successful largely in proportion to the perfection of the psychic processes involved. A clear head should precede the moving hand, or functioning vocal organs. The student should think technique before and after its actual execution. This is even yet, in spite of a great advance in recent years, the weakest part of the student's method of work. All that we know of science as well as the results of all rightly directed practice emphasizes the importance of this central truth.

Assuming that the psychic condition is satisfactory for the production of a definite tone—*i.e.*, that it is heard mentally, what follows before it is actually produced, before it becomes a tone from the physicist's point of view? What is the chain of physical, somatic, bodily or anatomical (to use several words that express similar but slightly different aspects of the same main idea) connections involved, and what is the nature of the physiological processes; in other words, what are the parts of the body involved and how do they act? This will be clearer if we first consider the mechanism concerned and its functions in a general way.

The instrument which is played upon, which finally gives rise to the tone, may be spoken of as that connected series of cavities for which we have no single term but which are generally named the resonance chambers when regarded from the physicist's point of view. To the musician they are the instrument, to the physiologist and anatomist a set of chambers communicating with each other. Plainly all the rest of the vocal mechanism exists for them, and too much stress cannot be laid on this fact. However excellent the state of training of the part below them this is of no avail except in so far as it can affect these resonance cavities.

How is this instrument played upon and how are these cavities made actually into resounding chambers? In the answer to this, in the recognition of the relationship of the three distinct parts of the vocal apparatus lies the one great fundamental conception of the manner in which tone is produced. To understand this clearly is to comprehend in its main outlines the whole subject of voice production in a scientific way.

Before a tone is heard vibrations of the atmospheric air must reach the ear. These are set up by the vibration of the air within the resonance chambers, and this again is effected by the mechanism below them—*i.e.*, by the movements of the vocal bands of the larynx which are due to the blast of air emanating from the lungs, this itself being brought into being by the movements of the chest, using the term in the widest sense, thus including the diaphragm, etc.

Breathing has for its object so far as phonation is concerned no other purpose than to so affect the vocal bands, that the resonance chambers really do resound. The question is how is this breathing best accomplished so that the instrument shall be most efficiently played upon? We cannot alter the anatomical structure of the instrument appreciably, but we can improve the functioning of the several parts of the whole apparatus. Breathing can be improved as regards power and control. More can be done with less expenditure of energy than originally if there be judicious training. How shall we train? As the outgoing stream of air alone affects the vocal bands, it is clear that we must aim to so apply and regulate this outflow that the desired result shall follow from the least possible expenditure of energy. How the air is got in is important only in relation to its expenditure. But the easier the supply is furnished the better. This law of the conservation of energy is one of the greatest importance, for all beings have but a limited supply of energy and our problem must ever be how best to husband this as a wise man should study how best to spend his limited income. One must not only consider what is called for in ordinary conversational speaking, or in singing in a small room, but also when the greatest possible efforts are demanded. In all cases when movements are concerned, indeed whenever activity of any kind psychic or physiological is involved the *law of habit* should be borne in mind—*i.e.*, one should so think and do that a habit may be established, for a habit implies, when a good one, that there is economy of both mental and bodily energy.

The aim of all training is to establish good habits—ways of doing things which will leave the subject with more capital to invest so to speak, as he wastes less. It follows that the same methods should always be used in trying to attain the same end. There are few subjects of equal importance so little considered by students of music in a conscious intelligent way. A clear conviction as to the foundation for close adherence to certain methods of doing things is an invaluable mental asset for any student.

The whole subject of breathing has been so fully considered in previous chapters—indeed more or less in all parts of this work—that it is not necessary to go into much detail now. The investigations of physiologists in the internal have only emphasised the author's teaching on this subject. The present position of the subject may be stated thus: (1) In inspiration the whole chest is enlarged, this involving the descent of the diaphragm. (2) The amount of mobility is much greater in the lower half of the chest. (3) This lower half of the chest and the diaphragm act together, constituting a special mechanism of great importance. (4) The abdominal muscles discharge a coöperative function. It follows that the advice of a present day famous tenor to "breathe low" is sound. Nevertheless, it must not be forgotten that inspiration begins above and that the upper chest has its functions also. It is not merely a region of support for the lower mechanism, important as this function is. The terms "abdominal" and "diaphragmatic" respiration have led to misunderstanding. Neither the abdominal muscles nor the diaphragm ever act alone in normal respiration, though they are important coöperative factors.

Breathing exercises should be based on broad views of the subject, and no part of the respiratory mechanism should be neglected.

Small an organ as is the larynx it is through it the energy of the expiratory act is transmitted effectively or the reverse to the all-important resonance chambers. This should be so done that there is no waste; in other words, that there be perfect co-ordination between the breathing and the laryngeal mechanism. The vocal bands must be so related in function to the expiratory mechanism that the outgoing blast of air shall be as effective as possible. There must be no waste of power—*i.e.*, of the expiratory blast through escape of air that accomplishes no purpose. The blast must be so applied to the vocal bands, or, in other words, they must be so adapted to the blast that there is no waste of energy. If the bands approximate a little too late there is waste of breath power. The bands must further so beat the air of the resonance chambers as to get the greatest possible result with the least possible expenditure of energy. As all these co-ordinations imply the action of many muscles in a related way, it is plain that intelligent and prolonged training is necessary; and if our scientific knowledge had no other result than to establish such a conviction on a sure basis it would be well worth while; but it is a light unto the feet of the student and teacher at every step, only it must be a clear light, not one seen through a mental haze. If there be failure the fault must not be set down to science but to ourselves.

It is ever to be borne in mind that when anything is done in the right way not only is there no pain, unpleasant feeling or evil after-effects, but when real skill has been attained through training, the result is accomplished with a sense of ease and all the accompanying feelings are agreeable. The singer need not know that he has a throat by any disagreeable reminder. At the same time a function may be correctly discharged but continued too long, so that weariness or positive fatigue with some evil consequences may follow. Fatigue always implies more or less poisoning of the system.

Of the resonance chambers, the mouth cavity, the pharyngeal cavity and the naso-pharynx, which may both be regarded as a part of the mouth cavity, and the nasal chambers, the latter may be considered the least variable in shape; nevertheless they can, by means of the soft palate, be to a large extent shut off from the other parts of this series of chambers.

The means by which the size and shape of the resonance chambers can be varied are chiefly the soft palate and the tongue, the latter being of the greatest importance. The changes in the shape of the mouth cavity necessary for the formation of vowels are due chiefly to the movements of the tongue, and the tongue is more largely concerned in the utterance of consonants than any other moveable part of the upper voice mechanism.

For practical ends it is important to realize that one speaks with the tongue; and if one believed that everything depended on this organ, other parts—including the outer mouth or lips merely to be kept out of the way—the result would on the whole likely be gain.

In the formation of vowels the result may be good when the lips take but the slightest active part, and the student is advised to practice vowel formation without the use of the lips. He is likely to use them enough in any case provided he ensures the formation of pure vowel sounds, and people seem to have an extraordinary facility for over-doing the use of lip movements, for getting the teeth in the way and thus spoiling tone, that was begun well, before it has escaped from the mouth. It may be observed that those who get their living on the streets by the use of the voice, and who use the voice much and often speak rapidly, and in spite of this are heard well, so construct their words that the lips are not seen to move to any appreciable extent except as the lower jaw moves. The lips seem to be always apart. It is not the amount of movement that is important but the kind of movement, especially its rapidity.

Muscular efforts for the production of consonants should be neat, decisive, sharp, rather than held ones, which tend to spoil the word as a whole. As a rule, one is safe in holding the vowel as long as possible and in making the time dwelt on the consonant as short as possible—*i.e.*, consistent with distinct and musical utterance.

The same applies to singing with even greater force. In speaking especially short pauses not printed in the text may be made to great advantage, and this is often better than dwelling on consonants. The mouth of the speaker and still more that of the singer should not attract the attention of the listener, so the less movement of the lips of a kind readily open to observation, the better. Besides such movements being unnecessary are a waste of muscular and nervous energy.

Singers are not warranted in departing to any appreciable extent from the pronunciation of words laid down as standard for speakers—*e.g.*, "shall" should not be sung as "sholl," and in such a word as "motion," the final syllable should not be made equally important with the first one. Singers should observe the laws of a good elocution; in other words, such treatment of the language of the song as an approved reader would employ. The author would go so far as to say that no singer should appear in public till he can utter every syllable as he sings so that it is readily recognised by the listener. At present such is rarely the case even with the best vocalists. All prospective vocalists should study utterance by the speaking voice first and continue it when the study of singing has been begun. The words of every song, etc., should be mastered in all respects before they are sung.

As the degree of success in singing or speaking depends so far as technique is concerned on a series of co-ordinations the condition of both the psychic and bodily mechanism as determined by training and the general health of the individual is of great importance; and it is not to be forgotten that the mind as well as the body is to be considered in all questions of hygiene.

FOOTNOTES

[1] The chapters on the Registers of the Singing Voice may be omitted by readers whose practical interest is confined to the Speaking Voice.